BREAKAWAY

The Inside Story of the Pittsburgh Penguins' Rebirth

Andrew Conte

Blue River Press
Indianapolis, Indiana

Packaged by Wish Publishing

Front cover photo by Andrew Russell, *Pittsburgh Tribune-Review*
Cover designed by Phil Velikan

Printed in the United States of America
10 9 8 7 6 5 4 3 2

Published by Blue River Press
A Tom Doherty Company

Distributed by Cardinal Publishers Group
www.cardinalpub.com

This book is dedicated to anyone who has ever wondered what happens behind closed doors.

Table of Contents

Prologue
December 21, 2005

Gambling executives paced the faded carpet of an old penthouse office at the eastern edge of downtown Pittsburgh. With the pop of techno music in the air, these men and women hoped to sell a slice of Caribbean lifestyle on the darkest day of winter. They had invited reporters here to look at colorful, poster-sized drawings of their $1 billion plans for a casino and hockey arena.

With the weak midmorning sunlight glinting off the stainless steel dome of the Civic Arena outside, the 1960s building looked like a spaceship that had landed amid hundreds of cars lining a parking lot. Built upon dreams of the future, the Pittsburgh Penguins' hockey rink would become a relic of history this day if team owners got their way. As a consultant looked out the 15th-floor windows, he did not gaze toward the team's home but pointed to the blocks below, where dilapidated red-brick buildings and surface parking lots rested amid dirt-gray snow. A towering stone cathedral, already a designated historical landmark, stood in the first block. A contemporary synagogue sat behind, with a turquoise roof.

The consultant beckoned his audience to imagine: "That's where it will go." The plan called for an island-themed slots parlor – among the largest anywhere in North America, with up to 5,000 machines. The casino with palm trees and a two-story waterfall towering at the center of its lobby would rake in so much money that its owners could afford to pay $290 million for an 18,000-seat hockey arena next door. The two buildings together would be so popular that a brand new neighborhood would spread across the vast parking lots surrounding the old arena. Sleek condominium towers and office buildings would stand above entertainment restaurants like Planet Hollywood and the ESPN Zone. The 28-acre community would reach out toward the downtown office towers with a massive grassy park capping a four-lane highway that would cut through the middle.

In the brightly colored drawings, the project already looked like a success. Faceless people moved toward the arena in groups of twos and threes and passed through the glass atrium at the building's entrance. Above it, pressed into the building's façade, a two-dimensional imprint showed an image of the team's greatest player, Mario Lemieux, a hall-of-famer who twice won the National Hockey League's Stanley Cup, the most-storied championship trophy in all of North American sports. Its sterling rings bear the names of every player who has lifted it in victory.

To bring the imagined world to life, the hockey team must take risks unlike those any other franchise ever had faced. Sports conform to tradition, rewarding those who stay within the lines and follow the rules. Success builds from little leagues to high schools to colleges, and for the select few, the pros – rising again from the minors to major leagues. Players become coaches and coaches become managers. The system builds on itself from within. Spectators remain on the outside, behind the barricades and in the stands, a safe distance from the action. Those who break the rules receive penalties. But this time, instead, the Penguins must write a new playbook to survive in Pittsburgh. Even then, no victory will be guaranteed.

1
Blackout
March 19, 2006

Sitting inside the long, narrow luxury box high above the ice, Penguins President Ken Sawyer looked out at his hockey team and its outdated arena, a building affectionately nicknamed the Igloo for its curved dome. The Penguins had been unable to score through the first period and a half, despite having the hottest new player in a generation. For once, the seats were more than half full. With the home team headed to the bottom of the standings again, management welcomed the thousands of fans who routinely travel with the Toronto Maple Leafs when they visit places like this where tickets were plentiful. More than 15,000 people came to watch the game, even though the Leafs were struggling, too, coming off seven road losses and unable to score, either.

Even from his vantage, Sawyer did not have the best seat in the house. Desperate for cash, the Penguins had sold the nicest luxury boxes over center ice and kept one on an end for the owners. With them out of town, Sawyer used the box to host a friend from Toronto. Looking down into the bowl of the arena, the team executive saw signs of a building needing maintenance. Rows of orange and blue stadium seats stretched across the original concrete of the lowest level, below layers of balconies added over the years to stretch capacity. In places, seats had been roped off where rainwater dripped through the roof leaves. Above the seats, luxury boxes had been squeezed against the arc of the ceiling, and Sawyer knew the elevators reaching them often malfunctioned, stranding people who had purchased the most expensive tickets. On the ice, dark spots appeared where fluid from the cooling system had leaked.

Abruptly, as Sawyer sat and watched, the building plunged into nighttime darkness as every hard-wired light switched off at once. The moment occurred so suddenly that a visiting player

1

later joked about fearing he had blacked out. In a concrete bunker just outside the arena walls, a power line feeding the building failed. Then when the backup power source kicked in moments later, a second surge knocked it out as well and caused a small fire in a control panel. Sawyer had one thought: "We need a new arena."

He was not alone. From the ranks of stadium seats below, home fans and visitors together started an impromptu chant: "New a-reen-a, new a-reen-a."

The nightmare of Pittsburgh's Civic Arena started with dreams. On a warm September Sunday in 1961, thousands of people waited on the arena floor as a shaft of sunlight exploded across them and an orchestra struck up the first notes of the Star Spangled Banner. It seemed in that moment that the world had turned to gaze on the gleaming stainless steel saucer at the eastern edge of downtown Pittsburgh. For those who had worked for years to reach this point, the stakes could not have seemed higher. Not only were they about to open a new arena for sports and Broadway-style theater, but civic leaders hoped, too, that they were opening a new beginning for the entire city. Pittsburgh powered the Allies to victory through World War II with steel for tanks, landing ships and all manner of war machines — quickly ramping up after the attack on Pearl Harbor to turn out more steel than Germany, Italy and Japan combined. But it also paid a steep price with soot-choked air, chemical-fouled waters and a growing reputation as a nice location for a factory but no place for an executive, let alone his wife and children, to spend more than a long afternoon. This moment, when the roof of the new public auditorium was supposed to roll back from darkness in two-and-a-half minutes to drench the audience inside with a mid-September sun and blue sky, could determine the Steel City's fate — whether it remained only the workhorse of industry or emerged as a place for scientific discovery, artistic creation and higher education. This moment, civic leaders believed, could show the world that their city had evolved. They had banked on it.

For more than a decade, local politicians and corporate executives talked about Pittsburgh's desperate need for not only a public auditorium but also a place that equaled the great architecture of history. These men of government and industry had seen the world as they had waged war on Nazi fascism across Europe, witnessing the marvels of Rome and Paris along the way. Didn't they deserve to have a significant structure in their own city, the very place that had forged that freedom with its riverfront factories? Looking for inspiration after returning home, they considered the Roman empire's ancient architecture: "The perfect reference here, I think, would be Rome's great Coliseum – a structure which, even stripped of its original marble facing, still projects a feeling of awe-inspiring force and elegance," one corporate leader said, standing beneath the half-built dome of Pittsburgh's new arena in 1960. Another man, even earlier, compared the project to another antiquity: "The Romans had something of the sort we propose in their Pantheon – a vast circular structure with a great aperture in its dome always open to the heavens, so that, as the Romans thought, their gods could enter." These Pittsburgh men then built the only dome in the world larger than the one over the Pantheon.

They imagined the layout of the public spaces of early Greece, too, and then designed a place for both large speaking events and sports competitions. Hadn't it been a shame, when General Dwight Eisenhower visited Pittsburgh in 1952, that the city had no gathering spot other than an armory built for the First World War? No city of international renown, they determined, could exist without a gathering spot for thousands of its citizens. Not even sports could be accommodated in Pittsburgh. The only venue large enough for indoor sporting events had been a former car barn that had been converted in 1895 for ice hockey. Even that building, euphemistically named The Gardens, had been demolished before work started on the new auditorium, leaving the city with no major site at all. It would be an embarrassment of the ages, another city father argued, if Pittsburgh could not build something better for itself: "What Greek exhumed to look at us and remembering the marble stadium of Athens," he said, "would not sneer at the greatest industrial city of the modern world?"

Construction of the Civic Arena engendered dreams of Pittsburgh's emergence. (Carnegie Mellon University Architecture Archives)

Reporters came to Pittsburgh from around the world to look at the Civic Arena during its construction. (Carnegie Mellon University Architecture Archives)

City leaders had considered the pyramids of Egypt's Luxor, as well, and pushed the limits of their own modern technology to devise a building that could change with the weather, that could open for starry nights and close to wind, rain and snow. More impressive still, like the pyramids that still bewilder modern engineers for their precision, Pittsburgh's new arena would hold up 3,000 tons of structural steel without a single interior support – hanging instead from a cantilevered arm with its roots buried far below ground and its length extending 205 feet above the center of the arena floor.

The world had paid attention to this endeavor – even if, at times, questioning the viability of the project. *Fortune* magazine devoted several pages to Pittsburgh's new public auditorium and then offered an admonition for other American industrial cities: "The great steel dome has a meaning that goes beyond Pittsburgh," it said. "If one of the drabbest and dirtiest of cities has been able to remake itself in shining pride, any city in the United States should be able to follow its example."

None of that attention would matter now, if the roof's six 300-ton movable leaves failed to budge. Already one embarrassing setback had occurred. Originally the arena would have opened with a weeklong celebration called Pittsburgh Progress. The world's greatest minds on city planning, architecture, science and culture would have gathered: Dr. Jonas Salk, the Pittsburgh scientist who had freed children and their parents from the fear of polio, would have talked about medical breakthroughs like his vaccine, and David Rockefeller, heir to the Standard Oil fortune, would have come from New York to discuss banking. As it turned out, Pittsburgh had not progressed as far as organizers might have hoped: The event was canceled when labor strikes delayed the arena's opening by three months. After that, city leaders settled for a simple opening of the roof, rather than showing off at a lengthy coming-out party.

Sitting now under the dome, some 5,000 spectators waited with anticipation while listening to speeches by the governor, the mayor and other dignitaries. Finally, as the conductor of the Pittsburgh Symphony lifted his baton, a worker in a small control room halfway up the stadium seats pushed the single button, set on a gray panel filled with switches, knobs and lights, that would roll back the dome. Sunlight burst through the widening crack between the first two moving panels as they slid smoothly open on tracks. A lawyer for the city's main business organization wept, overcome with relief and the joy of seeing Pittsburgh suddenly emerge.

Forty-five years later, the need for a new arena does not come as a revelation to Penguins management or the team's fans. Over the years, the Igloo made contributions with its silver dome shining like a "great Cyclopean eye," in the words of yet another founding father. By its very presence, the arena allowed Pittsburgh to draw a National Hockey League franchise in 1967. The building's nickname inspired the new owners to name their team the Penguins, keeping with the arctic theme. Then, before the new franchise could officially take over, its minor-league predecessor, the Hornets, of the American Hockey League, closed out the team's final season with a flourish – winning the Calder Cup championship on a goal 26 seconds into overtime. It remained the only professional hockey championship Pittsburgh ever won on the Civic Arena ice.

Despite the lofty hopes of its planners with their grandiose dreams, however, the arena almost immediately revealed problems none had foreseen. The building was designed not just for sports but as a stage for theatrical productions and classical music performances, and it failed to fit any of the purposes correctly. Famed conductor Leonard Bernstein brought the New York Philharmonic to the arena in 1963 – and vowed never to return. With the dome closed, musical notes bounced off the ceramic ceiling tiles, creating confusing echoes; with the roof leaves opened, sound simply escaped into the open air.

The Carol Burnett Revue opened the building with a week of shows in the summer of 1962, but stagehands quickly realized the Igloo's high, curved roof left no space for hanging props and curtains. And when the roof opened, a gust of cold air washed through the arena seats and whipped at the curtains on the stage. After just eight seasons, the city's Civic Light Orchestra, one of the original tenants for whom the arena had been designed, left. Organizers lost so much money because of the building's odd features, they decided it made more sense to go dark for two years until a downtown movie theater could be turned into their new home, rather than continuing to put on productions in the arena.

Eventually the arena could not draw major rock concerts, either. When the Beatles played at the Civic Arena[1] in September 1964, the "Fab Four" walked into the building carrying their instruments. Years later, something like that could never happen: Touring solo, Paul McCartney needs 16 trucks, eight buses and nearly 100 workers. Because the arena's original loading dock had not been built large enough to accommodate 18-wheeler trucks, the space had been turned into a tool shed with the words "Ye Olde Garden Shoppe" painted onto the cinder-block wall. That inconvenience meant roadies setting up rock-and-roll concerts had to truck equipment by hand through a labyrinth of too-narrow hallways to reach the main stage. Lights, speakers and pyrotechnics that hung from the ceiling prevented the roof from opening during even the smallest shows, such as a performance by James Taylor and Carole King. Many major artists simply refused to appear at the arena, and promoters started passing over the building, and often the city altogether, on national tours. Even though the Penguins ultimately received the right to collect revenue from concerts and events on nights when they did not have home games, the arena rarely allowed them to make as much money as newer buildings in other cities.

Other shortcomings at the Civic Arena seemed comical. When the circus came to town, animals were housed in the arena's lower level, below the audience seats. That created problems early on when the elephants learned to pull the fire alarms, causing rescue trucks to turn up at the arena repeatedly until someone finally figured out the reason for so many false alarms. Giraffes, kept outside with their long necks, ate the leaves from nearby trees.

---

[1] Originally called the Public Auditorium, the building was renamed the Civic Arena shortly after it opened because those shorter words fit better on street signs. Later, in 1999, Mellon Financial Corporation paid $18 million for 10 years' worth of naming rights, and it extended the marketing deal through 2010, after which the building was again called the Civic Arena. Throughout this book, the author chooses to refer to the building as the Civic Arena.

Even for hockey, the Civic Arena had flaws. Players complained about dark spots on the ice because lighting built into the dome created uneven shadows. During rain, the roof could not completely keep out the elements, allowing water to drip on fans in rows of seats that had to be blocked off. Concourses were too narrow for concession stands and too far removed from the action for fans to follow the game while getting something to eat or drink. Later, when the lowly Penguins finally started qualifying for the post-season, the building could not stay cold enough in the early summer heat, and arena managers hired refrigerator trucks to cool the building so the ice would not melt.

Then there was the night when the power failed. The audience apparently never really faced any serious danger, but those who had gone through the experience said it seemed amazing that with so many people suddenly pitched into blackness, no one panicked and caused a stampede. With two electricity failures in the one game, play had been stopped for 46 minutes. When the players returned to the ice for the final 27 minutes of regulation, including the entire third period, Toronto scored the game's only goal. That dropped the Penguins to 39 losses on the team's way to a second-to-last-place finish for the 2005-06 season.

Long before that night, Penguins owner Mario Lemieux had started taking the arena's shortcomings personally. Originally, he had never expected to own an NHL franchise, and now he had one that failed to win games and struggled to pay its bills in a building that made turning a profit seem almost impossible. Lemieux had started out as a player, and a special one at that.

Lemieux had been drafted in 1984, first overall, by a Penguins franchise that already had declared bankruptcy less than a decade before. In its first 17 years until then, the team had been owned by five different groups involving more than two dozen investors. Its first change-in-ownership sale came midway through the team's initial season. Lemieux had been heralded as someone who could turn around the fortunes of a hard-luck franchise that had rarely qualified for the playoffs and never lasted long when it did. For months before draft day, Penguins General Manager Eddie Johnston had been traveling to Montreal to check out the player many of the scouts considered the clear number-one pick. As selection day drew nearer, Johnston reportedly had been overheard practicing for the moment in his office, learning how to choose Lemieux in the player's native French as well as English. The desire to obtain Lemieux had been so great that some speculated later – although never with evidence – that perhaps the Penguins management had not set the team up to win down the stretch, in order to remain in last place so they could keep the top draft slot.

On draft day inside the Montreal Forum, the hockey arena in Lemieux's hometown, Johnston used the words he had rehearsed so many times to select the top draft pick. Sitting in the stands, Lemieux, 18 years old at the time, heard his name but did not move, staring stoically ahead. Because he had not agreed to contract terms with the team before draft day, Lemieux refused to visit the Penguins' table after his name was called or to wear the team's sweater. He told a Canadian television station that day, "I am not going to their table because the Penguins do not want me badly enough." Years later, Lemieux wrote in his autobiography that he could have handled the situation better: "Looking back, I wish I would have done it differently," Lemieux wrote.[2] "I was advised to do it that way, but sometimes you do things when you're young that you later regret. That was one of them."

The conflict did not last. Within days, Lemieux signed the richest rookie contract in history, worth $700,000 over three years. He appeared on the cover of *The Hockey News* that summer next to his jersey and under a headline that asked the question, "Can he salvage the Penguins?"

In his first game, on his first shift and with his first shot, Lemieux gave an immediate answer. Less than three minutes into his first game as a Penguin, against the Boston Bruins at Boston Garden, Lemieux stole the puck from defenseman Ray Bourque, a future member of the Hockey Hall of Fame. Then,

---

[2] Lemieux, Mario. *The Final Period*. Reich, Brisson and Reich Publishing. Pittsburgh, Pa. Pg. 41.

with his first shot in the NHL, Lemieux pushed the puck past goalie Pete Peeters. Lemieux finished the season with 43 goals, 100 points, a most valuable player award from the league's all-star game and the Calder Memorial Trophy for rookie of the year. None of those achievements had been enough to lift a team that still finished with the league's second-worst record, but it had been a start.

Lemieux eventually led the Penguins to salvation on the ice. He twice lifted the Stanley Cup, the NHL's championship trophy, and he racked up numerous other prizes: He led the league in scoring six times; he was named the league's most valuable player three times for the regular season and twice for the playoffs; he played in 10 all-star games, getting named the all-star MVP in three of them. Along the way, Lemieux also won the Canada Cup in 1987 by scoring the go-ahead goal in the final minutes of a best-of-three series against the Soviet Union, with Wayne Gretzky, known as "The Great One," getting the assist and then leaping into Lemieux's arms to celebrate.

Yet even in moments of greatness, Lemieux faced adversities. He briefly talked of retirement as early as 1992 when he missed 16 games that winter because of severe back pain. Already, he had undergone back surgery two years earlier, and health problems continued to nag him throughout his career. When he ultimately led the league in scoring during the 1991-92 season and the Penguins won a second-straight championship, Lemieux did not seriously consider giving up the game right then.

Away from the ice, the Penguins continued to experience frequent turnover in the owners' box. Even after winning the first championship in 1991, the Penguins had new owners again when a group of investors headed by Hollywood producer Howard Baldwin took over. Baldwin had been a founder of the World Hockey Association franchise that eventually became the Hartford Whalers and joined the NHL in 1979. When he came to Pittsburgh, Baldwin brought with him an intuitive flair for entertaining fans. The Civic Arena presented obvious problems, but Baldwin remained intrigued by the unique structure and the quirkiness of its retractable roof. His wife, Karen Elise Baldwin, eventually wrote the screenplay for a movie called *Sudden Death*, which came out in 1995 and featured

*Mario Lemieux celebrates the unusual feat of scoring five goals, five different ways, on December 31, 1988. (*Pittsburgh Tribune-Review, *James M. Kubus)*

martial arts actor Jean-Claude Van Damme saving an arena full of hostages from terrorists. The film fell into the genre of *Die Hard* action movies popularized by actor Bruce Willis, and it featured a brutal fight scene between Van Damme and the Penguins mascot in the arena kitchen, as well as an exploding marquis outside. "The ability of the roof to open was fun," Baldwin said years later. "If you look at that period of time, everybody was doing *Die Hard* this and *Die Hard* that. My wife, Karen, had the idea, 'What if someone ever really held an arena hostage?'"

In October 1992, four months after the team won its sec-ond-straight championship, the new owners rewarded Lemieux with the largest contract in league history, at $42 million over seven years. The team also guaranteed that Lemieux would remain the league's highest-paid player with an escalation clause that required the team to pay him at least $1 million more than any other NHL player. Lemieux deserved to make more money, Baldwin said. "We had won two Stanley

Cups. Check your records. Not many teams have done that. (Lemieux) was, without question, the greatest player in the world, in my mind." If Gretzky or some other hockey star won a raise above what Lemieux was earning, the thinking was that, Lemieux deserved to get one, too. "Then so be it," Baldwin said.

The Penguins' new owners filled out the team with so many high-quality players that the franchise nearly fielded its own all-star team in 1992. Four Penguins that year were named to the Wales Conference starting lineup: Lemieux, Kevin Stevens, Jaromir Jagr and Paul Coffey. The Penguins focused the following year on not only winning a third title but on dominating the league from start to finish, winning all the league awards and etching their names on the Stanley Cup one more time. Even among that group of stars, Lemieux stood apart not only as someone who could score goals and command the highest salary, but as a leader. "He would blame himself even when it wasn't his fault," said Tom McMillan, a former hockey beat reporter who wrote a book on the Penguins and edited another, and who went on to become the team's vice president of communications. "I always thought that he motivated himself that way. People thought he wasn't sophisticated with the media, but your teammates will go to the wall for you when that happens, when they know you are taking blame, if you're taking the pressure off them. He would say all the time, 'I'm paid the big money, I'm supposed to score the big goal.'"

The perfect season did not happen, for reasons that no one could have predicted. In January 1993 – five months after signing his record-setting contract – Lemieux went to a doctor to have a lump on his neck checked out. It turned out to be a form of Hodgkin's lymphoma, a cancer of the white blood cells. "To find out you have cancer – any type of cancer – is scary," Lemieux wrote years later.[3] "When they told me I had Hodgkin's disease, it was probably the worst day of my life. I mean, everything was going so well, I was playing some good hockey, we had a chance to win another Cup, there were no worries." The team issued a statement in which Baldwin stated the obvious: "This is not about hockey." It was about giving Lemieux the best chance to beat the disease. "You care about

[3]   Lemieux, Mario. pg. 79.

him as a human being, and that's all I cared about," Baldwin said years later. "I just wanted him to live a normal and productive life. If he ever played hockey again, that was a big, huge, massive bonus for the community and him, but the biggest thing was his health."

For six weeks in the middle of the season, Lemieux underwent radiation treatments. On the day of the last treatment, March 2, 1993, he returned to play in a game against Philadelphia and scored a goal. Almost unbelievably, Lemieux went on a scoring drive for the rest of that season – averaging more than three points a game for one 16-game stretch – and he won the league's scoring title in addition to the league's MVP trophy and top awards from the players association and hockey writers. It had been a stunning turnaround, even when the team fell short of another Stanley Cup championship by losing in overtime of Game 7 to the Islanders in the second round. After that season, Lemieux needed a second back surgery to repair the fibrous tissue that connects muscles. He started the 1993-94 season but again missed games so his back could heal. The Penguins finished on top of the division with 101 points and lost in the first round to the Washington Capitals. By then, Lemieux felt extremely tired, and doctors diagnosed him with anemia and fatigue. He had never really allowed himself to recover from the radiation treatments 15 months earlier, and then he had developed an infection from his back surgery. All the injuries had compounded to the point that Lemieux decided to sit out the 1994-95 season, which was shortened by a lockout, so he could recover. The team had agreed in Lemieux's contract that he would be able to decide whether he could play based upon his own "determination that he is not physically able to play hockey for an entire season at the level customarily associated with (his) exceptional and unique knowledge, skill and ability as a hockey player."[4]

The Penguins ownership group headed by Baldwin had decided to keep Lemieux at any cost. When he stayed healthy, Lemieux performed in ways that clearly defined him as one of the best – if not simply the best – to ever play the game of

---

[4] "Narrative statement in support of proofs of claim of Mario Lemieux," filed in U.S. Bankruptcy Court on January 25, 1999, by Lemieux's lawyer, Douglas A. Campbell.

hockey. As long as he was on the ice, fans would come to the games and the team almost always had a legitimate shot for a deep run into the playoffs. The problem became that as Lemieux experienced health problems, the team could not always count on him playing. "You were trying to find a way to keep him on the payroll, never knowing whether he would play or not," Baldwin said.

The owners, too, had added other players around Lemieux to keep the franchise playing at a high level. The Penguins had been fortunate to draft Jagr, the first Czech player to sign with an NHL team after the fall of the Soviet bloc in Eastern Europe, and as he developed into another legitimate star, the owners faced a dilemma about whether to keep him and Lemieux. "Economically you couldn't really do it," Baldwin said. "You couldn't trade Mario. Even if you were foolish enough to think it was a good option, no team would take him. He was in and out of the lineup with back problems. It was not his fault, of course. It was a curse he had to deal with." But if the Penguins traded away Jagr, who had value for other teams, and it turned out Lemieux could not play, the franchise would lose its two greatest marketing assets.

After taking a year off, Lemieux came back for the 1995-96 season. He hired a trainer and started conditioning four months before the games started. That year, again, he played at a high level. He won the league's scoring title and was named the regular-season MVP for the third time. Still, Lemieux felt he could not sustain the energy he had before. That summer, Lemieux met with Baldwin and agreed to play one more season, but he warned that it would probably be his last. The owners realized that Lemieux had been through a traumatic recovery ever since doctors had diagnosed him with cancer. Even with the time off from the game, Lemieux continued to experience debilitating back problems. Nevertheless, Baldwin desperately hoped that Lemieux would come back for as long as he could. "Of course we felt he had to come back and play," Baldwin said. "We wanted him to play. He was so important to the franchise. Everyone was being held hostage by his physical condition. That's not a criticism, just a statement. He was held hostage, too."

In February, at the Dapper Dan Dinner, an annual sports banquet in Pittsburgh, Lemieux announced that he planned to retire at the end of the season. He went on to win the scoring title for the second-straight season, and he played as a first-team all-star. Immediately after the season, the Hockey Hall of Fame voted to induct Lemieux without waiting the customary three years after retirement.

At the same time Lemieux was dealing with his health ailments, financial problems started growing for the Penguins franchise. The team could not really afford to pay the contracts for Lemieux and the other stars the owners had acquired to play around him. "The largest influence on profitability is player costs," the accounting firm Coopers & Lybrand wrote in a 1997 study of the team. The Penguins had averaged more than 16,000 fans a game and 20 sellouts over the previous six years[5], and revenues had increased to more than $41 million a year. More than two-thirds of that money came from ticket sales, while TV and radio contracts made up less than 20 percent, and advertising brought in the next biggest chunk at just over 10 percent. On the spending side, the accountants reported that player costs alone took up more than $31 million, or about three-quarters of the revenue. The team could not afford to keep up, losing nearly $25 million in 1995 and more than $30 million two years later. Coopers & Lybrand valued the franchise at no more than $95 million.

When Baldwin's group took over the franchise in 1991, it had been a blessing to get a team that had just won a championship and seemed ready to compete for more – but it had been a challenge, too. "The flaw in the business model then was that they won the Stanley Cup with a very low payroll," Baldwin said. "That's good but it's bad, too, because it means when all the players' contracts were up, they wanted to be rewarded for being the best in the world. We had a team that

---

[5]   The team had only nine sellouts during the 1994-95 season when the NHL had a 48-game lockout.

was one of the best teams ever, but it was paid for under old contracts, so to speak. We were left with the task of having to compensate them for what they had done or seeing them leave."

As the team's debts mounted, Lemieux agreed to defer more of his salary. After the Los Angeles Kings gave Gretzky a raise in 1993 – paying him $25.5 million over three years – the Penguins owed Lemieux more than $2 million under the contract clause that kept him as the league's highest-paid player. Lemieux pushed off that bonus until 2000, without interest. The team owed him another $2.7 million for the 1994-95 season, when Lemieux had taken off because of his injuries and had agreed to take his salary over four years. He was due to receive $4 million in rights payments that he allowed the team to delay in paying, and $1 million a year through the final four years of his contract. By 1998, the Penguins owed their star player $32,597,629. The franchise had failed to pay him a portion of his rights fees at the start of 1997, and then the following year it paid him only $1 million of the more than $2.5 million he was owed. The team wanted to defer more payments into the future, but by then Lemieux declined to renegotiate.

On October 13, 1998, the franchise, which had been through bankruptcy before in 1975, declared itself insolvent for a second time.

"They were a completely broken franchise," said Chuck Greenberg, a lawyer and close friend of Lemieux. When Baldwin took ownership of the franchise in 1991, his ownership group did not acquire the arena operations as well. Without enough money to keep up with the lavish salaries players had been promised, the team sold off key assets such as the television and radio rights to broadcasts, and even the advertising rights throughout the building. "It was the equivalent of being born without any of your internal organs," Greenberg said. "You're going to die. It's just a question of how long it takes."

Days after the Penguins declared bankruptcy, Lemieux and Greenberg were eating dinner in a private room at Morton's Steakhouse in downtown Pittsburgh with the player's two agents, Steve Reich and his uncle, Tom Reich. The four friends often had dinner together in those days, and the banter was lively as they considered Lemieux's options with the team in bankruptcy court, owing him tens of millions of dollars. In a moment that rarely happened when those guys were together, they all stopped talking, and the room fell completely silent. "For whatever reason, all of a sudden the four of us stopped talking at the same time," Greenberg recalled later. "There was this pregnant silence. We looked at each other, and we each realized that we were thinking the same thing: You know, we ought to buy this."

As the person owed the most money, Lemieux had three options: He could walk away from the Penguins and try to earn a salary by playing out the rest of his career in another city; he could watch the team be sold and relocated, while collecting a sizable payment as creditor; or he could make a play to take over the franchise. The first two options required little imagination, but Lemieux would have squandered his legacy in Pittsburgh. The third option, however, meant taking on uncertain risk. The four friends at dinner that night had enough money to pay their meal tab, of course, but they needed help to come up with the cash to purchase the hockey team. If they could interest enough investors in the plan, Lemieux might be able to convince a bankruptcy judge to give him ownership of the franchise. Even then, however, he might never make back the money he was owed if he could not manage the team any better than his predecessors. "We really had nothing except for Mario and all that he represented as a galvanizing force to inspire us, and the insatiable passion that we all shared to try to serve him and ultimately his partners and the city by preserving the team for western Pennsylvania," Greenberg said.

Before he could contemplate a takeover, Lemieux needed to come up with the money to pull the organization out of court and then to operate it. He still needed $20 million from a single investor when Tom Reich introduced him to a California billionaire named Ron Burkle. Although he had only a casual interest in hockey, Burkle had made his money by investing in lost causes – most often inner-city grocery stores, at first – and turning them into money-making operations. With an innate business sense, Burkle could make Lemieux's takeover bid stronger by ensuring that the new ownership group actually had a plan to pay the bills and get into the black. Burkle sent teams of assistants to Pittsburgh to check out the hockey franchise, conduct background research on Lemieux, and take a close look at the takeover proposal. They considered every detail, down to how much the team could charge for tickets and how it would try to sell them. Satisfied that the Penguins under Lemieux would have a viable business plan, Burkle put up $20 million toward the $60 million that Lemieux needed. Together the two men – the business insider who seemed to be able to see around corners into the future, and the hockey hall-of-famer who never panicked or seemed to forget even a minor detail – made a strong case for keeping an NHL franchise in Pittsburgh.

Burkle's investment also had the effect of convincing others it would be all right to back the team as well. "There was this enormous negative pall over the future of the team," said Sawyer, the league's chief financial officer for 14 years. "Even though it was a good team on the ice, the image of the team was really one that it was on shaky ground. You're trying to raise capital at that time when the stock market's flying high, and you're asking people to invest in a hockey team that's bankrupt, with the principle outward investor and owner being someone who is one of the greatest hockey players of all time but who has no business record. It took a leap of faith by a lot of people to invest." Burkle brought instant credibility. Lemieux had only a 10th-grade education because he had dropped out of school to work on his hockey skills, but Burkle's endorsement allowed him to make the case that the takeover plan had real potential. Lemieux picked up large contributions from a half-dozen other major investors, many of them local business leaders who could afford to put money into a hometown franchise. With the goal of building more local interest, Lemieux's backers also started the FOMs, or Friends of Mario, a group of Pittsburghers who each agreed to put up $200,000 toward the team. At that low level, the money would not mean as much to Lemieux as the moral support of having allies at his side. Finally, Lemieux raised the stakes himself by forgoing any payments from the bankruptcy judgment so that he would be at least as heavily invested as everyone who had put up cash. With all the money counted, Lemieux's group had raised $56 million.

Another reorganization bid came directly from the National Hockey League, which told the federal Bankruptcy Court it could offer only two alternative options: it would either reorganize the franchise in another city or dissolve the team and distribute its players among the remaining franchises. A third plan had been floated for a while, with Microsoft co-founder Paul Allen paying a deposit on an $85 million offer to buy the franchise and move it to Portland. Under that plan, Lemieux might have lost his legacy, but he would have made back most of the money he was owed.

*Mario Lemieux emerges from bankruptcy court on June 24, 1999, after the reorganization plan was approved. (*Pittsburgh Tribune-Review, *Chaz Palla)*

Ultimately Lemieux won out – getting the team, even though that did not solve all of its money problems. Sawyer was hired on the first day to run the front office operations. Lemieux's management team first negotiated a new television contract with the local Fox affiliate to recognize the high ratings the team had been drawing with its strong play on the ice. The Bankruptcy Court also awarded the new owners the naming rights to the Civic Arena. Baldwin's group had tried to sell the rights earlier, only to find out it did not really own them. Lemieux's group was able to sell the name for $18 million over 10 years to Mellon Financial, a local corporation.

The other key to the Lemieux takeover plan was his insistence that the team needed to get public help for a new arena so it could start making money rather than losing it. For the Penguins, arena costs ate up nearly a quarter of the team's non-player expenses, the worst home ice deal in the league, according to Bill Daly, the league's deputy commissioner. The Penguins paid $4.6 million a year in arena costs, or $1 million more than any other team without its own building. The arena had been a major cause of the team's problems, and if the new owners expected to not only come out of bankruptcy but to stay in the black, they had to figure out a way to lower their arena expenses and make more money from ticket sales, concessions and other game-day spending. "Most of the teams in the league had new arenas that generated higher revenue streams," Sawyer said. "Competitively around the league, we were at a disadvantage. Our market was small compared to the big markets, and then the other smaller markets seemed to all have new arenas."

Before Lemieux agreed to take over the Penguins, he and his supporters wanted public officials to say in writing they would use tax dollars to help pay for a new arena that would be built across the street from the Civic Arena. It quickly became clear that no one was ready to promise that kind of money. While they said they understood Lemieux's concerns, none of the politicians would take the chance of angering voters over an expensive new sports facility for a bankrupt hockey team. "We knew they were not in a position to make an absolute commitment," Greenberg said. "We wanted as strong a commitment as we could get, knowing it would not be the kind of commitment that could be enforced in a court of law." Looking for a word that gave the politicians the flexibility they needed but that also carried as much emotional weight as possible, Greenberg suggested they agree to "endeavor" to build an arena. "That really was more of a moral commitment that they were going to do everything humanly possible," he said. The politicians agreed, and the language was added to the terms of Lemieux's takeover plan.

Within their home market, the Penguins faced another disadvantage. Both the Steelers football team and the Pirates baseball team had received public help for new stadiums opening in 2001. Politicians had rallied to help pay for new stadiums even when voters rejected a referendum on the idea. Flaws at the Civic Arena would be cast in even darker relief. The Penguins, in the NHL's oldest hockey barn, would be competing for local fan dollars with teams that had state-of-the-art stadiums, featuring the latest high-tech gadgets and the finest finishes, granite and marble, rather than bare concrete. Modern sports buildings have open concourses and ample room for luxury boxes that provide all the amenities of a studio apartment, with a private bathroom, small kitchen area, a living room and private seats for watching the live action. Corporate sponsors expected that kind of space for hosting clients and rewarding employees. The new stadiums would have it while the Civic Arena would not. Since it opened, the arena had been expanded five times for hockey, building capacity to 17,000 seats from 10,500. Narrow luxury boxes were tucked above the roofline of the dome so that fans with those seats could touch the ceramic-lined ceiling as they climbed narrow stairs to reach them. "New stadiums attract fans and they also attract sponsors, and so long-term deals were being done for those stadiums for much higher dollars," Sawyer said about the football and baseball stadiums. "There are only so many dollars in the universe."

The new owners had no leverage, either. Previous owners had signed a lease at the Civic Arena that lasted for another seven years when Lemieux took over, removing any advantage that could be gained from threatening to relocate. Even the team's good play had become a liability, with players demanding more lucrative contracts because of their success. Chasing after the league's best teams would mean spending more money than the Penguins could afford. "We had to figure out a way to get from point A to point B, financial stability-wise," Sawyer said. "The writing was on the wall in terms of what we had to do. It wasn't brain surgery. You knew you couldn't compete at that time because it cost too much and the revenues couldn't be there in the older arena."

If Lemieux was going to salvage the Penguins one more time – and have any hope of recouping the millions of dollars he was owed by the franchise – he had to figure out a way to get a new arena.

2

Street Smarts
November 2, 2004

At every transition in his life, David Morehouse sat down and wrote a list of the things he wanted to accomplish – places where he might move, the kind of house where he would live, jobs he could do and his priorities. After serving as the traveling chief of staff for U.S. Senator John Kerry's losing presidential bid in 2004, Morehouse had many options. Over the previous 18 months, he had made and renewed hundreds of contacts in major cities from almost every state, among local Democratic ward bosses, businessmen and celebrities such as Jon Bon Jovi and Meg Ryan.

The downside to that high-powered life had been that through the final six weeks of the campaign, Morehouse had not been home to Boston once to see his wife or their 18-month-old son, Jackson. In the final days, people close to Kerry had contemplated the nightmare scenario of another close election like the one in 2000 that had turned for Republican George Bush only after the hand-counting of Florida's ballots with their hanging chads. To be prepared for another slim margin, the Kerry campaign wanted to immediately name the senior members of a new administration, and they asked top campaign staff to choose what jobs they might want. Depending on who would serve as Kerry's chief of staff in the White House, Morehouse either would be the administration's deputy chief of staff or the director of cabinet affairs. The deputy job offered more seniority and clout, but Morehouse found himself hoping for the cabinet affairs post, knowing it would offer a better chance for getting away from the office at reasonable hours to see his family. Unlike when he had worked on the two winning campaigns for President Bill Clinton or Vice President Al Gore's losing bid in 2000, Morehouse unexpectedly found himself just rooting for the campaign to end. He wanted to go home, almost more than he wanted to win. As it turned out, the election had not been as close as the previous one, but Kerry had not conceded until a day after the election ended and the final votes in Ohio were counted, giving the Electoral College edge to Bush again. At the top of his post-election list of priorities, Morehouse wrote that he wanted to spend more time with his family.

In the left-hand column of the sheet of paper, Morehouse wrote a long list of the places where he and Vanessa wanted to live. They enjoyed Boston, but they wanted to find a place where they could afford to buy a good-sized home to raise what they expected would be a family with at least several children. As the crowd man for Clinton's 1992 campaign and then as the advance man for the president the following four years, Morehouse had gotten to see more American cities than many people could name. Having lived in Washington, D.C., Los Angeles and Boston, Morehouse wanted the amenities of a major city; as a native of Pittsburgh, however, he also wanted a place small enough that it had close-knit neighborhoods and a high quality of life. His list included Austin, Denver, Portland – both Oregon and Maine – Seattle and Minneapolis, where Vanessa had grown up. Pittsburgh did not make the cut.

On the right-hand side of the paper, Morehouse wrote down a list of powerful contacts he had made through the campaigns, people who could help him find work. Until he decided what kind of job he wanted, Morehouse figured he would start a consulting business that helped people solve problems that required political solutions. He had a natural talent for dealing with elected officials, and he knew that would be useful to people with a variety of issues dealing with government. In that list, Morehouse wrote the names of people like James Carville, who had run Clinton's 1992 campaign; Paul Begala, who worked with Carville and served as an aide to the president; General Barry McCaffrey, who had served as the nation's Drug Czar when Morehouse worked in the Office of National Drug Control Policy; and Gore, the former vice president.

Near the top of the list, under the B's in alphabetical order, Morehouse had written the name of Ron Burkle, a California billionaire who had been a powerful campaign fundraiser for Clinton and had turned out to be one of the president's closest friends. Morehouse first met Burkle early in the Clinton administration when the president held a fundraiser at the billionaire's lavish Green Acres mansion in Beverly Hills, California. There had been many parties and fundraisers after that first one, and Morehouse most often served as the advance man, arriving days early to meet with Burkle and go over the detailed arrangements for each event. Most often, these events mixed the business of political fundraising with pleasure, such as a concert by the Eagles rock band in Burkle's backyard one night. Amid the stress of a nationwide campaign, staff workers could get a little giddy among the extravagance of Burkle's home. One night during the 1996 campaign, a White House spokesman had taken a Nestea plunge into Burkle's swimming pool while the formal party went on at another terrace of the sprawling complex. On orders from Leon Panetta, Clinton's chief of staff, Morehouse and others took the man inside, got him dried off and into some borrowed clothes without any of the campaign contributors noticing.

After Clinton won re-election that year, Morehouse decided not to go back to Washington, and Burkle helped him find a job in Los Angeles. Because of his experience in the drug policy office, Morehouse wanted to work for DARE, the Drug Abuse Resistance Education nonprofit, and Burkle served as its chairman. Morehouse landed a job as the organization's deputy director, and he helped turn around the agency amid criticism that it didn't work. He knew firsthand from the federal government that simple messages warning about the dangers of drugs often worked best. It had been a revelation to him that Republican Nancy Reagan's "Just Say No" campaign had been effective. Too often, kids started using drugs because they did not realize how harmful they could be.

Now eight years later, Morehouse planned to call on Burkle again. He figured the businessman might be one of several people willing to pay him a retainer to deal with a myriad of political problems, and that would support the consulting business. Before heading out to California, Morehouse heard from one of Burkle's assistants that the billionaire might want help with his hockey franchise, the Pittsburgh Penguins. Morehouse had grown up sneaking into Penguins games when he could not afford a ticket. He and his friends had discovered a number of ways to get into the Civic Arena. Sometimes they would pitch in to buy one ticket, and the person who went into the game would open one of the many doors to the outside and let everyone else into the arena. Other times, they would walk up the ramps that wrapped around the city-side of the building and climb over a low wall to reach an outdoor smoking lounge. From there, they could walk right into the game with all of the paying fans. Despite being a fan of the hockey team and having worked for years with Burkle, Morehouse had no idea until then that the Democratic backer co-owned the Penguins.

On the flight to Los Angeles, Morehouse thought that helping the Penguins might be one of the things Burkle would want him to do. But when he got there and they sat down to talk in the restaurant of The Beverly Hills Hotel, Burkle said he needed Morehouse exclusively and that he wanted him to move back home to Pittsburgh to work with the Penguins. Elected officials had promised to endeavor to help pay for an arena, and that money had never come. Burkle wanted Morehouse to figure out what had gone wrong and how they could fix it.

The idea of returning home had never occurred to Morehouse, but now that Burkle made the offer he started getting excited about the prospect. When he discussed the plan with Vanessa, Pittsburgh started looking even better, at least as a temporary option. David's mother, who still lived in the city, had just turned 80, and she would get to see her grandson more often. Pittsburgh had some of the country's lowest housing costs, so they would be able to rent a three-story brick house on a college campus in the city's nicest neighborhood, a place that reminded them of Cambridge, Massachusetts. If they got an itch for a major city, they were never more than a 90-minute flight from New York, Philadelphia or Washington, D.C. Morehouse called Burkle and agreed to take on the assignment for one year.

Pittsburgh had changed in many ways from when Morehouse and his family had first moved into a red-brick, three-bedroom Cape Cod in the city's Beechview neighborhood nearly a half-century earlier. He had been born in 1960, and they had been the only family on the block of Pauline Avenue without an Italian surname like the D'Alessandros, the Colosimos, the Salernos and the Tambellinis, whose cousins ran several well-known local restaurants. Beechview had been the kind of place where people had moved when they looked to escape the squalor of their urban neighborhoods. Eventually it, too, had become a destination for Italians coming straight to the United States.

Pauline Avenue had been thick with so many children that it could be hard to find a seat on the swings at the park near the top of the hill, and young people roamed the small neighborhood without their parents constantly looking after them. Instead, children had been free to run through the woods across the street, building shacks among the trees and warring with the kids who came down from the other side of the forest, among the homes on Palm Beach Avenue. In one memorable fight, a boy threw a two-by-four that struck the 6-year-old Morehouse in the forehead. Blood ran down his face like water so he could not see, but still he had not started crying until one of the neighborhood moms saw him and let out a panicked cry. Another time, in the fourth grade, Morehouse and his friends walked to the end of the street with older boys, hopped on a street car into the city, and went to see a wrestling event at the Civic Arena – all without a parent's supervision.

It had been here in the neighborhood, too, that Morehouse learned in grade school to stand up for himself: A bully had been harassing him for weeks, telling Morehouse that he literally could not walk in front of the boy's house. Then one day the bully stole Morehouse's baseball mitt, and that made Morehouse more angry than afraid. He punched the bully in the nose, causing it to bleed, and then Morehouse watched in shock as the boy dropped the mitt, crying as he ran away. "I remember when it happened, this was like a revelation: If I had just done that, I wouldn't have had to run from him all these years," Morehouse recalled years later. "It was like, 'Oh, that's all you have to do if someone is picking on you: You just punch 'em back and they don't pick on you anymore.'"

At St. Catherine's Catholic grade school, Morehouse had been smart enough to get placed with the brightest kids, but that group did not include all his friends, and so he did whatever it would take to fall back with the rest of them, goofing off and not paying attention in class. It was as if he could not slow down his mind enough anyway to keep up with the classroom lectures, and so he would daydream and then do poorly on the exams when it came time to recite what he was supposed to have learned. His ambition had been to grow up to be an athlete, like Johnny Unitas, who had come from a nearby neighborhood and then gone on to become perhaps the greatest National Football League quarterback ever. "I remember consciously doing poorly on a test so that I could move back into the group with my friends, and that was in third grade," Morehouse recalled. "From that point on, I was just like a kid who tried to be funny in class." By the second grade, Morehouse's parents had split up, his dad moved out of the house, and his mom started working six days a week, often 10 hours a day. In the late-1960s, older boys from the street would burn their draft cards on the sidewalk, and drugs started appearing in the neighborhood. Hypodermic needles turned up from junkies who had gone into the woods to shoot up and then dropped them on the ground. During a pickup basketball game one day, a not-much-older boy dropped a plastic soap box from his pocket and pills of all sorts of colors and sizes spilled out across the blacktop.

The most successful adults in Beechview seemed to be the ones with union jobs: the drivers for *The Pittsburgh Press*, the steamfitters, who worked on heating systems for commercial buildings, and the boilermakers, who ran the pipes for large industrial projects like power plants. Those guys were the ones with the nicest cars and the swimming pools in their backyards. After graduation from South Hills Catholic High School in 1978, a few of Morehouse's friends went off to college, but most just stayed at home. Pittsburgh's steel industry had started a freefall by then, and almost none of the young guys could find a job. Midafternoon any day of the week, guys would crowd into Pauline Parklet, waiting to get into a game on one of the two basketball courts. The games got so serious at one point that Morehouse used his free time to organize a summer basketball league, complete with T-shirts and neighborhood spectators. The group of players included Tim McConnell, who went on to gain local fame as a championship-winning high school basketball coach, and Greg Gattuso, a football player at Penn State who became an assistant coach at the University of Pittsburgh and the University of Maryland.

Morehouse figured his best shot at making something of himself would be to land a union job, too. A neighborhood guy, "Ironhead" Gualteri, served as the business agent for the Boilermakers Local 154 on Banksville Road, a main four-lane street heading into downtown. Gualteri had put many Beechview guys to work, and Morehouse hoped to be one of them. Every morning for weeks, Morehouse waited while Gualteri had breakfast at the Eat 'n Park restaurant across the street and then walked over to the union shop. Gualteri's brother "Tinhead" would tell Morehouse to get lost. Even if he was a guy from the neighborhood, they had no jobs to offer. Card-carrying members could not find enough work. Still, Morehouse kept coming, showing up every morning and asking whether they didn't have some job for him. The Gualteris finally got so sick of seeing this kid every morning that they broke down and told him to show up for a union training school.

Two years later, Morehouse was still working as a boiler-maker trainee when he reported for a night-turn job doing repairs at the W.H. Sammis Power Plant in Stratton, Ohio. He joined a group of guys working on scaffolding 30 feet off the ground. Lines of pipes had bowed, and their job was to tack weld them to a beam running overhead to straighten them out. As usual, none of the guys had tied off with ropes, because they would be moving around on the platform, and also because the union guys looked down on anyone who seemed that concerned about their personal safety. As Morehouse reached overhead with a welding lead in his hands, the lateral beam broke from its welds and started spinning in his direction. He quickly ducked, and his hard hat fell off as the beam flipped over and struck him on the side of his head. Instead of falling backward off the scaffolding, Morehouse collapsed straight down onto the boards. He woke up hours later, not remembering a thing about the accident, at a hospital in East Liverpool, Ohio. The doctor on call stood over him, asking him his name. Morehouse knew his name, but he could not find the words to say it. In a moment, his career as a boilermaker had ended. He eventually regained his words, but balance problems lingered for years, and he could not go back to working with heavy equipment in precarious places again.

If he could not get a union job, Morehouse followed the other leading path for neighborhood guys who did not go to college – political patronage. By then, his mother had been working in the Allegheny County Register of Wills office, and his uncle, Sam Tiglio, served as the Democratic Party chairman in a city where that's the only party that matters. With his mother ready to retire, the register's office had an opening and Morehouse got the job. "It was definitely patronage," Morehouse later recalled. At the same time, he cracked the code to his education, enrolling in the local community college and finally figuring out how to get A's: Pay attention in class, do the homework, and pass the exams. His first good grade had been as eye-opening as when he punched the neighborhood bully in the nose. Morehouse earned an associate's degree and enrolled at Pittsburgh's Duquesne University, but he soon dropped out before earning any credits because of a brief medical relapse.

An even bigger awakening occurred when Morehouse went to a political rally in the Pittsburgh suburb of McKeesport to hear the Arkansas governor who was running for president. Clinton was still running at a distance behind Senator Paul Tsongas of Massachusetts and former California Governor Jerry Brown, among others. As he listened to Clinton, Morehouse started hearing the call to action that he had been seeking. Here was someone talking about jobs – the economy, stupid – and changing the federal government after 12 straight years of Republican administrations. "I heard him and it inspired me," Morehouse recalled. "I thought he was the answer to what I thought was problematic in government." Morehouse went back home and started volunteering for the campaign right away, driving a van in the motorcade whenever the Arkansas governor came to western Pennsylvania and volunteering in the staff office the rest of the time. Someone there suggested that Morehouse would be good at doing advance work for the campaign. Morehouse had no idea what that meant, but the person explained that the job entailed traveling around the country to places where the candidate would be visiting and making all the preparations for the campaign rallies. That sounded pretty amazing to a kid from Beechview who had never really been much of anywhere. He used the connections from his mother and uncle to fill out his thin resume with a letter of recommendation from Pittsburgh Mayor Sophie Masloff, the city's matriarch.

When the campaign did not respond right away, Morehouse followed the same tactic he had used with the union job: he called every day and asked them to send him out on a campaign stop. Like the boilermaker union, the Clinton aides relented, perhaps just to stop him from calling. They sent him to Philadelphia as a crowd man, with the job of getting as many people as possible to turn out for the candidate. By now, Clinton had been nominated by Democrats at their national convention, and the general election race remained tight with the incumbent President George H.W. Bush and third-party candidate Ross Perot. Morehouse worked with college students and union members in Philadelphia to get out a huge crowd. He did so well, the campaign sent him to Cleveland a few days later, and he turned out another large audience. Pretty soon, Morehouse had gained a reputation as the rookie crowd guy, someone with a natural ability for bringing out legions of campaign supporters wherever he went. By election day, Morehouse had worked his way so far into the campaign's inner circle that he was invited to be in Little Rock when Clinton won the presidency.

In the heady days after the election, the campaign told him to thumb through the yellow book of Schedule C jobs for appointees, to figure out what kind of work he would want to do in the new administration. Morehouse chose the Interior Department, even though he had never been to a national park; the Defense Department, even though he had no military experience; and the drug policy office, something he knew about from his days in Beechview. When he showed up at the Pentagon for what he thought would be a job interview, he sat with seven other campaign workers. Each person was asked what they wanted to do. The first guy, a close friend from the campaign, picked legislative affairs. Put on the spot a moment later, Morehouse picked that office, too. In the first days of the administration, he worked on issues such as military base closures and whether gays could serve in the armed forces. That job didn't last long. With Clinton going out on the road again – now, as the president – Morehouse went ahead of him to set up events. The first trip was to San Jose, California, and Silicon Valley. Morehouse no longer had to generate crowds but now focused instead on getting the right backdrops and making sure the appropriate people were invited to participate. Almost anywhere Clinton went, Morehouse either traveled with him or a couple days before him. He saw the country and a good part of the world that way.

Later, Morehouse left the Pentagon for work in the Old Executive Office Building, next to the White House. He served as the deputy director of advance in the White House, and one of his jobs was to compile the manifest for everyone permitted to travel on Air Force One. It had been a thrill one day to call his mom from aboard the president's airplane – even if she did think it was just a hoax. With a White House access pass, Morehouse never grew tired of walking through the corridors of the building, and he passed through an underground tunnel on his way to lunch at the Old Ebbitt Grill on 15th Street one day when he saw a steamfitter welding pipes. One of Morehouse's buddies pointed at him in a dark suit and told the welder about how this White House staffer used to do that kind of work. The man stopped working, flipped up the shield on his welder's hood, and said, "Oh yeah, what kind of work did you do?" Morehouse said he had been a boilermaker. The man turned away and said, "Boilermakers can't weld." Never one to back down from a direct challenge, Morehouse took off his suit jacket, asked the guy for his welding gear, and then did a quick repair on the pipes. "So if anything ever explodes down there, you'll know it was my weld," Morehouse said years later with a chuckle.

During Clinton's first term, Morehouse also worked in the Office of National Drug Control Policy, serving as the director of strategic planning and the acting assistant director for drug policy. His experiences from the old neighborhood helped, giving him a passion for letting kids know the danger of drugs. He worked on promotional messages, getting the first public service announcements into movie theaters and hammering home the simple message about just saying no. When he was campaigning for Kerry years later, that job in the drug policy office led to an awkward media interview when a reporter for *Rolling Stone* magazine showed up dressed as a Viking and cornered Morehouse to talk about the work he had done trying to keep kids off drugs. Morehouse no longer worked for the drug policy office or DARE, so while the moment certainly registered as an awkward one, it did little to embarrass him.

Street smarts had been enough for Morehouse to go from working the night shift welding pipes in a power plant to working in the White House and then serving as the de facto second-in-command for the nation's anti-drug programs. When Morehouse left the Clinton administration in 1997 and went to work for DARE in Los Angeles, he had earned only that associate's degree from the community college back in Pittsburgh. Since then, he had counseled a president, run multi-million-dollar programs, and negotiated with some of the world's top corporate executives and wealthiest business people. None of those experiences conferred college credits, however, so Morehouse was startled when a close friend suggested he apply for a graduate program at Harvard University's Kennedy School of Government. Morehouse had written numerous letters of recommendation to the school, vouching for people who had worked with him – and for him – throughout the Clinton years, but he had never considered trying to get into the program himself. He had assumed that someone with only two years of community school education simply could not get into any Ivy League graduate program, and certainly not one as competitive and selective as the Kennedy School of Government. With nothing to lose, he followed the advice, studying for the entrance exams, writing the application essays, and using his thick Rolodex to submit impressive letters of recommendation. President Clinton agreed to write one of the required letters backing Morehouse, and McCaffrey, the nation's drug czar, wrote another.

Morehouse got in to Harvard, and then immediately started sweating about whether he belonged. On the first day of classes, he sat in a large lecture hall and listened to classmates introducing themselves. They included an Army general and a cabinet minister from Taiwan. Morehouse became convinced more than ever that Harvard had made a mistake, but when the work actually started, he realized that the same rules he had learned at Allegheny County Community College – paying attention in class, doing the homework, and studying for exams – worked here, too. He earned A's in classes on negotiating and leadership and received nothing lower than a B in any class. "I was so afraid of failing," he said, "I just put extra work into it."

By the time Morehouse came back to Pittsburgh in 2005 at age 45, the city was not the same one he had left. The smokestacks of his youth had been replaced, with one former steel mill turned into a high-tech corridor for leading robotics and software companies and two others turned into shopping malls. The Homestead Mill, once the site of an expansive factory that produced steel during World War II, was torn down in the 1980s and sold for scrap that could be recycled in mini-mills for new products. After sitting as a flat, barren moonscape for another decade, the land had been transformed into a lifestyle mall with popular restaurants, a movie theater and dozens of shops amid apartment buildings and offices. Many of the city's residents had departed, too: Pittsburgh's population had dropped by half from 660,000 residents when Morehouse was playing in the woods across from his Pauline Avenue home. Some of the first things he noticed about the old neighborhood around his mother's house were that the number of kids had plummeted and the rules definitely had changed. Few parents anymore would allow their 10-year-old son to ride the trolley into the city with older boys to attend an event at the arena.

Yet other things had remained the same. Political patronage still offered a reliable career for many young people with family members and neighbors involved in the Democratic Party, which continued to control city government. No Republican had been elected mayor since before the New Deal. The Grand Old Party typically fielded candidates who made strong policy arguments and considered it a moral victory if they picked up more than a third of the vote. Many of the people Morehouse had clerked with at the Register of Wills still worked there.

Morehouse's political connections remained fresh. Every time he passed through Pittsburgh with one of the national campaigns, he kept up his local contacts. Although Kerry represented constituents in Massachusetts, he had run his presidential campaign largely out of Pittsburgh, the home of his wife, Teresa Heinz. She had inherited a fortune from the Heinz ketchup company when her first husband, Senator H. John Heinz III, a Pennsylvania Republican, died in a plane crash near Philadelphia in 1991. Pennsylvania would be an important swing state with 21 electoral votes, so it didn't hurt to play up the connection to Pittsburgh in a failed attempt to help Kerry appear at home among blue-collar voters. At one early point, Morehouse had even talked with Pittsburgh officials about holding the nominating convention in the city that year, floating in riverboats to make up for a shortage of hotel rooms.

All of those connections back home turned useful again as Morehouse tried to gauge whether the city's hockey team could win any support for an arena. Burkle and Lemieux, in particular, believed that they had been promised public money for the building, just like the Steelers and Pirates had received for their new stadiums. The hockey owners had been unable to get politicians to put that cooperation in writing then, and after the owners brought the hockey team out of bankruptcy, no one seemed eager to help them any longer.

Part of the problem was that the elected officials who ran the city and county had grown up in an earlier era. They idolized the Steelers teams that won four Super Bowls in the 1970s. They adored the Pirates that won the World Series in 1960 by beating the Yankees on a dramatic Game 7 walk-off home run by Bill Mazeroski and then came back to win two more championships in the 1970s. Pittsburgh had taken its title then as the City of Champions. When Lemieux and the Penguins won two Stanley Cups, the older generations had cheered on the victories, but they had not cherished them in the same way. Bob O'Connor, a city council president who briefly served as mayor for six months before dying from brain tumors in 2006, had season tickets for the Steelers and sat with the fans even when he could have used a luxury box controlled by the public authority that owned the building. Born six months after the Allies' D-Day invasion of Europe in World War II, O'Connor exemplified this outdated thinking about the city's sports teams. When the Penguins' owners started making their case for an arena, O'Connor once turned to a reporter and said, "It's not like it's the Steelers." Another time he told the Penguins executives he wouldn't "lose one vote" in Hazelwood, a depressed city neighborhood in his council district, if the team left Pittsburgh. Hockey didn't matter to guys of his generation.

Another setback was that the politicians had ruined all of the public goodwill when they pushed through a one-percent county sales tax to pay for the football and baseball stadiums. Voters had rejected a referendum to use tax dollars on the buildings, and then-Pittsburgh Mayor Tom Murphy, the predecessor to O'Connor, had gone to the state capitol in Harrisburg and worked out legislation to use public money anyway. He compounded the public's anger at one point by boasting that the city had won help for the stadiums with a stealth bill that lawmakers had passed without knowing what the legislation contained. That ploy backfired, but the legislature came back the next year and approved stadium measures for Pittsburgh and Philadelphia anyway. The stadiums got built and the fans loved them, but many taxpayers never forgot the anger over how the deals had been worked out by lawmakers after the measures failed at the ballot box. After that, it would be harder than ever to get the public behind paying for another sports complex – and few politicians wanted to take up the cause of trying to persuade them.

A bigger problem for getting an arena had emerged in the years since elected officials said they would help Lemieux. The city did not have enough money to pave streets or pay police officers. "The city was broke," said Ken Sawyer, who was the team president at the time. "How could they justify spending money on a team or an arena, even though the old arena was on its last legs?" After decades of delaying improvements and borrowing against the future, Pittsburgh had allowed its debts to grow so large that they ate up bigger parts of the annual budget. Instead of lobbying for another sports palace, Murphy was going to Harrisburg these days seeking support for a new tax on commuters. Thousands of people came into the city each day from the nearby suburbs but they paid little for the public services they used. State lawmakers were threatening to put the city into receivership with two oversight boards, and Murphy's legacy as a three-time mayor hinged on coming up with enough money to balance the budget. If he would be pushing any secret legislation or twisting arms behind closed doors this time, Murphy would be trying to win help for a new tax on suburbanites and not a hockey arena.

The Penguins franchise failed to help itself, too. By 2004, the team had finished at the bottom of the Atlantic Division three straight years, never earning more than 69 points in a season. On top of that, in 2004 the NHL and its players seemed headed for a lockout. Sitting in her city hall office one afternoon, Councilwoman Barbara Burns explained that while she could see the need for a new arena, particularly as a way to help keep another generation of young people from leaving the city, she would not attempt to make that case as long as the labor dispute continued. With the potential for going dark over an entire season, the league would be unpopular with even its strongest supporters. That would not be the time to argue with an angry electorate about why they should help pay for a hockey team's new home.

Morehouse made the rounds among his political contacts, and he came to a blunt conclusion: despite what they had been told during the bankruptcy proceedings, Burkle and Lemieux could not count on any public money for an arena. "The one thing that I helped with was for a hockey team to understand that the political realities change," Morehouse said years later. "It wasn't necessarily that they were lied to. It was that the realities changed. They change every day. It wasn't personal. It was just that the city was on the verge of bankruptcy … and the landscape changed. So now the question is, what to do?

No public funding. (The Penguins) don't have the money. We hadn't made money since bankruptcy. And we know that we can't survive in the old building. The economics don't work."

That did not mean the team owners had no options. In a report to Burkle and Lemieux, Morehouse made his assessment of the political situation. Then he laid out two possible scenarios for saving the franchise:

One, the owners could simply move to another city that already had a newer arena or would be willing to build one. Kansas City officials had just decided to build a state-of-the-art venue, even though the city would not have a major league tenant to play in it. Other cities, too, would be willing to work with the Penguins.

Two, Burkle and Lemieux could roll the dice on using casino money to build an arena. State lawmakers had just legalized slot machines a year earlier, and bidders would be required to submit their proposals before the end of 2005. Television sports reporter John Steigerwald had first floated the idea of using slots money to pay for an arena but the proposal had not gone anywhere. Now billions of dollars would be pouring into Pennsylvania for casino projects, and each bidder would be trying to out-do the others and win the license in a subjective process. It would be the riskiest decision of all, but the Penguins could try to get some of that casino money for the arena.

3
The Next One
July 22, 2005

The Penguins' owners wanted out of the game. Given the long odds of trying to win the license for a casino and then using the profits from it to build an arena, they decided to take the easy money if it came. Ever since Mario Lemieux and Ron Burkle took ownership of the Penguins in 1999, their ownership group had been living almost year to year, doing whatever it took to pay the bills and stay solvent. One team insider likened the team's attitude in those days to "turtling," or pulling up inside a protective shell to keep from getting hurt. By early 2005, with no hope of public help for a new arena, the team's owners had become too frustrated to keep going.

That year, in particular, had been tougher than most. As a franchise in a relatively small market, the Penguins perennially lost top players to bigger markets under the National Hockey League's free agency system, in which teams could pay as much as they wanted to lure players away from franchises that didn't have enough money to compete. For years, the Penguins had been a team that simply could not pay the highest salaries. In 2001, the team had traded away Czech superstar Jaromir Jagr, a key player on the Penguins' championship teams a decade earlier, when it became apparent they could not afford to keep him. After trading to get him, the Washington Capitals signed Jagr to the league's highest salary ever at $77 million over seven years. There had been others: Robert Lang, a center, went to the Capitals as a free agent during the following off-season; Alexei Kovalev, a right wing, was traded to the Rangers in 2003 with three other players for four lesser-known players and nearly $4 million in cash; Martin Straka, another forward, was traded that fall to Los Angeles for two prospects. "The NHL was struggling with its economic structure," Ken Sawyer, who was the team president at the time, said later. "There

*When the Penguins traded star player Jaromir Jagr to the Washington Capitals in 2001, he signed the league's richest contract at $77 million. He and Mario Lemieux fight for the puck during a game in 2005, after the Capitals traded Jagr to the New York Rangers. (*Pittsburgh Tribune-Review, Chaz Palla)

was minimal sharing of revenues among the teams, and player salaries were going up at a huge rate every year. Revenues were not going that fast. ... These were our stars but these were things we needed to do. They were having great success on the ice, and the way the salaries were going, you just couldn't pay those salaries. You would be losing money and jeopardizing the future of the team in Pittsburgh."

Fixing the league's problem would not be painless. The owners wanted a cap that would limit how much even the richest teams could pay in salaries for their entire roster. Small market teams, like Pittsburgh, could compete if they made enough money to spend up to the limit, while those in the richest markets would be limited. The system would give almost every franchise at least a chance, and league officials figured that kind of parity would give more fans across North America a rooting interest in the games. Everyone would benefit. Players, however, saw that a cap like that would limit how much they could expect to be paid. Under the free agency system, salaries had continued to rise. Whenever a star like Jagr won a record-setting contract, some other player would inevitably come along later and receive more money. Even the players near the bottom of the system had seen their wages increase. That difference over money had created a stalemate. Unable to reach an agreement, owners had locked out players for the entire year. No one got paid for the 2004-05 season, but no one made money, either. It had been another year of financial losses for the Penguins owners.

During that dark year, Lemieux and Burkle had started exploring the idea of trying to find a casino partner, when they received an offer for a buyout. William Del Biaggio III, an heir to family money who went by the nickname "Boots," wanted to buy the Penguins. He had met Lemieux through golfing years earlier, and Del Biaggio had used whatever few connections he had to make bigger ones to get as close as he could to his sports heroes. Already he had been a partner on the purchase of a minor league hockey team in Omaha, Nebraska, along with Lemieux, Mike Eruzione, captain of the United States 1980 "Miracle on Ice" Olympics gold medal team that had defeated the Soviets, and Luc Robitaille, an NHL hall-of-famer who played a season in Pittsburgh and then won the Stanley Cup with Detroit. Among those guys, Del Biaggio often seemed to be more of a groupie than an actual investor. This time, he appeared to have the money.

With a purchase agreement to buy the Penguins, Del Biaggio set up an office in Pittsburgh at the team headquarters inside Chatham Center, an office complex near the Civic Arena that had been built around the same time and with similar ambitions. With a charming smile and the appearance of wealth, Del Biaggio quickly became known among the local doormen and waiters at local hotels and restaurants for his generous tipping. The first step in taking over the team had been to reach a tentative agreement with Lemieux and Burkle, and once that had happened, Del Biaggio had 30 days to work out the details for his purchase. By July 21, time had run out, and Del Biaggio still had not finalized the agreement. Everyone in the team's executive offices figured he needed just a little more time to complete the sale.

That same day, a Thursday, the NHL Players Association ratified a proposed contract that included the salary cap and allowed games to finally resume for the 2005-06 season. That moment, alone, had set off celebrations among the Penguins executives, because many in the front office believed it meant the franchise would have a chance to compete, no matter who owned the team. Pittsburgh still would need to increase its revenues to be able to afford spending up to the salary limit, but at least the team no longer risked losing players to another franchise that could spend anything to sign away the top talents. By Friday afternoon, the league's board of governors planned to vote in New York on the ratified contract, and then one person from each team would attend a lottery to determine the order for that year's amateur draft. Because of the lost year, the order could not be set by the previous season's results, with the worst teams picking before those who had gone the deepest into the playoffs. The Penguins had finished at the bottom of the league during the 2003-04 season, but that no longer mattered. Every team would have a chance at the top pick in a lottery.

Having the top draft pick always confers an advantage, but some years it can be more valuable than others. In the 2003 draft, the Florida Panthers had the top pick, but they traded it to Pittsburgh, which wanted to take Marc-Andre Fleury, a goalie with the potential to someday be a major presence in the net. The following year, teams vied for the top pick with an eye on Alexander Ovechkin, a Russian player considered the top in the world. Despite their last-place finish the previous year, the Penguins did not automatically receive the top pick, because the NHL had changed its rules for setting the draft order. When the team had drafted Lemieux in 1984, there had been unproven charges – as often occur in any league when a hot prospect is available the next season – that the Penguins management had set the team up to lose just to lock in last place, and in return, the top pick. The league had shifted to a lottery system in 1995, meaning that teams with the worst records would receive a high pick but would no longer be guaranteed the first choice even if they finished last. In the 2003-04 season, the Washington Capitals finished one place ahead of the Penguins but then won the lottery to get Ovechkin. The Penguins, instead, chose another Russian, Evgeni Malkin, who had come to the United States for the draft and then returned home to play for his team there.

For years, hockey insiders had expected the 2005 draft to be dominated by Sidney Crosby. Once or twice every generation, a prodigy comes along with the potential to change the direction of a franchise. Lemieux had been that type of player in 1984 when he came to the Penguins and helped transform the team from one with a rich tradition of rarely making the playoffs into one that won two championships and vied for the Stanley Cup almost every season for more than a decade. Lemieux had not carried the franchise all by himself, but he had been a catalyst for team managers to build around. A few other players had been like that in the history of the NHL – Wayne Gretzky in Edmonton, Bobby Orr in Boston and Gordie Howe in Detroit, among others. With Gretzky, who was known as "The Great One," the Oilers entered the NHL in 1979 and then won the Cup four times.[1]

Crosby had been marked as "The Next One" even before age 16, when Gretzky famously told *The Arizona Republic* newspaper that the teenager might someday break his records and was the best player he had seen since Lemieux. The recognition only helped solidify the reputation of a player who already had started making a name for himself on the ice. Donald "Dee" Rizzo, a hockey talent scout who happens to live in Pittsburgh's Greenfield neighborhood, first went to see Crosby when he was just 13-and-a-half and still had a little baby fat in his cheeks. A friend in Canada had tipped him off to the young star and encouraged him to come north to watch Crosby's team,

---

[1]   After Gretzky was traded in 1988, the team won one more championship in 1990, led by Mark Messier, but then did not return to the Stanley Cup final until 2006 when it lost to the Carolina Hurricanes.

the Dartmouth Subways, a midget hockey team in Nova Scotia, play against one of the league's better teams, the Royals from Calgary. Crosby scored a hat trick, and Rizzo struck up a conversation with the player's dad, Troy. The next summer, Crosby and his father traveled to Los Angeles for a camp hosted by Rizzo's firm. Only 14 at the time, Crosby ended up playing with older boys who already ranked among the best in North America. What made Crosby great was that he had a strong work ethic to keep improving, he made the other players around him stronger, and he had an innate sense for the game that only a few of the very best players seemed to possess. "I've only seen a few players in my life do what he does," Rizzo said years later. "Even at a young age, Sidney knows what he's doing with the puck even before he has it. I've seen Mario do that. I've seen Gretzky do that. Just a few. They're so far ahead of the game. He knows before the plays happen. He slowed the game down to where he thinks out exactly what's going to happen."

Crosby had a knack for winning championships, too. At Shattuck-Saint Mary's School in Minnesota, where he went to play against older and more-experienced competition, Crosby led the team to a national championship in 2003. The next year, he was drafted first overall by the Rimouski Oceanic, in the Quebec Major Junior Hockey League, one of three leagues that make up the Canadian Hockey League. In his first season, Crosby scored 135 regular-season points – the most in the CHL by a 16-year-old since Gretzky. With 168 points in his second season, Crosby averaged 2.51 points per game over his CHL career – second only to Lemieux. He was named the Canadian Hockey League's rookie of the year the first season, and he received the most valuable player award both years, while finishing as the scoring champion each time. His team record for scoring a goal or an assist in 37 straight games still stands.

Perhaps just as remarkably for his reputation, Crosby embraced the attention from fans. Late in his junior career when it became clear to even casual hockey fans that he would be the first pick in the NHL draft, Crosby showed up with some teammates in the arena parking lot one morning before an Oceanic game with boxes of donuts from Tim Hortons. Players had returned from a road trip to see fans lined up all night waiting for playoff tickets. For Crosby, the moment had nothing to do with his playing ability but said everything about the player he had become. "He's always been very mature for his age, being in a national spotlight at a very young age and being able to accept it as he has," Rizzo said. "All great players have a self-confidence about themselves. Crosby is not cocky at all, and that's the thing that makes him so great, but you have to have that confidence. All the great ones have that confidence about them. They want that. They accept that challenge. They rise to it. Sid doesn't say it, but you can see it in his eyes."

Because the NHL had not played any games in the 2004-05 season, every team would have a chance to win the top pick in the draft lottery. Every franchise received three pingpong balls, but then the league removed balls from some teams that had owned the top pick in one of the previous four seasons or that had made the playoffs in one of the previous three seasons. The Penguins were one of four franchises – along with the Buffalo Sabres, Columbus Blue Jackets and New York Rangers – that did not lose a ball and had a 1-in-16 chance of winning the top pick. Pittsburgh had chosen Fleury as the top pick in 2003, but it had traded up with Florida to choose him, so the Penguins were not penalized. Ten teams had two lottery balls, with a 1-in-24 chance, and 16 teams had one ball, with a 1-in-48 chance.

Still, no one with the Penguins organization came to work that morning thinking the team would win the Crosby lottery. It had been enough just to get the new collective bargaining agreement so that games would resume for the fall and the Penguins would have a chance to keep the stars the team had signed in the previous years. Sawyer, the team president, and Craig Patrick, the general manager, had traveled to the league's offices in New York. Sawyer had gone to the board of governors meeting, where team officials had approved the new collective bargaining agreement. Immediately after that vote, Patrick had gone to a secluded room where one person from each team would be on hand to watch the pingpong balls get selected to set the draft order. The year before, Sawyer had been the one team representative in the room when the Penguins lost the top pick to the Capitals, so the two men decided Patrick should be the one to go into the lottery room this time. Earlier that day, the general manager had stopped at St. Patrick's Cathedral in midtown Manhattan, as he does on most trips to New York City, and he held a four-leaf clover in his hand for luck. From where he sat in the third row, Patrick could see where the pingpong balls would come out of the lottery machine, but he started talking with the other team representatives around him and stopped paying attention to the action at the front of the room. He had no way of sharing the news, anyway, because the league had confiscated every executive's cell phone so the results would remain secret until a televised show later in the afternoon. If anyone in the room needed to go outside — to use the restroom even — they had to walk with a league escort to ensure no one would talk.

Back in Pittsburgh, team executives tuned in to the lottery broadcast to watch the results just like everyone else. David Morehouse, the consultant hired by Burkle to figure out whether the franchise could win help for a public arena, sat in a conference room with Del Biaggio, the presumptive new owner, and a couple other people, to watch the results. Ted Black, a team lawyer, wandered out of the office to get some lunch and then walked across the street to the Civic Arena, figuring players and coaches might be getting together to watch the results. The building was mostly empty, except for reporters holed up in the media area below the stands in the dark, concrete interior of the building. They were going to watch the draft on a closed-circuit television feed. Down the hall, Black found head coach Ed Olczyk in his office alone. In a twist of fate, Olczyk had been drafted into the league himself in 1984, two picks after Lemieux had gone first overall. Olczyk had gone to the Chicago Blackhawks, but he had played with the Penguins for one season and part of another toward the end of his career. After retiring in 2000, he had worked in Pittsburgh as a color analyst for the team's television broadcasts, and three years later he made the unlikely jump from the broadcasting booth to the players' bench as coach.

Meanwhile, the NHL had parked a satellite truck in front of the Crosby family's home. Knowing that he was a lock to go first in the draft, Crosby sat on a high wooden stool in the wood-paneled basement game room decorated with framed newspaper clippings and photographs on the walls. Rows of shelves behind him held trophies, medals and more photographs. He wore shorts and a black t-shirt with the logo for Reebok Hockey, one of his corporate sponsors along with Gatorade. Crosby had grown up dreaming of playing for the Montreal Canadiens. That team had drafted his father, Troy, as a goalie in the 12th round, also in 1984 – 239 places after Lemieux was picked that year. Even so, Crosby had an eye on Pittsburgh, too. He had skated with Lemieux the previous summer at a camp in Los Angeles, and Rizzo had been talking up the benefits of coming to a place like Pittsburgh, with a rich sports heritage and fans who had sense enough to give even a star some privacy. "Pittsburgh takes to certain guys," Rizzo said. "With his work ethic, I knew he would win them over. I know our town. I know we love guys who work."

At the same time, in the Pittsburgh suburbs, Lemieux sat in a doctor's office waiting room with his oldest daughter. He already had agreed to sell the team anyway, so he didn't plan to watch the draft lottery.

While the results were known to league officials, the NHL wanted to hype the draft order as much as possible on ESPNews and the Internet, to drum up interest among fans after not having any games for a year. The broadcast started with the bottom third of the draft order, with the last envelope holding the winner. Penguins executives watched with interest to see how soon the franchise name would be called out by Commissioner Gary Bettman and added to the draft board in New York. Sitting in the league offices, surrounded by officials from each of the other teams, Sawyer braced himself for the worst. "My fear at first was how disappointed I would be if we heard our name first, which meant we were last," he recalled later. "To me, that was like, 'That's not fair.'" Olczyk, sitting back in his office, had a copy of *The Hockey News* on his desk, and he crossed off the name of each team as it was called. During the commercial breaks, he and Black tried to figure out how the Penguins' odds increased as fewer teams with three balls remained in the running. When Bettman got down to the final 10 teams, the Penguins still had not been called, and the lottery started getting very interesting.

When the results came down to two teams – Pittsburgh and the Anaheim Ducks, which had two balls in the lottery – the broadcast went to a commercial break. Sawyer was invited to stand on a stage next to Brian Burke, the Ducks general manager, so the television cameras could catch their reaction when the winning franchise was named. Sawyer felt a calmness wash over him with the irrational relief of knowing his team had three pingpong balls in the lottery, one more than Anaheim.

Inside the Civic Arena's media room, television camera crews started pointing their lenses and bright lights toward team spokesman Tom McMillan, who had been sitting in the room to watch the results with reporters. At first, he couldn't figure out what was going on, why all the camera lights had turned toward him, and then he suddenly realized that he was the highest-ranking team official in the room, and the cameras would capture his reaction to the results – either way. He thought to himself, "Don't do anything that's going to get you on a blooper tape forever." Down the hall in the coach's room, Black knelt on the floor in front of a television with his fists balled, arms raised and face scrunched up in anticipation. Inside the Penguins offices, Morehouse quietly waited next to Del Biaggio.

After the commercial, Bettman stood at a podium in New York, held up a white envelope, and said, "The number one overall selection belongs to … the Pittsburgh Penguins," as he unfolded the paper to reveal the team's logo inside. Sawyer took one step back, almost as if he was falling.

McMillan, conscious of the cameras on his face back in Pittsburgh, stood up, pumped his fist and quickly walked out of the room before he could embarrass himself. A television reporter later asked him where he had gone so quickly, and McMillan answered, "I was going outside to scream." In the coach's office down the hall, Black reflexively blurted out, "We just got a new arena." He sprang to his feet, hugged Olczyk, and they started jumping up and down around the office. When Bettman announced that the Penguins had won the draft, it seemed like payback for all the years of frustration, a team insider said. It appeared to be a sign that Lemieux and Burkle had been right six years earlier when they took the risk of bringing the team out of bankruptcy with the goal of keeping the hockey franchise in Pittsburgh. Good fortune had finally turned in the team's favor.

At the Crosby home, the questions started almost right away about whether Crosby felt he could save the Penguins franchise like Lemieux had done a generation before. "Definitely there's pressure there," he told reporters in those first moments.[2] "My first goal is just making the team, and after that, we'll see how things go." Asked what he knew about Pittsburgh, Crosby, of course, mentioned Lemieux and how they already had practiced together. Then he mentioned Rizzo, the agent who had spotted him five years earlier and had become a family friend in that time. "I have a friend in Pittsburgh, Dee Rizzo," Crosby said. "Rizz, if you're watching, maybe I'll see you next season." Rizzo, who was following the Canadian broadcast on a computer feed from his home in Greenfield, felt stunned that Crosby had remembered him. Within 24 hours, more than a thousand of Rizzo's friends from across North America had called his cell phone and left a message of congratulations. "That's just the kind of kid he is," Rizzo recalled later. "He's a good person. You have to root for him, because he's good people."

Penguins officials, meanwhile, frantically tried to reach Lemieux. He had turned off his cell phone when he went into the doctor's office with his daughter.

Five hours before the televised announcement, Patrick had been talking with the people next to him when the actual lottery started. He did not notice that the Penguins' ball came out

---

[2] "Patrick: It's a very, very lucky day." by Karen Price, *Pittsburgh Tribune-Review.* July 23, 2005.

first until Lou Lamoriello, the general manager of the New Jersey Devils, tapped him on the shoulder and congratulated him. Patrick's eyes welled with tears as he looked up. After years of losing players that the team could not afford to sign to new contracts and getting less-than-equal trades in return for giving up stars, the Penguins had a chance for rebirth. "After what we went through – what the city of Pittsburgh went through – I thought we deserved that pick," Patrick said later.

After the draft, Del Biaggio ran around the Chatham Center offices high-fiving and hugging Penguins employees. The team he planned to purchase had just won the rights to draft a player who could change the fortunes of the franchise and turn the losing team into a playoff contender someday. What Del Biaggio had not realized was that his deal actually had just fallen apart. Winning the Crosby lottery changed everything, and it meant the terms of the sale would have to change. "The deal wasn't quite done, and obviously circumstances changed," Sawyer said. "This was like suddenly you were selling a piece of land and you just discovered gold underneath." Del Biaggio had a chance to close the deal before the lottery, but he had waited while doing his due diligence, and the opportunity had evaporated. One executive who walked through the team offices that afternoon and saw Del Biaggio thought to himself that the prospective owner looked like a fan celebrating, not someone appreciating that his purchase agreement had just blown up. It was almost a "be careful what you wish for" situation, the executive thought to himself.

Amid the hoopla in the team's executive suite, Morehouse quietly slipped away into his office, a tiny former closet without windows. He quickly banged out an e-mail to Burkle: "Whatever deal you had just changed," he wrote. "The Penguins won the lottery, and the player that is available is a once-in-a-generation player."

Later that afternoon, Lemieux found out about the draft results and finally spoke with reporters. He took a few soft questions about Crosby, about what it had been like to play with him at the camp in Los Angeles, and what it would mean for the Penguins to get someone of that ability to play in Pittsburgh. Lemieux understood instinctively what the moment meant. He had been through this before, as the player drafted to save a dying franchise. It was as if he were reliving history but from a new perspective, as the owner of the team in financial trouble who would have the opportunity to take the best player in the world. It would be remarkable, Lemieux responded. At the end of the interview, a reporter asked what getting Crosby would mean for Lemieux's ownership of the team. The owner chuckled, almost as if he had forgotten that he had agreed to sell the Penguins: "We'll have to talk to Boots, but we'll see."

Within days, the Penguins were off the market. Burkle and Lemieux had never talked with each other about what they would do if the team won the rights to draft Crosby. The odds had seemed too slim to consider, at least from the point of view of making a business decision. Sure, Crosby could end up in Pittsburgh, but it was more likely that he would go somewhere else. Even in the final moments, it had seemed that he might go to Anaheim. Then the conditions changed. "Remember the context," McMillan said. "Everything was bleak, bleak, bleak, bleak. We had lost a year of hockey. What's the future of hockey? The future of the team? Can't sell the team. Can't get a new arena." No one had dared dream – at least not for anything more than a private, fleeting moment – about what it would mean to win the Crosby lottery. Then they won it.

Independently, the two owners seemed to reach the same conclusion: They would make a play for an arena. If Del Biaggio ever had a real chance to buy the Penguins, the moment had ended.[3]

---

[3] Years later, team officials had to wonder whether Del Biaggio really ever had the money to buy the Penguins. In 2009, Del Biaggio admitted in federal court that he had falsified investment papers so it seemed he had the collateral to borrow $25 million to purchase a major stake in the Nashville Predators NHL franchise. As it laid out the case against him, the U.S. Securities & Exchange Commission charged that Del Biaggio had used investors' money as "his personal checkbook to pay home mortgage and decorating expenses, gambling debts, credit card bills." He was sentenced to eight years in federal prison and required to pay $67.5 million in restitution to his victims.

Penguins head coach Ed Olczyk talks with Mario Lemieux and Sidney Crosby during a game in 2005. (Pittsburgh Tribune-Review, Chaz Palla)

Sidney Crosby and Mario Lemieux share a laugh during practice at the Mellon Arena in September 2005. (Pittsburgh Tribune-Review, Chaz Palla)

Crosby's arrival in Pittsburgh also affected Lemieux as a player. He had returned to the ice in 2000 after a three-and-a-half-year retirement. Just as he had done the first time, Lemieux made his mark right way, scoring an assist 33 seconds into his first game. Lemieux had decided to come back to the game because he finally felt healthy enough to play again, and because he wanted his son, Austin – who had been born prematurely in 1996, weighing just two pounds – to see him play in the NHL. Lemieux also believed he could help the team. As much as his return would excite fans and help sell tickets, the decision had never been calculated to make money, insiders said. Before Lemieux could return to the ice, however, he had to receive the league's permission for an owner to suit up with his players. The NHL had only one requirement: that Lemieux could not trade himself to another franchise. During that first half-season back, the Penguins reached the Eastern Conference finals in 2001 and lost to New Jersey. But after that, even with Lemieux, the franchise had faltered, finishing last in its division and out of the playoffs in each of the three years before the lockout. If Lemieux ever wondered whether it had been the right decision to come back after his retirement, he suddenly had an unequivocal answer. Suddenly it all made sense. He would stay on long enough to play with Crosby, literally passing the puck to the next generation.

Lemieux reached out to Crosby in one other significant way. When he had first come to Pittsburgh and hardly spoke any English, Lemieux stayed with an American family that treated him like he was one of their sons. Lemieux paid the favor forward before, opening his home for a time to Fleury when he came to Pittsburgh in 2003. On the day the Penguins officially drafted Crosby a week after the lottery, Lemieux extended an offer for Crosby to come live with him as well. Unlike Lemieux a generation earlier, who had refused to acknowledge the Penguins when they drafted him, Crosby stood with the team and wore its sweater. He also accepted the invitation for a place to stay.

Despite the Penguins' sudden good fortune, the team still needed a place to play. If local politicians were unwilling to help pay for a new arena, the Penguins would have to take their chances on coming up with the money themselves. That meant rolling the dice on casino gambling. Now Lemieux and Burkle would find out just how far Lady Luck might take them.

4

Gold Rush
July 5, 2004

Pennsylvania Governor Ed Rendell sat at a desk inside the winner's circle at Philadelphia Park, wearing a sober business suit and tie. He had come to the racetrack 20 miles north of the city to visit the stall where that year's Triple Crown near-miss, thoroughbred Smarty Jones, rested in his early retirement. With one stroke of his pen, Rendell accomplished what so many people had dreamed about but no other leader had been able to accomplish – legalizing slot machines in the Quaker State.

Literally overnight – at about 3:00 on the morning of July 4th, a day earlier – state lawmakers had passed a sweeping piece of legislation that suddenly transformed Pennsylvania into the nation's largest new gambling venue, with up to 61,000 slot machines. The industry would raise $1 billion a year, the politicians promised, for pet projects across the state without needing even a single penny from taxes. The same residents who threatened to vote out anyone who called for higher taxes gladly would waste away hours in a casino with an electronic debit card plugged into a slot machine, with 55 cents out of every lost dollar going to the state and local towns. Some of the loudest complaints came months after the slots vote, when Rendell walked into a Pittsburgh bingo hall to call out letters for the game — and the senior citizens inside demanded to know how long it would take for any of the casinos to open.

With 12 million residents and two major population centers, Pennsylvania had long been in play for politicians and gambling executives eager to pump the state for dollars. As slot machines moved outside of Las Vegas and Atlantic City in the 1990s, elected officials nationwide could hardly believe their luck: by legalizing the machines, lawmakers could fill state coffers while keeping residents happy. The original idea had been riverboat gambling, under the working theory that constituents would be more tolerant of casinos surrounded by a body of water. The quaint image of Tom Sawyer floating down the Mississippi among paddle-wheeling casino boats had sold river towns throughout the Midwest on gambling, starting with Iowa in 1989. That the image had been perverted so that some of the newest casinos were not even on rivers but moored on manmade lakes, with each sitting like a castle surrounded by a moat, hardly mattered.

Riverboat gambling seemed to many like a logical fit for Pittsburgh. South of the city, the Monongahela River cuts through an industrial valley lined with the salted earth and hulking frames of former factories. To the north, the Allegheny River drops down from the foothills of the Allegheny Mountains through rural areas and Pittsburgh's tonier suburbs. At The Point, a prow of land where waters from the rivers mix, muddy brown and green, to form the Ohio River, early European settlers had come on conquests seeking to control the frontier. The French first built a small log outpost there in 1754, Fort Duquesne, and then destroyed the building as the British advanced during the French and Indian War. Military leaders believed at the time that the army that commanded the confluence also controlled western expansion, as the Ohio River feeds into the Mississippi River and ultimately the Gulf of Mexico at New Orleans. The British built Fort Pitt, a larger embattlement than the one the French had abandoned.

Two hundred and fifty years later, gambling executives had their own ambitions for the three rivers. Long before lawmakers voted to approve slot machines, Harrah's Entertainment, a Las Vegas-based company with 85,000 employees on four continents and revenues of more than $10 billion a year, worked out a deal for space at Station Square, a former train depot in the city's Southside neighborhood, which had been turned into an entertainment destination during the 1980s and now housed a Hard Rock Café and nightclubs. On the North Side, the owner of the Gateway Clipper, a fleet of tourist barges decked out to look like riverboats, bought up land for docking gambling boats. These companies had been pioneers, taking a risk by staking out land on an unfulfilled promise of riverboat gambling. The state remained through the 1990s, after all, a place where blue laws still prohibited residents from purchasing beer, wine or hard alcohol on Sundays or holidays, such as Election Day.

That all changed with the inauguration of Rendell in 2003. As a rule, Pennsylvanians do not elect anyone from Philadelphia to the state's top job. The City of Brotherly Love already imposes outsized influence, and the commonwealth's farmers, coal miners and industrial workers look warily upon Philadelphia. No matter. That sort of unwritten rule does not apply to Rendell. Gregarious and quick-witted, he possesses the confidence to take decisive action in a moment and to face reporters without flacks running interference, often letting journalists run out of questions before he cuts off their access. As the mayor of Philadelphia in the 1990s, Rendell used the job as a platform like no other leader of an American city. He embraced the moniker "America's Mayor" as he turned around Philadelphia with a close attention to cutting crime so wealthy suburbanites would feel safe staying in the city after dark, shopping at high-end stores and moving into new condominiums. With typical bravado, Rendell did all that as a reporter watched his every move, having granted complete access during his first term to a writer named Buzz Bissinger. The resulting book, *A Prayer for the City*, portrayed Rendell as a gun slinger with a natural talent for showmanship and a heartfelt streak of sincerity. Once, after the mayor had stayed up all night in his office to wait out striking workers, an aide cleaned up the spot on Rendell's sofa where he had briefly slept. Before reporters arrived to interview him, Rendell messed up the pillows again, knowing that his sleeping near his desk would show his commitment to the city and make a better story. Another time, Rendell drove out in the middle of the night to be with the grieving wife and children of a city police officer who had been shot and killed.

In Harrisburg, Rendell employed a similar free-wheeling style by setting big agendas and worrying less about the details or who would carry them out. His plans for the state called for massive spending on social programs such as education and children's health insurance, as well as on infrastructure for replacing rusting bridges and repaving potholed roads. He needed money and lots of it. In the past, those kinds of programs meant that politicians had to raise taxes and risk upsetting voters, but Rendell had an eye on gambling. In places that already had legalized slot machines, players felt almost better about themselves knowing that some of their lost money might end up paying for budget items such as new playgrounds and police officers' salaries. Gambling companies seemed to be willing partners too, so eager to rake in dollars that they would agree to give a generous share in tax payments to any place willing to legalize their industry. An elected official like Rendell could reap all the benefits of raising money with little of the negative backlash; rather than being upset, residents were likely to applaud the officials who made it all possible.

Pennsylvania actually came late to the game. After riverboats first appeared in places like Iowa and Missouri, other states followed with their own iterations designed to skirt existing rules and avoid offending sober-minded voters. At one end of Pennsylvania, Delaware allowed video lottery terminals at the state's race tracks. That state's constitution strictly prohibits slot machines, but these games were ruled to be an extension of the lottery – even though gamblers recognized them as slots. On the other side, West Virginia allowed a similar extension of the lottery, first at tracks for dog and horse racing, and then, in one small town, at small cafes where owners could install up to five machines each. Within a decade of legalizing the lottery machines, almost every laundromat, car wash and ice cream store in the mill town of Weirton had a mini-casino. Rendell's pitch was simple: Pennsylvanians already were gambling, but they were losing their money in neighboring states. If the commonwealth legalized casinos, too, more than $1 billion a year of that money would stay home, coming into public accounts through a hefty 55-percent tax on casinos, among the highest in the nation.

Gambling remained a tough sell. Over the July 4th holiday in 2004, while most Pennsylvanians were concerned with picnics and fireworks, state lawmakers huddled under the capitol dome in Harrisburg. Democratic leaders took a two-page bill on horse racing and replaced it with a 146-page tome that outlined every detail of what could become the United States' largest legalized casino district outside of Nevada. Opponents to the law tried to make noise, but almost no one was listening. In that vacuum, lawmakers greased a bill that would not only bring billions of dollars to the state but would also have the potential to make multi-millionaires of some well-connected political players. Philadelphia would get two casinos, and Pittsburgh would get one. Each of the state's six race tracks would get a casino. Two other licenses for large casinos with up to 5,000 machines each would be up for grabs at any other location in the commonwealth. Finally, the law included narrow language for two smaller casinos with up to 500 machines at resorts, favoring destinations in a rural area east of Pittsburgh.

To round up the votes needed to pass the sweeping legislation, lawmakers sweetened the bill with handouts for various constituencies. The language included money for lowering school districts' property taxes, buying new equipment for volunteer firefighters, reviving the horse-breeding industry with prize money for Pennsylvania-born offspring, building a Philadelphia convention center and a Pittsburgh hotel, and paying down debts at the Pittsburgh airport. The only major project across the state that lawmakers seemed to leave out of the bill was a new hockey arena for Pittsburgh.

Passage of the slots law set off a gold rush, with political insiders, gambling companies, developers, land owners and investors courting each other to see who could make the best marriage to win a slots license. Unlike states that permitted a free-for-all for everyone who wanted to open a casino, Pennsylvania set strict limits on the location, number and size of its slots parlors. Licenses would not be awarded to the highest bidders. Instead, elected officials would appoint a panel of people who would choose which companies would be permitted to build a casino based on secret, subjective criteria. Each license for a large casino would cost a flat fee of $50 million.

Suddenly, it seemed, anyone with a bit of juice in the General Assembly knew a group of private investors who wanted in the game. Almost every major gambling company across the country wanted a stake in Pennsylvania. The potential market could be huge. Even before slots were legalized, Harrah's had estimated that Pennsylvanians accounted for more than two million visits a year to casinos in other states. Philadelphia ranked as the nation's fifth-largest market, even though its residents had to drive over the border to Delaware or Atlantic City to reach the nearest legal slot machine. Rendell promised that keeping Pennsylvania's gamblers close to home could be worth $3 billion a year. Gambling executives seemed to believe the take could be higher.

That promise of big money brought out extravagant proposals from casino bidders. Las Vegas Sands – the owner of The Venetian, a $1.5 billion resort that transformed 120,000 square feet of the Las Vegas Strip into an odor-free version of the sinking Italian city of its namesake – wanted to build a casino out of the rusting hulk of the former Bethlehem Steel Works. In the Pocono Mountains, another proposed casino resort hotel would rise up 30 stories like a skyscraper from the rolling forests. Yet another plan would put a $300 million casino at the edge of Gettysburg's Civil War battlefield, drawing southern gamblers up across the Mason-Dixon Line. Celebrity bidders drawn to the state included developer Donald Trump, members of the 1990s R&B group Boyz II Men, Mo-Town crooner Smokey Robinson and the owner of the Philadelphia Flyers hockey team.

If the Penguins' owners hoped to wring enough money out of legalized slot machines to build an arena, they needed to find a gambling partner. Already many of the biggest names had been claimed or had settled on deals so singularly impressive that they neither needed nor wanted to partner with the hockey team. David Morehouse, the Penguins' consultant, came up with an audacious-sounding proposal: Any company that wanted to partner with the Penguins could use the team's name and fan base to rally support for its bid, but in return, the gambling company would have to pay for an arena. The gambling company's commitment would have to be complete. It would not be enough to pay a portion of the cost of an arena or promise future revenues, he argued. For the plan to work, the company would have to put up all the cash for an arena so taxpayers would not have to pay anything. That pitch would be so sweet, no elected leader could turn it down – or he would immediately look suspect if he did. "The goal was simple," Morehouse said years later. "Come up with an idea that was so good that no one could with a straight face say 'No' to it."

The Penguins vetted more than a half-dozen gambling companies as potential partners. Morehouse talked with Neil Bluhm, a Chicago hedge fund billionaire who already had invested in running two Canadian casinos and had his eye on building his own in Pennsylvania. The hockey team looked at Boyd Gaming. With a massive casino in New Jersey's Atlantic City, Boyd considered opening a Pennsylvania casino to offset its losses in case Rendell happened to be right about residents choosing to lose their money closer to home. Caesars Entertainment had been considered as a potential partner for the Penguins as well, until it was purchased that summer by Harrah's Entertainment, which already had plans for a competing Pittsburgh casino. The Penguins rejected some partners because they did not seem to have a legitimate chance to win, and others because they did not offer enough in return. One bidder promised $100 million toward an arena that was expected to cost $290 million, while another would have paid half the construction costs. Either would have left the Penguins still scrounging for more money. Morehouse insisted that the arena had to be completely free to taxpayers for the proposal to succeed.

One bidder agreed. Executives at Mississippi's Isle of Capri Casinos had been eager – perhaps even desperate – to expand into the Pennsylvania market, but they lacked the local connections of a company like Harrah's, which had locked up its location a decade earlier. Isle's executives had been opportunistic before. Bernie Goldstein had started the company in 1990 when Iowa legalized slot machines, and he had expanded from operating barges and recycling scrap metals into running riverboat casinos. A map pinpointing the company's holdings years later traces its roots, along the Mississippi River south from Marquette, Iowa, down through Missouri, Mississippi and Louisiana. When the company relocated its headquarters to the spring break destination of Biloxi, Mississippi, Isle became best known among gamblers for its red parrot logo and a commitment to bringing faux island life to tired river towns. By the time it bid on a Pittsburgh casino, Isle had been moderately successful, with 15 midlevel casinos in six states and the Bahamas.

With riverboat gambling at the company's core, Isle executives saw that a major Pittsburgh casino – bringing in an estimated $350 million a year – would extend their brand to the east. With that kind of revenue, company executives believed they could afford to pay $290 million for the arena and still make a profit on the casino. The development would cost a lot of money, but cash came cheap while lenders had billions of dollars and needed projects in which they could invest. By partnering with the Penguins and Mario Lemieux, Isle could make a unique argument, too, that its casino would provide an unmatched civic benefit. "It wasn't that much of a leap of faith," said one company insider. "It was going to give us a leg up on everybody else. We were solving these issues for the city and the state, and we were doing it by partnering with a guy who's got a good reputation."

The Penguins checked out Isle's offer and found that it had the backing of lenders who would make good on the promise. People on both sides of the bargain, from the team and the gambling company, believed they could make an offer no reasonable person, not even a political crony in the state capital, could refuse. "We found Isle of Capri, which was prepared to take a very bold step and say, 'If we get the license, we'll pay for the arena,'" said Ken Sawyer, the Penguins team president at the time. "Remember, this was the number one complaint: 'We don't have any money for an arena; we don't want public money for an arena.' So here was a group that said, 'We'll pay for it.' … It then gave us a pretty strong statement out there; how do you turn this down?"

Chasing that dream of steady returns, Isle's executives arrived in Pittsburgh on the winter solstice in 2005, touting a laidback outlook and promising an artificial paradise for the city's gray, snow-slushed streets. Sawyer and Isle's top executive, Tim Hinkley, met inside the team's offices at Chatham Center early in the morning and signed the agreement that would link their fortunes to the outcome of the state gambling board's decision. Their partnership, called Pittsburgh First, promised to build an 18,000-seat arena next door to a casino with up to 5,000 slot machines. The two buildings would be separated by a narrow corridor to satisfy the league's concerns about protecting the integrity of the game by keeping it distinct from gambling. To get the money flowing as soon as possible, Isle planned to set up a temporary casino with 1,500 slot machines in a tent on the parking lots next to the Civic Arena. The building would have a fabric roof with a real façade, looking to visitors like a permanent building. A third partner, Nationwide Realty Investors, which already had built a privately funded arena in Columbus, Ohio, proposed to develop the property under and around the old Civic Arena with offices, apartments, retail shops and restaurants. Twenty-eight acres that once held a maze of narrow streets alive with shops and apartments had been leveled for parking lots a half-century earlier, and it would be restored again. In all, the project would invest more than $1 billion in an area that had never lived up to its promise. "That was what I always pushed back on, an unqualified argument that was way better than anyone else's proposal," Morehouse explained years later. "It included jobs. It included tax revenue. It included development. It included an arena. It included revitalizing an area that needed to be revitalized. It included money going into a blighted neighborhood, not just around the development. And it included the taxpayers not having to pay anything for it. It was literally one of those ideas that you couldn't with a straight face, as an elected leader, say you didn't support – so the leaders who didn't looked suspect."

After signing the paperwork, the executives walked next door and rode an elevator to an empty office on the penthouse floor with windows overlooking the development site. Reporters, who had been walking around the room looking at renderings of the proposed development, started taking their seats among rows of cushioned folding chairs as Sawyer walked to the podium. A bank of television cameras sat at the back of the seating area on a riser, with their lenses and bright lights pointed at the stage. Morehouse waited at the back of the room, away from the cameras. After years of serving presidential candidates, he knew how to work behind the scenes to steer reporters with a bit of inside information or the right sound bite.

Without a new arena, the Penguins would leave Pittsburgh, Sawyer warned. With the team's lease at the Civic Arena about to expire the following year, it could start looking for a new home in just six months. If it seemed like the Penguins had a real chance to get an arena in Pittsburgh, the team would extend its lease at the old hockey barn for one additional year to finalize the terms of the deal. If not, the team could very well end up leaving with its young prospects and its potential promise of future championships when the rental agreement ran out. The arena would be the final piece, the missing link that would keep the Penguins in the city. Pittsburgh First would let that happen.

"Obviously if we win this license, it's not too late," Sawyer said in a calm, even tone that hinted at his Canadian roots. "We'll be here. Not only will we be here, but it will be tremendous for the city and for us. But this is what has to happen."

If it didn't, the stakes would be high for Lemieux, the team and its fans. Sawyer issued an ominous warning: He could make no promises about where the Penguins would be playing if any group other than Isle of Capri received the slots license. "If we don't succeed here, absolutely there's a risk this team will have to leave town," he warned. It had not been an idle threat. If the Penguins could not get an arena now – with taxpayer money or through the Pittsburgh First partnership with Isle of Capri – the hockey team would have to relocate. "The arena was the missing link that would keep us in Pittsburgh and also result in us making a commitment to Pittsburgh, which we wanted to do," Sawyer said later. "But we didn't want to make a commitment if we didn't know what our future would be."

Failure also would have consequences for the city, team executives warned at the unveiling. More than building just an arena and a casino, Pittsburgh First would right a wrong that had taken place in a community of first-generation immigrants, a place predominantly housing blacks when the bulldozers knocked down the first structure in 1956, a two-and-a-half-story brick row house at 1206 Epiphany Street. That morning at 11:00, city officials gathered to hear a brief eulogy marking the destruction of a building that had been erected just after the Civil War, and then headed off to the William Penn

Hotel downtown for lunch. In the wake of that day, thousands of people had been forced to move out of the Lower Hill District to make way for the Civic Arena and the development that had been planned to follow. The Reverend Jim Simms, a Baptist pastor and former county politician, stood up at the Pittsburgh First podium to project in his deep baritone what this development would mean for that neighborhood. He appeared that morning as a paid consultant for the Penguins, as someone who could present the neighborhood's perspective and reach out to the remaining residents over the plans for redevelopment. "The Lower Hill was devastated," Simms said in a preacher's rhythmic cadence. "The community was dislodged, and there was almost a diaspora of people who had to leave the Lower Hill. The Civic Arena now sits upon that site. We have an opportunity today to correct that."

Even if Isle of Capri clearly had the best plan – and that would be open to debate – the casino company would not automatically get the slots license. Under Pennsylvania's byzantine selection process, the decision would come down to a vote by politically appointed members of the state's Gaming Control Board. States such as Mississippi allowed as many casinos as the market would bear, creating clusters of competing properties in Tupelo and Biloxi. Other places auctioned off licenses to the highest bidder, letting market forces determine who had the most money to invest, or at least the largest appetite for risk. Pennsylvania lawmakers agreed that the board members alone should have absolute and final say – pending appeals to the state Supreme Court – about who would get each of the 14 licenses. The board's staff would investigate each bidder to make sure no partners had a recent criminal past and to confirm whether each group could raise the money to build a casino if it won. Then the members would choose whom they liked best by any subjective measure, and they would choose the winners in secret, literally behind closed doors inside a state office building.

Board members became king makers. Each slots license would be like a license to print money. The bidder, the bidder's children and the bidder's grandchildren's grandchildren could expect to make money in perpetuity from owning a slots license in Pennsylvania. State regulators estimated that conservatively the state would get more than $1 billion a year in taxes, and the owners would rake in nearly as much, paying their employees and operating expenses and then counting their take. To build support for his project, one bidder sold off shares as small as 0.125 percent – and, yet, by one estimate, that small shaving still might be enough for each owner to make at least $50,000 a year forever.

Because of that inherent power, state lawmakers gave a lot of thought about who would control the new industry – so that everyone across the capital would have a stake. Rendell, who had to sign the slots law for it to take effect, would get to pick three members of the new Gaming Control Board; leaders of both the Republicans and the Democrats in both the state House and Senate each would select one as well. Any decision by the board would require agreement among the four legislative picks and support from at least one person chosen by the governor.

The members came from positions of power. The governor chose an old friend from Philadelphia to serve as the gambling board's chairman – Thomas A. Decker, a lawyer for Cozen O'Connor, a firm with 20 offices across North America and one in London. Known to everyone simply as "Tad," Decker had received his undergraduate degree from the University of Pennsylvania, coming out three years after Rendell in 1968. Sharp and cynical, Decker kept members on task to rigid deadlines.

Rendell still had two more picks. He used one on another friend, Mary DiGiacomo Colins, a Philadelphia County judge. Rendell had hired her to work in his office when he had been Philadelphia's district attorney. She, too, had come out of the University of Pennsylvania, in 1970, and received a master's degree at Villanova University, where Rendell earned his law degree. Twice elected as a county judge, DiGiacomo Collins has the stern countenance of a school principal that no one wants to cross.

For his third pick, Rendell chose Sanford Rivers, an assistant vice president of enrollment at Pittsburgh's Carnegie Mellon University, who spent 15 years working weekends at a second job as a head linesman in the National Football League. He officiated at Super Bowl XXXIII in Miami and wears a championship-style ring from that 1999 game between the Denver Broncos and the Atlanta Falcons.

Members of the General Assembly picked the four remaining board members. House Speaker John Perzel, a Philadelphia Republican, chose the head of the Temple University Health System, Joseph W. "Chip" Marshall, who said he would keep his $740,000-a-year job and work for the state on the side. Officials in other states might receive an honorarium to serve on a gambling board (plus soup and a sandwich in Illinois, if the meeting lasts through a mealtime). But Pennsylvania paid each member $145,018 (plus $5,000 extra for Decker, the chairman). The board's executive director, at $180,011, meanwhile, made more even than Rendell or the state's Supreme Court chief justice.

House Democrats chose one of their own for the gambling board, state Representative Jeffrey Coy, who had served 11 two-year terms in the General Assembly before resigning. In addition to salary, each gambling board member received $650 for car payments. On Valentine's Day 2006, Coy picked up a new Cadillac sedan, with the state agency paying about two-thirds of each monthly payment. Other members picked out their own cars: a General Motors Yukon XL, a Mercury Mountaineer, a Buick Lucerne and a Chevrolet Impala, among them.

Senate President Pro Tempore Robert Jubelirer, a Republican from Altoona, in the western half of the state, had opposed the legalization of gambling. Still, he had to pick a gambling board member, and he chose Kenneth T. McCabe, special agent in charge of the FBI field office in Pittsburgh. Tall and broad with a soft voice and relaxed demeanor, McCabe resigned his post and took a slight pay cut to serve on the board.

On the Democratic side of the Senate, Minority Leader Robert Mellow from Lackawanna County in the state's coal-rich northeastern corner, picked a Scranton attorney named William P. Conaboy. He chose not to give up his full-time job as vice president of a company that provides rehabilitation and home healthcare services to disabled people. That ultimately turned out to be a wise move.

Pennsylvania's new slots industry drew hundreds of people seeking jobs, including Kevin Eckenrode, whose mother's cousin happened to be married to Conaboy. When he applied to the state gambling agency, Eckenrode listed the board member as a reference. Then after receiving a $33,000-a-year job as a press aide, Eckenrode rented a 23rd-floor penthouse apartment in a building overlooking the lights on the statehouse dome. In celebration, he and his girlfriend stayed up drinking one night, slept in late the next day and then went out drinking again that afternoon. When they came back to the apartment, Eckenrode's girlfriend wanted fresh air, so she opened one of the apartment's large oversized windows and climbed onto the sill. The temperature had cooled in the late-February evening after reaching into the low 50s that afternoon, and the clouds had cleared away. On the sidewalk below, an off-duty National Guard lieutenant was walking toward the apartment building when he looked up, saw a woman falling, and called 911. Police charged Eckenrode with his girlfriend's death, and a Dauphin County jury convicted him of involuntary manslaughter.

Conaboy resigned from the gambling board within a month of the incident. He was replaced by Ray Angeli, the president of Lackawanna College in Scranton, who also kept his day job.

The Penguins were not the only bidders for the one Pittsburgh slots license. Detroit businessman Don Barden had strung together a chain of casinos that included riverboats in Indiana and Mississippi as well as a building in Colorado and a highrise casino hotel in downtown Las Vegas. He wanted to locate a casino on Pittsburgh's North Shore, near the Steelers' football stadium. The Penguins had considered Barden as a potential gambling partner, but team executives believed he did not have enough money to build the project and no real shot of winning.

Harrah's, meanwhile, had spent years preparing to locate in Pittsburgh just on the chance that lawmakers would someday legalize casinos. The Las Vegas company had partnered with a Cleveland developer, Forest City Enterprises, which did not need the Penguins' help to seek a casino license. More than a decade earlier, Forest City had wagered on redeveloping the Station Square train depot into an entertainment destination with an indoor shopping mall, restaurants and nightclubs. The property had been a key part of Pittsburgh's recovery story, giving residents optimism just as its steel mills were closing. Harrah's and Forest City had worked out a deal then that if Pennsylvania ever legalized slot machines, they would make a play for developing a casino on that site. "It was, without question, a dream team," said John Verbanac, a public relations consultant hired by the bidders. "On top of all that, it had a location for a casino that, frankly, had been envisioned for over a decade. Those guys had the pockets and the perspective to go anywhere but really saw Station Square as Pittsburgh's place to play. ... I won't call it hubris, but there was a great deal of confidence among the Forest City and Harrah's team that that team and location would be successful."

Sitting between the Monongahela River and cliffs leading to Mt. Washington, a scenic overlook 400 feet above, the Station Square site had some limitations, but the two companies had cultivated connections throughout Pittsburgh and the state. The partners had been so successful at laying the groundwork for their bid that many observers believed they had the best shot at winning the license.

Forest City's holdings across Pennsylvania included two hotels, four shopping malls and nine apartment buildings, and it had gained a reputation for building or restoring properties when no other developer would get involved. The company remained a family-owned business, starting with Albert Ratner, co-chair of the board, Charles Ratner, the president and CEO, and five other Ratners serving as board members, executive vice presidents or both. Many of the company's private projects had a public component, such as tax breaks or direct grants, that helped the family leverage a profit from an otherwise uncertain situation. The family contributed, too, toward politicians. Pennsylvania set no limits on how much any one person could give to a politician's election campaign, and in the two years before seeking a slots license, executives at Forest City and an affiliated management company gave more than $140,000 to candidates across Pennsylvania. Before that, when Rendell first ran for the governor's office in 2002, Albert Ratner and others connected to the company gave him more than $100,000. "We're very active in making sure we've got good government," Robert McGurk, the company's regional officer in Pittsburgh, said at the time of the casino bid.

Now the family wanted to bring casino gambling to Pennsylvania. Under the terms of its deal with Harrah's, the gambling company would run the casino, and Forest City would own the casino license. At Station Square, the family had locked up another powerful local interest in the Pittsburgh History & Landmarks Foundation. As a measure of its influence, the nonprofit historical society had recently killed a proposal by the mayor to raze blocks of dust-caked storefronts in the downtown's commercial district to build a new shopping mall anchored with a Nordstrom department store. The nonprofit argued the project was heavy handed, and its opposition to the project gave credibility to a small group of property owners who wanted to hold out. Having the foundation behind a gambling proposal could be equally powerful. Around the time it had worked out the Harrah's partnership in the early 1990s, Forest City also agreed to pay History & Landmarks a $25 million endowment and $1 million a year in community development money if the developer ever won state approval for a casino at Station Square. The foundation became a strong ally.

Forest City also sought out two of the city's top Republican and Democratic political donors as partners. Even in a city rich with connected Democrats, Ratner found a rare partner in Charlie Zappala, someone with political connections and deep personal ties to powerful leaders. Zappala maintained boyish looks even into his 50s, with an easy smile, thick, dark-colored hair and tanned skin even in the depths of winter. His nephew Stephen had been elected Allegheny County's district attorney. Charlie's brother – and Stephen's father – had served as chief judge on the state Supreme Court, which would rule on disputes over the gambling licenses. On his own, Charlie had given more than $86,000 for the campaigns of mostly Democratic public officials in the state. With his wife, he gave $25,000 to Rendell in his run for governor.

Even in Pittsburgh, anyone seeking business with the state needs to know a few Republicans. The Ratners also reached out to a leading donor across the aisle – Bill Lieberman, a corporate insurance broker. Lieberman, who wears a gray beard and often a bowtie, had contributed more than $60,000 to Pennsylvania candidates. Most went to Republicans, but he also gave $1,000 to Rendell's campaign. Zappala and Lieberman each received a nine-percent stake in the proposed Forest City casino.

Even with their personal connections and close political ties, the Ratners still did not want to miss any angle, and so they brought in Steelers hall-of-fame running back Franco Harris. It's impossible to overstate Pittsburghers' allegiance to the player who delivered the most famous play in the city's football history, the Immaculate Reception. In a 1972 playoff game before the team ever won a Super Bowl, the Steelers were losing in the final seconds to the hated Oakland Raiders, coached by John Madden, who went on to become even more famous as an announcer and video game promoter. As time ran out, Steelers quarterback Terry Bradshaw heaved a long pass that went long down the field, bouncing off the shoulder pads of another player and flipping into the air. Inches before it touched the ground, Harris appeared seemingly out of nowhere, caught the ball off his shoelaces and carried it into the end zone untouched for the 12-7 victory. The Steelers lost the following week to the undefeated Miami Dolphins, but Pittsburghers remember that play as the moment that led to a football dynasty. At Pittsburgh International Airport, two statues greet visitors: one of a young George Washington, who led the British troops to the original site of Pittsburgh during the French and Indian War, opening up westward expansion across North America and giving rise to the city; and one of Harris catching the ball against the Raiders. Visitors often stop to get their picture with the Harris statue. The Ratners offered Harris a four percent stake in the casino and a job handing out $1 million a year in projects for disadvantaged residents, if they won the license.

Even to a casual observer, the Ratners had formed a powerful bid, with strong ties to casino gambling, state politics and local sports fans. But did their advantage go further than that? Sitting on a panel at a luncheon hosted by the Press Club of Western Pennsylvania, Pittsburgh Mayor Tom Murphy chastised the room full of reporters for ignoring the truth as he saw it. "It's no secret," Murphy said about the gambling bids. "The word is out. The fix is in, in Pittsburgh." Pressed to name the insider, Murphy backtracked. "And get sued?" he asked. Reporters in the room knew he meant Forest City.

The members of the Forest City group immediately felt the impact of what Murphy had just done. The group obviously had strong political connections to a lot of insiders among both political parties in Harrisburg, but the Ratners had been equally cognizant that under the rules established by state lawmakers, any influence they might exert would be prohibited by rules designed to prevent interference – and the penalty for violating that process would be severe. "We always viewed the reality of how politics intersects with gaming as a one-way ticket to a federal penitentiary," Verbanac said. "If you have looked at the history of gaming and its legalization across the country, wherever gaming went somebody went to jail. There's a lot of money at stake."

When members of the state Gaming Control Board heard what Murphy alleged, they wanted to know whether he had the proof to back it up. Decker, the board's chairman, McCabe, the former FBI agent, and Rivers, the NFL referee, went to City Hall within days. Sitting around a long table in the mayor's conference room, a ceremonial space with a fireplace and photographs of every Pittsburgh mayor since Ebenezer Denny in 1816, the gambling board officials demanded to know what Murphy could prove. Under the rules set up for the board, each of the members appointed by the legislature had to agree on a winner along with at least one of the three picks of the governor. If the fix really existed, McCabe said, he had to be one of the collaborators – and he did not know anything about it. He insisted they call the U.S. Attorney to open an investigation if Murphy had evidence. "You made this statement, so let's prove it," McCabe said to the mayor. "If the fix is in, that's illegal. I'm not going to be part of this." Murphy backed down, saying he had heard rumors but had no real evidence. He publicly retracted the statement and apologized. No one ever provided evidence that a fix existed.

The damage already had been done. Because of the sordid history of gambling and politics, any accusation – and especially one by an elected official at a public forum – created a stain that easily spread and would be nearly impossible to remove. The impact of Murphy's words was indelible. "It was stigmatizing from day one," Verbanac said. "A statement of that nature when it came to gaming was so easy. It was like saying a person with a vowel on the end of their name is a member of the mafia. It was so easy to say: gaming, big corporations, big money, the political donations – the fix is in. It was cheap and it was easy, and it was unfortunate." Some might have suspected the other gambling bidders had put Murphy up to making such an accusation, but members of the Forest City group eventually came to believe the mayor had done it out of his own affinity for building stadiums and arenas. Already the city under his administration had put up a football and a baseball stadium, and if Isle of Capri won the license, it could get an arena, too.

Like many others, Morehouse had heard similar rumors about Forest City. He did not know whether a "fix" could exist, but the partnership between Harrah's and the Cleveland developer had a long, head-start advantage in terms of making plans and getting to know political insiders. In a strategy memo to his bosses, Morehouse wrote that Forest City basically had occupied the inside game. The Penguins only option then, he had argued, would be to play an outside game. The team's fan base offered an opportunity that neither of the other bidders could match. If the Penguins and Isle of Capri could build excitement among the team's fans, they could pressure elected officials and, perhaps, somehow sway the independent gambling board as well.

"The idea was to try to avoid battle on that ground, the ground of their choosing," Morehouse explained later, "and to try to battle on the ground of our choosing. While they had the inside game, we decided to run an outside public campaign." He planned to take the lessons he had learned as a political insider and as a strategic planner who had earned a master's degree at Harvard University and apply them to the campaign for a slots license. The outcome of this vote would not be determined by an electorate of citizens but by the hand-picked members of a secretive board of insiders. Political leverage might be applied anyway.

"You pick the ground you fight on," Morehouse said, "and you take your strengths and maximize them and take their strengths and minimize them. You turn their strengths against them. So it's not going after their weaknesses. It's turning their strengths against them."

With his accusation in front of a room filled with reporters, Murphy already had turned the greatest strength of the Harrah's-Forest City alliance against them, making their political connections appear to be suspect. Meanwhile, Penguins backers on their own had started to build a grassroots campaign to bolster the strength of the team's greatest asset, its fan base. Two Pittsburgh men started their own website, SlotsforMario.com, where they ran a petition drive and organized fans to come out for protests and rallies.

Compared to the years of work Harrah's and Forest City already had invested, the Penguins were just getting started – and they would have little time to catch up.

5
Cashing Out
January 19, 2006

Darkness fell on Route 90-East Beach Boulevard where the pavement ran with the Gulf of Mexico on the right and Mississippi beachfront towns on the left, from Pass Christian 24 miles to Biloxi Bay. It had been half a year since late August, when Hurricane Katrina washed six miles inland with 120-mile-per-hour winds and a 27-foot storm surge. Power remained off in most places, and few lights showed from the calm waters or the communities of homes and businesses. Nine out of every 10 buildings were destroyed here, and daylight revealed one-story homes shifted off their foundations, with walls torn away to show the wooden framing, like skeletons beneath. Blue tarps served as roofing for many of those structures stout enough to remain homes. Casino barges that once brought tourists to drop their money in slot machines sat beached on the land, exposing their once-submerged hulls so that they stood four and five stories high. One barge designed to look like a Spanish galleon rested on the sandy beach, a ghost ship with boards ripped from its sides and its masts standing empty. A moonless nighttime hid the damage, with only stars above and occasional headlamps from a passing car.

In the distance, a lighted, seven-story red parrot clung to the side of a 12-story hotel, shining as a beacon to both tourists and locals. Below its feathers, light streamed across a covered driveway where valets stood ready to take the keys from drivers of cars, SUVs and pickup trucks lined up waiting to enter. Calypso music played from speakers built into the steel-framed canopy. Through the doors of that building, it seemed as if the storm had never happened. Rows of slot machines created mazes of flashing lights and a cacophony of beeping sounds. Vacationing seniors sat next to construction workers burning off a few evening hours after a day of laboring in the sun. Others crowded around the gaming tables or lined up nearby at an all-you-can-eat buffet with carved roast turkey and beef stationed next to piles of fresh fruits and a lush salad bar. Men wearing khaki slacks and island-formal shirts sat with women in beach-casual dresses at a steak restaurant that looked out toward a thin, tree-lined barrier island. A man who travels the country selling batteries, razors and odd items to independent convenience stores sat at the bar telling stories over icy glasses of American-brewed light beer.

Just 119 days after Katrina landed, on the day after Christmas, the slots came back on at Isle of Capri Casinos' flagship building. The casino featured 950 slot machines, 550 hotel rooms and two-story palm trees wrapped in white lights. Like the first seedlings after a forest fire, slot machines were bringing life back to Mississippi's Gold Coast. If it seemed odd that games of chance had returned when people across the street still couldn't move back into their homes, Governor Haley Barbour would tell you with a slow, deep Southern drawl that repairing the casinos first brought back tourists and jobs. The casinos were the ones that could access easy cash from lenders and investors without waiting for government help. That, in turn, gave local folks a chance to earn a living while rebuilding their lives.

Besides the casinos' economic benefits, folks cleaning up from the deadly, destructive storm needed a diversion. If reality loomed outside with seemingly insurmountable odds, the casino odds remained the same: slot machines spin through 2 million number combinations every second, paying out roughly 90 cents for every dollar played. For tourists, the money lost allowed them to believe they were aiding the recovery, too, and not just in town to gawk at the storm damage.

In the darkest moments, even as the storm lashed against their casino barge and filled the first floors of its land-based hotel with sea water, Isle's top executives already knew what they would do: rush back and be among the first to reopen at least a stripped-down casino. Tim Hinkley, the company's president, proudly told the story. He wore a red turtleneck and khaki pants, about as formal as the company's Caribbean dress code allowed. With gray hair, a moustache and round glasses, he looked more like a university professor than a casino company

Tim Hinkley, president of Isle of Capri Casinos, stands outside of the company's casino and hotel in Biloxi, Mississippi, in January 2006. (Pittsburgh Tribune-Review, *Joe Appel)*

*Isle of Capri's casino in Biloxi, Mississippi, stands next to the end of a bridge destroyed by Hurricane Katrina. (*Pittsburgh Tribune-Review, *Joe Appel)*

executive. The storm hit on a Monday in August and by that Friday, Isle made payroll to the two-thirds of its 1,200 employees whom it could find. The company handed them turkeys on Thanksgiving, and it offered them their jobs back by Christmas. The company's aggressively hopeful gamble paid off when it reopened as just the second casino to come back after the storm.

Hinkley promised that same attitude for a Pittsburgh slots parlor. If Isle won the license to open a casino there, he said, it planned to first put up a tent that would bring in gamblers within weeks rather than the year or more it would take to construct a lavish new resort. The company already had agreed to lease space in the parking lots surrounding Pittsburgh's Civic Arena. The games would be the same, and they would generate money right away – both for taxpayers and to help pay for the construction of Isle's permanent casino across the street.

Yet even as Hinkley stood on a parking pad outside the Biloxi casino making his pitch into a video camera, the landscape shifted again around the gambling company. In Pittsburgh, Mario Lemieux, the Penguins owner and star player, ended a team practice session by calling an impromptu press conference. He had changed his mind again. He wanted to sell the team.

On the morning of the announcement one month earlier, when Isle executives unveiled their bid for a $1 billion casino gambling complex in Pittsburgh's uptown neighborhood, Lemieux was supposed to stand with them. He had been there in the team's offices earlier that morning when the two groups signed a contract agreeing to work together through the bidding process. However, when the executives walked to the building next door and rode the elevator up to the penthouse office to meet with reporters, Lemieux never appeared. He had been there for a moment after coming up in an elevator with team President Ken Sawyer. Then when they stepped into the hallway outside the room where the event would occur, Lemieux felt a fluttering inside his chest. For months he had been experiencing episodes when his heart would unexpectedly start racing, and he had started feeling one at that moment. "Suddenly it came on, and he just said, 'I can't do this,'" Sawyer recalled later. "He was prepared to stand up there, but he got off the elevator and said, 'I have to leave.'"

Lemieux had been diagnosed with atrial fibrillation, a common irregularity of the heartbeat that affects 2 million Americans, but one also that would prevent him from continuing to play hockey. It turned out selling the team would only be part of the plan. A week after making that announcement, Lemieux, at 40, retired from hockey a second time. He told Crosby about the decision at breakfast one morning and then let the world know a day later. Neither move had been part of the original strategy to get a casino license, but many circumstances had changed in just a few weeks. At a press conference in the arena's Igloo Club restaurant, Lemieux said neither the sale of the team nor his retirement from the game should affect Isle of Capri's casino bid. It would not affect his commitment to the city, either. "I intend to stay here a long time, no matter what happens in the future," Lemieux said. "I'll always be a Pittsburgher … My heart is always going to be here." In case anyone still doubted, he reinforced his feelings one more time: "I've always been committed to Pittsburgh, and that hasn't changed."

Mario Lemieux announces his second retirement on January 24, 2006, as author Andrew Conte prepares to ask a question. (Pittsburgh Tribune-Review, *Chaz Palla*)

Lemieux's heart was no longer in the casino-arena bid for other reasons, too. Despite the overwhelming enticements included in the Pittsburgh First proposal – an offer that was supposed to be too good to refuse – few critical lawmakers had lined up behind the proposal. The elected officials who supported it immediately were the state lawmakers and members of city council who always backed the team. None of the major players – not the governor, the county executive or the mayor – had openly endorsed the Isle of Capri plan. They had not backed any of the other bidders, either, but none of them would provide a free arena. "There might have been some disappointment that there wasn't instant reaction by the governments," Sawyer said. "That was probably disappointing at the time."

Selling the team now also brought a financial motive for Lemieux's ownership group. As long as the team had some chance of getting an arena, even a one-third shot at winning the casino bid, the franchise had more value than when it had no arena plan at all. Before drafting Crosby, Lemieux had agreed to sell the Penguins for $120 million, and already some analysts believed the value had increased by $50 million or more.

Finally, Lemieux had vowed all along that he would not be the one to move the Penguins out of Pittsburgh if he had another option. He would rather sell the team, he said, than relocate. "I'm not going to be the one to move the franchise," Lemieux told reporters after announcing his decision to sell the team. "There's a possibility that could happen if we don't get the license and the arena doesn't get built." Sawyer backed him up at the time: "I hope none of you expected Mario to own this team forever. He's done more than he should, and more than he was asked to do, and teed us up perfectly in the community to jump in on a great opportunity."

Back in Biloxi, the news of Lemieux's plans came as a shock to Hinkley and the other Isle of Capri executives. They had built their proposal around a promise to keep the Penguins in Pittsburgh, and they had counted on having Lemieux as the sympathetic face for their bid. Now he wanted out, and that seemed to change everything. Sitting inside the steak house at his newly reopened Biloxi casino, Hinkley talked with a reporter the morning after Lemieux announced his intention to sell, and the gambling executive tried to put his best spin on the new development as the sun rose outside over Biloxi Bay. Isle's plans, he said, would not change: "The deal was always looked at from a long-term standpoint. It transcended ownership."

If Lemieux's announcement caused anxiety in Biloxi, it unexpectedly brought joy to Hartford, Connecticut. Nine years after the Hartford Whalers left Connecticut in 1997 as part of the NHL's expansion into the Sun Belt, the franchise – renamed the Carolina Hurricanes – brought the Stanley Cup to its new home in Raleigh, North Carolina. Alan Victor, a diehard fan, never really recovered from the betrayal. He and a half-dozen of his hockey buddies still gathered on Saturday nights sometimes, wearing their blue-and-green replica sweaters with the Whalers logo on the front and the names of former players on the back. That the team never won the Cup during its 18-year run in the insurance capital of the world makes its former fans all the more bitter.

It came as big news, then, when two of Hartford's biggest developers announced competing plans to purchase the Pittsburgh Penguins. Like the Whalers diehards, these men had remained hockey fans long after the franchise had departed. Unlike the others, they were in a position to do something about it.

Sam Fingold, 34, operated a development company in Hartford that embraced the kinds of projects that make local political leaders happy, once spending $45 million to turn a vacant department store building into student housing for the University of Hartford. Larry Gottesdiener, meanwhile, represented the sort of developer that city leaders can't afford to hate. He owned more of downtown Hartford than anyone else, with his empire covering more than 1.4 million square feet and valued at more than $500 million. Most of his buildings sit near the Civic Center, the Whalers' former home. Getting the Penguins for the arena would be the first step to winning approval for a new building and giving people a reason to stay in Hartford at night after office hours.

Despite their ties to Hartford, Fingold and Gottesdeiner started out by saying they would keep the Penguins in Pittsburgh – as long as Isle of Capri won the rights to open the casino. In that case, the team would get a free arena, and the initial investment would pay off for any new buyer who flipped the Penguins to someone who actually wanted to keep them in the Steel City. If Pittsburgh failed to build an arena, each developer had plans to move the team to a more lucrative site. For Gottesdiener, Hartford made all the sense in the world. He already owned the property around the old arena, and he had promised to help build a new arena if the city ever had a professional team that could move into it.

Fingold's strategy did not turn so clearly in Hartford's favor. He lived there but had grown up in Toronto. A lifelong fan of hockey, he had rooted for the Whalers but did not have a deep emotional connection to the franchise. When he looked at the Penguins, Fingold saw the team more as an investment, a way to make a name for himself while reaping untold profits from a franchise in a league on the mend. If the old adage about buying low and selling high were true, the NHL could hardly get lower, and the Penguins were among its lowliest franchises, playing in the league's oldest arena and regularly missing the playoffs. With Crosby on the roster, along with the other top draft picks that came from so many losing seasons, the team also had the league's best potential upside. If Fingold could scoop up the team for $175 million or less and move it to a city that cared enough to build a taxpayer-funded arena, he could resell the franchise in a few years and make a killing. In the meantime, Fingold could impress his kids while living out a lifelong dream of owning an NHL franchise.

Privately, NHL Commissioner Gary Bettman reached out to Fingold and told him the league did not want the Penguins to move anywhere if it could be at all avoided. No one from the NHL would say that publicly, but the back-channel discussions indicated that Bettman wanted to do everything possible to keep the team in place. Fingold was fine with that stipulation, but he remained unconvinced that Pittsburgh could find a way to replace the Civic Arena if Isle of Capri did not win the casino license bid. Even when Dan Onorato, the Allegheny County executive, called Fingold and promised money for an arena, it remained unclear how the politician would keep his word. "Everybody said, 'Yeah, we'll build you an arena in Pittsburgh,' but nobody was quite sure how it was going to get funded," Fingold said later. "That makes you a little nervous. The last thing I wanted to do … was move from Pittsburgh. It's a great sports market. In reality you wanted to stay there. The question was, how were you going to get the money to build it? At the time, Pittsburgh wasn't in the greatest shape and didn't have a ton of money."

If he couldn't get an arena in Pittsburgh, Fingold would move the Penguins to Kansas City. With the Royals in baseball and the Chiefs in football, Kansas City already had two major league franchises. That left the long winter months between the Super Bowl and baseball's opening day. Before the nation's financial crisis, corporate executives had money to spend, and Kansas City politicians felt their town needed a major league arena to fill the void. With the blessings of taxpayers, Mayor Kay Barnes pushed for a state-of-the-art arena with the philosophy that if you build it, surely some major league franchise will play in it. Business leaders had stepped up, agreeing to buy every luxury box in the arena, even though no one had any idea who might play there or whether they would be competing on ice or a basketball court. The building, too, had every amenity, from a shiny, reflective exterior that evoked a clean modernistic future to expansive spaces for lucrative concessions. Still, no team had come, even as construction neared completion.

Win or lose, Fingold figured he had a sure bet. If he could somehow buy the Penguins, the team either would get a free arena in Pittsburgh paid for by Isle of Capri, or if that did not happen, he could move the team to Kansas City with a new, free arena there. "My outside opinion is, this doesn't look good for Pittsburgh," Fingold warned during his courtship of Lemieux and the Penguins. "The old story of too little, too late."

Late in the evening of August 5 – eight months after the Penguins announced their partnership with Isle of Capri – Fingold could hardly contain his glee. He had just laid out a

$10 million down payment and signed a letter of intent to purchase the Penguins from Lemieux and Burkle for $170 million. In private, Fingold bubbled over with excitement about the opportunity. In public, he said all the right things to calm the concerns of Pittsburgh hockey fans, issuing an official statement that called the Penguins "an important part of Pittsburgh's sports landscape." Only if Isle of Capri won the license would they remain there. Around this same time, Fingold had been touring the Civic Arena as the prospective buyer when he stepped around a corner and ran into Kevin Stevens, a left wing who played two stints with the Penguins and who had recently been hired by the franchise as a scout after retiring as a player. Fingold bubbled over, blurting out that he often played as Stevens in hockey video games. Stevens cackled his distinctive high-pitched laugh. "I was astonished by the size of him," Fingold recalled years later, still savoring the moment. Fingold, as owner, also would be the team's number one fan. "Owning an NHL team is kind of like Xbox for adults," he said. "You know it would be kind of fun to play around. It would be fun to interact with the players. How much interaction you actually have, I don't know."

Across Hartford on the night that Fingold sealed the agreement, Gottesdeiner could console himself by rationalizing that these types of deals almost never work out, at least not on the first try, without any snags. He would have been right: Fingold ultimately backed out of the purchase agreement. He had come to believe the same thing that would scare off other potential suitors: the NHL planned to do almost anything to prevent the Penguins from moving. For Fingold, the NHL's insistence on Pittsburgh changed the stakes. He no longer had a backup plan with a new arena in Kansas City if Isle of Capri did not win the license. With that off the table from the league's perspective, Fingold saw that anyone who purchased the team would be left trying once more to negotiate with public officials for a new arena in Pittsburgh. Fingold figured those terms were too difficult, and he asked the Penguins' owners to give back his deposit. Lemieux and Burkle returned the $10 million and put the team back on the sales block.

Gottesdeiner remained in the hunt, but by now other bidders had emerged as well. All said they would keep the Penguins in Pittsburgh – if Isle of Capri won the rights to open a casino. Nearly every one of them also had a backup plan for some other city if the casino bid failed. Most bidders preferred to work behind the scenes. That meant the stakes were a lot lower if the deal fell through. As Del Biaggio had learned when he failed to purchase the Penguins before the Crosby draft lottery, sports insiders looked harshly on anyone who came close to buying a professional franchise but could not close the deal for any reason. By keeping their interest and the details of any proposal quiet, most bidders figured no one would know exactly how close they came – or not – to actually becoming an owner. Andy Murstein, the taxi cab medallion king of New York City, was not one of those guys.

Murstein's bid for the Penguins depended on building public support. Just as Lemieux had hired Morehouse to pry the casino license away from the state by enrolling legions of Penguins fans to sign petitions, show up at public hearings, and attend rallies favoring Isle of Capri, Murstein drew up a similar strategy. "I couldn't believe that anyone in their right mind was looking to buy this and move it," Murstein said later. "From the outset, we tried to separate ourselves from other bidders by stating that we would guarantee to keep the team in Pittsburgh." To buy the Penguins, he enlisted partners to help raise at least the $150 million he would need to make a serious offer. More importantly for his plans, he sought out high-profile investors who could build some excitement with the public. Although he was from out of town, Murstein had done his research and come up with two potential co-owners any Pittsburgh sports fan could respect: Dan Marino and Mark Cuban.

Marino had one of the few names that could make Pittsburghers scowl at the Rooney family, which owned the Steelers football team. Before heading off to break nearly every National Football League passing record as a first ballot hall-of-fame quarterback for the Miami Dolphins, Marino played in the Pittsburgh neighborhood of South Oakland, at a field with patchy grass, overlooking the Monongahela River and just a short throw from the Roman Catholic church he attended. Marino had stayed true to the city, choosing to attend the University of Pittsburgh when he could have gone to college almost anywhere in the country. There, in the same decade that the Steelers won four Super Bowls and the Pirates twice beat the Baltimore Orioles for two World Series titles, the Panthers won a national championship in 1976. Marino came to campus three years later and led the university to three one-loss seasons. As its credentials as the Steel City were just starting to fade, Pittsburgh took on a new moniker as the City of Champions. Marino, a hometown kid, was part of that pride. Players such as the Pirates' Willie Stargell or Steelers' Terry Bradshaw had come from out of town and made Pittsburgh their homes. Marino had come right off the streets and never planned to leave. However, the Rooneys did not see it that way, even though they needed a quarterback to succeed Bradshaw. When it came their turn to pick in the 1983 NFL draft, the Steelers left Marino on the board and took defensive tackle Gabe Rivera instead. Halfway through his first season, Rivera was paralyzed in a car accident north of Pittsburgh. Marino, taken by the Miami Dolphins six picks later, went on to set NFL marks for passing yards, completions and touchdowns. At the same time, the Steelers went 25 years without winning another championship. Steelers fans never forgot.

Cuban, meanwhile, represented everything that many Pittsburgh sports fans wished the owners of the Pirates baseball team could be: committed to the team and willing to spend almost any amount to win. With his black hair and tight-fitting t-shirts, Cuban grew up in the Pittsburgh suburb of Mt. Lebanon. Just 10 minutes from downtown, the neighborhood of tree-lined streets and Tudor-style brick homes has the reputation for being a haven for upper-level managers, lawyers and bankers. Not every top Pittsburgh executive lives there, but many of the people who answer directly to them do. Like many Pittsburghers, its residents are fiercely loyal to family and hometown sports. Cuban moved away, striking it rich during the dot-com boom, and then, in the fashion of every boyhood dream, he took the money and sank it into a sports franchise, buying the Dallas Mavericks basketball team. Unlike Ron Burkle, the Penguins' billionaire co-owner, Cuban let everyone know about his ownership by standing courtside in Mavs gear.

Adding Marino and Cuban to his team, Murstein hoped to stir Pittsburgh fans emotionally and to make it difficult for Lemieux to sell the team to anyone else if he wanted to remain in the city himself. Unlike the other bidders, Murstein was making a public stand in favor of Pittsburgh, suggesting that he would keep the hockey team in the city even if Isle of Capri did not win the casino license. "We knew from the start this was a good deal," Murstein said. "Pittsburgh is a great sports city and you knew the fans would support them. It had all the makings of a winner."

The Penguins never seemed to give Murstein a chance. As much as they loved using their own hometown appeal to try winning the slots license, they hated having someone else turn the strategy against them.

Murstein was not the only one seeking a hometown advantage, anyway. Jim Renacci, a former Pittsburgher who had moved to Columbus, figured his roots might be worth a discount when it came to buying the Penguins. Renacci made it big in nursing homes across Ohio, and he used the money to invest in an arena football team, the Columbus Destroyers. With his money and a sports team, he acted like a small-time Cuban. His team of investors for the Penguins included George Karl, a Pittsburgh native and coach of the Denver Nuggets basketball team. Renacci's bid was smaller, too – believed to be millions less than what others offered.

After months of false starts and public drama over potential buyers, Lemieux and Burkle finally felt like they found a buyer they could trust: Jim Balsillie, the founder of Research in Motion, the Ontario company that makes BlackBerry phones. Like the Hartford bidders, Balsillie swore that he would keep the Penguins in Pittsburgh under the right conditions. With his personal jet, Balsillie said he would commute to games from his home in Hamilton, Ontario, catching a flight after work, showing up in Pittsburgh in time for the game and flying home

*Jim Balsillie, right, the founder of Research in Motion, shows off a Penguins logo on his BlackBerry phone as Mario Lemieux stands next to him. (*Pittsburgh Tribune-Review, *Christopher Horner)*

that night. For someone with his money – estimated by *Forbes Magazine* at $1.7 billion at the time, which placed him among the world's 500 richest people – Balsillie said flying to Pittsburgh was no bigger a deal than a normal guy driving in from a distant suburb. To prove his point, Balsillie came down to Pittsburgh a couple of times, and not to sit in a luxury box, either. He sat in the Igloo's club seats, near the ice and among the fans. Few doubted, however, that Balsillie really wanted a team for Hamilton. Like Fingold before him, Balsillie reached a sales agreement to buy the Penguins and put out the $10 million down payment.

One week before state gambling regulators were scheduled to decide who would get the Pittsburgh casino license, Balsillie flew to Harrisburg to make a final pitch for Isle of Capri to win the casino license. Testifying under oath inside an auditorium at the State Museum building, Balsillie pledged his allegiance to Pittsburgh, saying he would keep the Penguins in the city if Isle of Capri won the slots license. "There's no wiggle room" if Isle wins the license, he told the commissioners, sitting on a stage at the front of the auditorium. "This gives ironclad certainty to everything. That's the beauty of the plan and the policy integrated. Yes, the team is there for sure. The arena is built for sure. We're there for sure. Everything's for sure."

Balsillie said he could not make any guarantees if either of the other bidders won. No deal had been worked out to pay for an arena without Isle's $290 million, except for some rough concepts. If a profitable agreement could be worked out, he would keep the team in Pittsburgh. No one could promise that would happen, but Balsillie said he felt "great harmony" with league officials about his plans to purchase the Penguins. On the way out of the hearing, Balsillie stopped to talk with reporters. He held up his personal BlackBerry to show that he had downloaded the team logo as his wallpaper. No one, he said, was a bigger fan or more committed to the Penguins' success.

Two days later, Balsillie was gone. He said he no longer wanted to purchase the Penguins. After the hearing in Harrisburg, Balsillie sent a letter to Lemielux and Burkle saying he wanted out of the deal. The team owners believed that he was trying to leverage a better price at the last minute. They also started to suspect that Balsillie's real intentions were to move the team to Hamilton as soon as he could. Lemieux and Burkle had been adamant that whoever purchased the team had to agree to make at least a strong effort to keep the team in Pittsburgh, even if Isle of Capri did not win the slots license. Balsillie said privately after pulling out of the purchase agreement that he had been concerned over the NHL's insistence on keeping the team in Pittsburgh. Bettman, the NHL commissioner, told Balsillie he wanted the franchise to stay. Lemieux and Burkle could agree to sell the team to whomever they wanted, but the deal had to be approved by the league and its 29 other owners. As Bettman went over the final details of Balsillie's purchase agreement, he inserted a new wrinkle: Whoever bought the team would have to stay in Pittsburgh until there was absolutely no chance for a new arena. If Isle of Capri did not get the casino license, the new owner would agree to let Bettman do the negotiating. Pittsburgh had proven itself as a hockey town in the early 1990s, not only turning out to support the Penguins but also getting its youngsters to lace up their skates to play the game. They might do it in Hamilton, too, but the league already had a team in that market — the Toronto Maple Leafs. Clearly the Pittsburgh fans would support the Penguins because they already had. Bettman and other league officials were not ready to give that up easily.

Balsillie figured he could not afford to cede so much control to the league. If Isle of Capri won the slots license, the team would be worth keeping in Pittsburgh, even if it meant he had to commute to games by plane. If it did not, and the odds were better than even that one of the other two bidders would win the license, the team would be worth less to Balsillie in Pittsburgh. The league's proposed strategy of insisting on keeping the team in the city and refusing to consider any other location would eliminate any new owner's leverage to demand help for an arena. Rendell and state lawmakers could simply continue to hold out, knowing the Penguins never would leave. Balsillie walked away from the Penguins.

Late at night on the Friday after Balsillie sent the letter terminating his purchase agreement, Lemieux, his lawyer-friend Chuck Greenberg and another friend Tom Grealish were e-mailing back and forth among themselves on their BlackBerrys, talking strategy. Lemieux had taken control of the team's destiny, deciding that he and Burkle no longer intended to sell the team. "We're feeling pretty good about ourselves, and the emails among us are flying fast and furious on the BlackBerrys," Greenberg recalled. "Of course, BlackBerry is owned by Research in Motion, which is Jim Balsillie's company." Greenberg suddenly realized the connection and sent a note to the other two: "You know, it just occurred to me, but RIM probably has the technology for Balsillie to be reading our emails right now." There was a pause, and then a reply popped up from Lemieux: "Well, Jimbo, if you're reading this…" And then he indelicately told the Canadian billionaire to mind his own business.

With five days to go until the state gambling board awarded the Pittsburgh casino license, Lemieux and Burkle owned the team whether they liked it or not. Selling the Penguins during the casino process had been a gamble: If Isle of Capri won the license, the team would be worth more than the $175 million anyone might pay; if it did not, and the Penguins had to return to the Igloo with its leaky roof, broken seats and narrow concourses, no one would pay that much money and the value could plummet. To split the difference for the guaranteed money, the owners needed to complete the deal before the gambling regulators chose a winner. That hadn't happened. Standing behind a podium at the Civic Arena, Lemieux said he felt shocked and offended that Balsillie had backed out of the deal. He planned to keep the BlackBerry mogul's deposit money because he believed the Canadian billionaire had breached their agreement. "The deal with Mr. Balsillie is dead," Lemieux said.

Gottesdiener, Fingold, Murstein and even Del Biaggio, along with a couple new bidders, said they might still be interested in buying the team. But there would be no time to reach a new deal before the gambling board ruled on Pittsburgh's one casino license. For now, Lemieux's future rested with its seven members.

6

Leaving Russia
August 12, 2006

Born four years before the collapse of the Soviet Union, Evgeni Malkin grew up in what had been a closed city. Designed in the 1930s as the Pittsburgh of Russia by Soviet dictator Josef Stalin, Malkin's hometown of Magnitogorsk was considered so vital to the Soviet empire that the communist leaders kicked out all foreigners before World War II and then prohibited them throughout the entire Cold War. Located near a mountain made almost entirely of pure iron ore, an oddity of nature, Magnitogorsk stands as a city of smokestacks and heavy industry, ringed by drab concrete apartment buildings filled with legions of workers to man those factories. Few Russians had access to Westerners or their democratic ideas throughout much of the 20th century, but the people of Magnitogorsk, near the boundary of what is now Kazakhstan and at the edge of Siberia, knew even less than most. Malkin was born into this grim, smoky place, but he had grown up at a time of *perestroika*, a period of awakening. First the Soviets lifted the ban on outsiders, allowing the first hints of the Western world to drift into this insular place. Then, abruptly, the Soviets disappeared altogether. The government-owned factories fell into private hands. The well-connected, who always had managed to get the best apartments and the thickest cuts of meat, started to become the wealthy. Capitalism replaced communism, and the children of Magnitogorsk could measure themselves against the children of the world for the first time. Their city had been built as a model of great American industrial metropolises, and its residents now wanted similar standards of living.

Malkin, like so many young boys in his hometown, dreamed of playing in the National Hockey League. Days were filled with playing hockey, and though they could not see any of the world's best players on television, boys seemed to know all the latest exploits of Wayne Gretzky, Mario Lemieux and other North American stars. It seemed every boy's favorite team, of course, had to be the Detroit Red Wings with its lineup of the "Russian Five" – Sergei Fedorov, Vyacheslav Fetisov, Vladimir Konstantinov, Vyacheslav Kozlov and Igor Larionov – who won the Stanley Cup in 1997. "Of course I read the paper, but we just couldn't watch," Malkin said in a rare interview about his childhood. "We knew the score of every game, but we couldn't see them."

Unlike almost any of the other boys in Stalin's steel city, however, Malkin had the ability to play in North America. His hockey skills had been recognized and rewarded in ways almost unthinkable a generation earlier. Ten or 20 years earlier – among his hockey-playing father's generation, even – Malkin could have hoped, perhaps, of playing someday for the Soviet national team. He might have joined in their closely guarded barnstorming trips across North America, proving the strength of the communist system against the finest players in the NHL. That would have been the closest he might get, and no more. Skating with those players, rather than against them, would have been unthinkable, except for those Russians daring enough to defect from their homeland. But Malkin did not grow up in that age. He had started playing hockey at a time when scouts from around the world had the ability to gauge his talents. By age 17, Malkin had become an international phenomenon, known to fans throughout North America as perhaps one of the greatest potential players of his generation. After the collapse of the Soviet Union in 1991, Russian hockey players could go anywhere in the world and many of them did, choosing to join NHL teams rather than staying close to home.

For all that evolution, Malkin could have been forgiven for feeling that time had turned back to the Cold War days of his parents as he landed at the international airport in Helsinki, Finland, on August 12, 2006.

Malkin had arrived in Finland with his hometown hockey team, Metallurg Magnitogorsk, the Steelers of Russia's Ural Mountains. He had grown up with this team through his teenage years, playing so long for the franchise that its managers seemed like his own family. Both his father and his brother had played for the organization, so, in fact, Malkin had blood ties to the Metallurg, too. Now that his team had come to Finland for a series of warm-up matchups before the start of the Russian Superleague season, Malkin prepared to walk away from this birthright.

Already he had been drafted to play in the NHL for the Pittsburgh Penguins – but the Metallurg had his passport, so he had been unable to simply catch a plane and leave on his own. Now as more than two dozen players and coaches disembarked from the plane, the team had to give every player his passport to move through customs. Malkin held his papers tightly in his hand as he picked up his bags and then officially crossed over onto Finnish soil. On the outside, he appeared to all as if nothing had changed. Inside, his heart raced at the thought that nothing would ever be the same.

Safely inside the airport terminal, Malkin slowly dropped back as his teammates headed for a bus that would carry them to the hotel where they would be staying. As they walked out of the building united in jocular banter, Malkin simply turned away. His Canadian agent waited nearby with a Russian-to-English translator. The player quickly found them, and together they ducked out of the airport into a waiting car and then disappeared. For five days, Malkin and his small entourage hid in a rented apartment under the watchful eyes of bodyguards, waiting. The Russian needed a visa to enter the United States, but he would not be able to request one until the embassy opened on Monday morning. Until then, he would wait with his cell phone turned off and no safe way to communicate with the outside world without giving away his escape plans. He watched Finnish television and scanned the Internet for stories about his disappearance.

Seven time zones away, a bleary-eyed Penguins executive woke up at his house in the Pittsburgh suburbs. Reports out of Russia had been conflicted in recent days, with some saying the Penguins second overall draft pick wanted to stay with his team in Magnitogorsk and others saying he had quit to play for Pittsburgh. The executive went to his laptop computer and started looking at the Penguins fan chat rooms. NHL hockey had become a favorite sport in Eastern Europe after the fall of communism, and the Penguins had Russian fans who would translate the country's newspaper headlines and post them in English. Right away, the executive found the latest news: the Metallurg had landed in Finland – and Malkin was missing. The executive called out in excitement to his wife in the other room: "I can't believe they did it."

Even as he was drafted into the NHL two years earlier, Malkin had trouble realizing the dream. First, he missed the NHL combine for prospective players in Toronto because it conflicted with his team's post-season training in Turkey. Then, when he traveled three hours by plane with his family to the United States Embassy in Moscow to pick up their entry visas, they learned the American government had blocked their visit. Paperwork had been misplaced or lost. The trip would be delayed a few more days, until his agents resubmitted the paperwork after a weekend of uncertainty and found a compliant embassy official who happened to be a casual fan of hockey.

When he finally arrived in Raleigh, North Carolina, for the draft, Malkin had a video camera in hand to capture every moment but he still did not know exactly where he might play someday. He was almost certain he would go second – after the overwhelming favorite, Alexander Ovechkin, a fellow Russian. That meant he would most likely end up in Pittsburgh, if the Penguins wanted him. The team had finished last in the NHL standings the previous year, winning just 23 games and collecting 58 points, one fewer than either the Washington Capitals or the Chicago Blackhawks. That gave the Pens an almost 50 percent chance of winning the top pick. Instead, the Washington Capitals, with a 14.2 percent chance, won the first choice. Because they could not fall more than one slot, the Penguins ended up choosing second. In a twist of fate, that slip in the draft later benefitted the team more than anyone knew at the time: The following year, after the NHL lockout, the Penguins were awarded the greatest chance of winning the top pick, because they had fallen out of first place in 2004. That meant they had a better chance of drafting Sidney Crosby than if they had gotten Ovechkin the previous year.

Better yet, scouts already were predicting that the second pick in the 2004 draft could turn out to be as good or, perhaps in the long term, even better than the first. "We lost the lottery, but we knew that year there were two players, 1 and 1-A," said Ken Sawyer, who was the Penguins team president at the time. "We couldn't go wrong. So we drafted Malkin. Now getting him over here wasn't going to be something that was easy or immediate. But we certainly knew we had a superstar in the making."

Malkin was so lanky – officially 6 feet, four inches and 200 pounds – that reporters marveled at how he had possibly come from his two diminutive parents. They, in turn, marveled at their son's chances, wherever he was drafted. Less than 24 hours before the draft, Vladimir Malkin and his wife sat at a glitzy reception for their son and other prospects, where agents handed out small gifts such as a camera, cell phone and a Sony Playstation 2. It hadn't seemed so long ago, they said, that their son had been sleeping with a hockey stick in his bed at age 3, or that at age 12 he had broken his leg and then removed the cast on his own so he could play in a tournament without his doctor's permission. "That's just an example of how passionate he is," they told a reporter. [1] "It brings tears to our eyes."

Despite rumors that persisted until the morning of the draft, the Penguins did not trade away their pick and took Malkin with little suspense or drama. No matter what happened that season in the NHL, Malkin planned a return to his team in the Ural Mountains. He needed at least another year playing with his countrymen before coming to Pittsburgh. As it turned out, Ovechkin returned to Russia, too, as all the draft picks – along with dozens of NHL veterans – looked for places to play during the 2004-05 season lockout, a first for any of North America's major professional sports leagues. Malkin had not gone to the NHL, but suddenly the league came to him. Sergei Gonchar, a Russian defenseman who had played for the Wash-

---

[1] "Malkin family soaking up every minute." by Karen Price, *Pittsburgh Tribune-Review*. Saturday, June 26, 2004.

ington Capitals and Boston Bruins, signed with the Metallurg during the lockout, along with Petr Sykora, a Czech right wing who already had won the Stanley Cup with New Jersey.

The next year, when those NHL players returned to North America, Malkin stayed behind. Still committed to his home-town team, he missed the chance to compete with Ovechkin and Crosby for rookie-of-the-year honors in the 2005-06 season. The Penguins had not been too concerned about Malkin's decision to stay in Russia for another winter, figuring it would give him more time to develop into an NHL-caliber player. Dave King, a Canadian who coached Malkin for the Metallurg, wrote a book about the experience and said it had been a wise move for Pittsburgh to let their draft pick stay in Russia to continue growing without the pressure of the NHL and playing so far from home. Although Gonchar and Sykora were gone, two former NHL players, Dmitri Yushkevich, who had been drafted by the Flyers in 1991, and Igor Korolev, who had been drafted by the St. Louis Blues the following season, had signed with the Metallurg. They became like big brothers to Malkin in his hockey growth. "They were constantly helping Malk with his game," King said. "Like, 'If you're gonna play there, Malk, you've got to do this, you've got to do that, you've got to be good at this.' So it was a really good situation for him." That season with the Magnitogorsk, Malkin played 46 games, scoring 21 goals and earning 26 assists.

The Penguins were not quite ready for Malkin, anyway. The team had miscalculated the impact of the year-long lockout on the speed of the game, and executives had not retooled enough to build a faster, leaner roster to complement the skills of their new star, Crosby. The year had been complicated, too, by Lemieux's unexpected retirement halfway through the season. The Pens won only 22 games that year and finished with 58 points, the league's second-worst record, just ahead of St. Louis. It had been, in the words of one beat reporter, "one disaster after another."

Instead, Malkin stayed in Magnitogorsk, unable to leave for fear of letting down his family, his friends and the team owners. They had encouraged him to stay with the promise that if he played just one more year with the Metallurg, they would let him go to the United States. The reality was that

Malkin had come of age at a time when Russian capitalists had started amassing huge sums of wealth, and his country-men were growing tired of seeing their best players leave the country to play for the NHL. Russian ice hockey had never been a minor league for North America, but ever since the collapse of the Soviet Union, that's exactly what had happened. As long as Russia's oligarchs, or wealthy businessmen, had bank accounts as large or larger than their American counterparts, they wanted to compete for their country's top hockey talent.

Malkin might have made more money in Russia, but he wanted to play in the NHL and to be around the world's best players. King said Malkin's expectations were raised again after he played on the Russian national team in the winter Olympics at Turin, Italy, in February 2006. "He learned a lot of things at the Olympics and saw the North American players so motivated, so focused," King said in an interview. "It was just a real good situation for Malk to understand there is another level and that's a great level to be at. To be on the ice and competing against these guys, I'm sure he thought, 'Geez, this is where I have to be. This is another cut above.'"

Malkin said years later that he had been surprised the Russian coach had selected him for the national team, and then he had wandered around the Olympic village with his mouth hanging open at the spectacle of the international event and the opportunity to meet so many top players. The moment had been so overwhelming that it almost seemed scary. "Everything was a surprise for me," Malkin said. "I was not understanding what was going on and not understanding the Olympics." The experience had a lasting impact on his perception of what it would take to compete if he ever made it to North America. The Russians lasted as far as the semifinals and finished in fourth place, but it had seemed to Malkin that the players had had a great chance to win, and it gave him a taste for playing among the best.

The issue of Malkin coming to the United States had been complicated by the lack of a transfer agreement between the NHL and team owners in Russia: a standing policy for transferring players from the Ice Hockey Federation of Russia expired in August 2006. That eliminated any chance for a routine exchange between Malkin's old team and his new one. It also allowed for uncertain expectations by the owners of the Metallurg. They did not want to lose their top star, and if they did, they certainly expected to be compensated for the loss.

Four days after the transfer agreement expired on August 2, the Metallurg team owners invited Malkin and his parents to a 9 p.m. meeting with team officials at a lakeside business center outside of Magnitogorsk.[2] There the team's president, Viktor Rashnikov, appealed to Malkin's nationalistic pride and his loyalty to his hometown in a desperate bid to keep him playing in the Russian Superleague just one more year. When he refused, Rashnikov thanked Malkin and his family and left the room. But when the family walked outside to head back to their apartment, the team president stood there waiting for them. Rashnikov suggested that he and another team official return home with Malkin and his family to continue the negotiations at their apartment. It was an offer the Malkins apparently could not refuse. "They didn't want to give up," Malkin told a reporter after the ordeal. "They hoped very much that the contract would be signed at that point at our house."

And so the talks continued, late into the night and early into the next morning. Malkin's agents in the United States knew the player was supposed to meet the Metallurg officials earlier in the evening, and when they tried to reach the family to see how the talks had gone, they got Malkin's mother on the phone. She whispered that she could not speak louder because the Metallurg managers were in the next room with her son. The agent pleaded with her to tell Malkin that he could simply walk away from the negotiations, but she did not intervene. In the family's living room, Gennady Velichkin, the Metallurg's general director, talked with Malkin and implored him to reconsider his plans to leave for America. He played to Malkin's feelings of loyalty to his hometown team, the one that had first recognized his talent and had then turned him into an international superstar. The Metallurg had just built a new arena, and Malkin could make it his own. In the modern Russia, play-

[2]   This narrative draws on an exclusive interview conducted with Malkin by Karen Price of the *Pittsburgh Tribune-Review* in late August 2006. Price was the first American reporter to speak with Malkin after he arrived in the United States that month.

ers no longer had to leave the country to realize their ambitions for sports domination. Malkin could stay in Magnitogorsk and still build his reputation. "I think he felt so obligated," King said in an interview. "You know how people can lay the guilts on you: 'You owe us something. We put a lot of time and money into you. We have a new arena. We really need you.' I don't blame the people in Magnitogorsk. He was an important guy to that team, and they wanted him back."

The talks continued like that until 2:30 in the morning. Malkin finally cracked. He gave in to the demands and signed a contract to stay one more year with the Metallurg. As the team officials left his family's apartment, Malkin walked into his bedroom with tears in his eyes. "I was very upset," Malkin recalled later, "because it was not my choice to sign that year with Magnitogorsk." He had simply weakened under the constant pressure from team's owners and executives who made their case every day, telling Malkin that even if he left for North America, the Penguins never would let him play in the NHL.

The next morning, Malkin realized that he could not go through with the commitment he had made. King, the Metallurg's Canadian coach, said he had expected Malkin to leave for the NHL and had been surprised, too, by his decision to sign a contract extension. Malkin had signed the agreement in the early hours after midnight, and later that day he went into the Metallurg offices to meet with King. "I was very surprised he was staying, and I could tell right away he wasn't real happy. He wasn't Malk. He was usually a happy guy with a big smile, and on our team he was really a guy with lots of humor, a really upbeat guy. You could tell he was troubled."

Also that morning, Malkin reached out to Gonchar, the defenseman who had played with the Metallurg and the Russian national team. Gonchar had signed a $25 million free agent contract to play in Pittsburgh for the Penguins. All the pieces seemed to be falling into place, except that Malkin would not be there to complete the puzzle. "I'm sure he felt like (Metallurg) helped him a lot," Gonchar told reporters.[3] "I don't know what to say. Maybe that's why he couldn't say no. When you feel like you're part of a family, maybe it's hard for you to reject

[3] "Gonchar believes Malkin was pressured." by Karen Price, *Pittsburgh Tribune-Review*. August 22, 2006.

them, even if he was only thinking NHL at that point. It's hard to say no when it's a family member, and even though it's not a family member asking him to sign the deal, he was there forever. He grew up there. Everyone in the organization knew him."

Malkin also made a call to his American agents, pleading for their help. He needed a way out.

A loophole in the Russian law allowed anyone to give two weeks' notice to get out of a written contract after signing it. With his agents' help, Malkin did just that, informing the Metallurg of his intentions to leave the team and travel to the United States. Still, he could not exactly leave Mother Russia. The Metallurg held Malkin's passport – and the team wasn't giving it back. Malkin could give notice, but he could not leave the country on his own. With his team scheduled to play its pre-season games in Finland the following week, however, the Metallurg owners would have to hand Malkin his passport. Given the chance to walk away, the young hockey star planned to take it.

On the way to Helsinki, the Metallurg stopped in Moscow for an exhibition game against a new team in the Russian Superleague. Malkin had performed as always, scoring two goals and an assist, but King noticed that his star player seemed different, that he had perhaps taken the words of advice seriously. "You could tell he wasn't happy, but when he stepped on the ice, he couldn't help himself. He played hard. He just played hard all the time. He played so well, but I could just sense this guy wasn't happy. I thought that this was going to be really interesting."

After the game, the team packed up for the flight to Helsinki, where the Metallurg was scheduled to play in the Tampere Cup, an annual tournament. When the team played in the city of Tampere the year before, King was spending some down-time checking out the city and ran into two of his players, Malkin and Nikolai Kulemin, another native of Magnitogorsk. Both 19 years old, they had been born two-and-a-half weeks apart, and they had come up together through the Metallurg system. They shared the dream, too, of playing some day in North America. As the players walked up to King, they showed him that they had just been shopping at a hockey store and had filled bags with t-shirts, hats and other gear bearing the logos of NHL teams. "They were pretty excited, because they were going to be able to wear some NHL stuff," King said years later. "You knew right away, these are young guys and they're dreaming about that league. I thought, 'They're just like our kids. They're just like the North Americans. They're living a dream, too. They want to get there.'"

Now as King came back to Tampere with the Metallurg for a second time the following year, he had to wonder when the two young stars would make their move to North America. Malkin had been drafted by the Penguins but had decided not to leave for Pittsburgh, and Kulemin that year had just been drafted by the Toronto Maple Leafs, but he had stayed in Russia, too. After the team plane landed, the players picked up their luggage and headed for the team bus, when King heard a commotion behind him. "We're getting on the bus with all our equipment, and my translator tells me they can't find Malkin," King said in an interview. "My first thoughts were, 'Holy geez, I wonder if this is it.' Everybody was stressed out going back into the airport, looking for him and looking for him. I recognized right away that this is what's happened, he's going to leave." Metallurg team officials waited around 45 minutes or longer, searching frantically for Malkin, but he could not be found. Several planes were scheduled to leave Helsinki for New York and other international cities at that same time, and many people figured Malkin might have gotten on board one of them.

When Malkin disappeared, no one but his agents knew exactly where he had gone. All they would say was that their client had gone somewhere safe, and that he was not in Russia.[4] NHL officials were of no more help: "The league would not offer the player assistance, financial or otherwise, in a situation like this," deputy commissioner Bill Daly said. "It's a mat-

---

[4] "Agent: Malkin safe, won't reveal whereabouts." by Karen Price, *Pittsburgh Tribune-Review*. August 22, 2006.

ter between the player and his former Russian club. We do, however, support the player's right to make personal choices consistent with his rights under applicable law."

As a guessing game started – where in the world is Evgeni Malkin? – news reports out of Magnitogorsk only added to the uncertainty and international intrigue. One story in *Pravda*, a national newspaper of Russia, quoted Malkin's parents saying their son had broken down and they could not reach him because his phone had been turned off. "My son simply snapped, and his nerves did not hold," Vladimir Malkin was quoted as saying. "In the last moment, they persuaded him to stay (in Magnitogorsk), though his mind was already in the NHL. I understand him, but I don't support him. It was a childish act." His mother echoed the concern, saying her son simply could not withstand the pressure to sign with his hometown team – but that he had been miserable about the decision. "Afterward he told me, 'Mom, (the Penguins) have already been waiting for me, and I promised,'" the newspaper quoted her as saying. "He left for camp in Finland very disgruntled." The Malkins could sincerely say that they did not know any details of their son's plan to escape. He had decided not to tell anyone but a couple of his closest friends what he wanted to do, and as long as he remained in hiding, Malkin could not call home to let his parents know that he was all right. That decision proved to be the right one when the Metallurg's general manager called Malkin's mother to find out where the team's star player had gone. "They said, 'What's going on? Where's your son?'" Malkin said in the only interview he has ever given on the subject of his escape. "My mother said, 'I don't know,' because I had not talked to my mom beforehand. A couple of guys knew, but not all of them, of course."

People around the world did not know what to make of this sudden, unexpected drama, either. Karen Price, a Penguins hockey beat writer for the *Pittsburgh Tribune-Review*,[5] had been writing about the sport for more than a decade, and she could not make out the truth in the barrage of reports. "You

---

[5] Karen Price sat for an interview with the author on October 7, 2010. As the hockey beat reporter for the *Pittsburgh Tribune-Review*, she conducted much of the original reporting on the Penguins drafting Malkin. The author is grateful for her original work and her gracious assistance.

think, Oh my god, has this kid wandered off into the woods of Russia and just lost his mind," she recalled later, "and we're never going to hear from him again?"

Speculation started to center on the idea that Malkin could turn up in Toronto. An agent had told one paper, *Soviet Sport*, that Malkin already had a Canadian visa when he left for Finland. King speculated on a radio sports talk show that Malkin could be holed up in Toronto with Ovechkin. Gossip about Malkin actually showing up in Canada became so rampant that the rumors started to take on a veneer of truth unsupported by reality. Four Pittsburgh reporters at the direction of their editors rented a car and drove across the Canadian border with a mug shot of Malkin, only to be mocked by border guards, police officers and anyone they stopped. "Seriously? That's why you're here?" one Toronto police sergeant said in a typical retort.[6] "If I knew where he was, I could sell it to the papers for a lot of money." As the dejected group headed back to Pittsburgh after a day of getting kicked out of the NHL headquarters, the offices of the players' association and a local hockey rink, word broke that Malkin had finally reappeared – in Los Angeles.

On the highway south of Buffalo, the reporters – three men and one woman – stopped at a Days Inn, rented a room for three hours, and walked into the hotel with laptops and bags of camera equipment. They needed a place to file their stories for the newspaper, but their presence created a stir among the staff at the front desk.

Metallurg officials were outraged by Malkin's decision to go against his newly signed contract and the team. His disappearance and then reappearance in North America with a pending contract to play in the NHL had been nothing less than "sports terrorism" and the "theft of the century," one team manager told the Russian press. They expected compensation in the tens of millions of dollars for losing their star player

[6] "Malkin search yielded few clues." by Mark Houser, Karen Price and Carl Prine, *Pittsburgh Tribune-Review*. August 23, 2006.

and threatened to sue the Penguins if Malkin signed a new contract. "We've put so much effort, resources and money into Malkin's development as a player," Velichkin told a reporter for Reuters.[7] "He was our gold diamond, our prize possession. He had a contract with us. We were building the whole team around him, and now he is gone."

The threats coming out of Russia turned so vitriolic that they actually scared off one of the potential investors looking to buy the Penguins. Sam Fingold, the Hartford developer who had placed a $10 million down payment to buy the Penguins, backed out of the deal partially because of concerns about whether he could relocate the team to Kansas City if needed. Another reason was that he had started looking over his shoulder. Fingold had just finished having breakfast in Los Angeles with Sidney Crosby's agent one morning, when he received a phone call from his father, who had been planning to put up some of the money to purchase the team. "He was like, 'Do you really want to mess with these Russians?'" Fingold recalled. "They were threatening they were going to sue this, they were going to sue that." He worried about what might happen. "There was a lot of money involved, and you had a star player who skipped out in the middle of the night," Fingold said. "The whole thing was a little weird. That kind of freaked me out."

As angry as Metallurg's owners sounded, they seemed eventually to accept that Malkin needed to leave to fulfill his destiny. Despite the tough talk, Malkin ultimately was allowed to go and play for the Penguins. "Everybody knew it was the right thing for him," King said. "It isn't like the organization gave in right away to it all, but I think that they recognized what was going on. They knew for sure he wanted to go to the NHL. It wasn't a fun time for the people in the organization, but I do think they recognized this was what Malk should do."

After Malkin left, King lasted only eight games into his second season as the Metallurg's coach, when he was fired with a 3-4-1 record. Kulemin, Malkin's teammate, stayed in Russia two more years before joining the Maple Leafs in 2008.

---

[7] "Malkin's team says they'll take Penguins to court." By Karen Price, *Pittsburgh Tribune-Review*. August 19, 2006.

By the time Price sat down with Malkin for his first American interview after disappearing in Helsinki, he had been transported to a place as far away from his home in the Ural Mountains as imaginable. He sat in the lobby of the Loews Hotel in Santa Monica, California, wearing shorts and a t-shirt, with the Pacific Ocean stretching out to the horizon behind him. Already he had skated with NHL players at the Toyota Sports Training Center in El Segundo, California, found a favorite place for breakfast in Venice, and developed a routine of swimming in the hotel pool, with its view of the ocean and its palm trees and its sleek deck chairs for sunbathing. The change from Magnitogorsk's isolation and endless factories had been stunning. Malkin recalled feeling nervous about how the following days and months would play out. The biggest surprise, he said, had been the American people. Most of them did not know who he was but welcomed him anyway. "It was so different," Malkin said years later. "The people in America, they all smile."

Sitting in the sunshine for that first interview, Malkin spoke through a translator and said he had never been concerned for his personal safety but had worried that people might put pressure on his family back home. So many residents of Magnitogorsk knew both his family and the team's officials that Malkin felt safe that nothing physically threatening would happen to his parents or siblings. Still lawyers had shown up at their apartment, trying to get his mom and dad to sign statements to undermine Malkin's story and force him to come back home. No matter what, he did not plan to return.

Years later, Malkin still marveled at the stress of leaving home under so much secrecy and pressure. "Now maybe it's a good story," he said, "but it was a tough situation."

The excitement of coming to the United States quickly turned to anxiety about joining the Penguins. Under the NHL's rules, Malkin did not have to negotiate a salary because it would be capped at under $1 million, with incentives and bonuses that could bring the total value to $2.85 million. A bigger concern was how the new team would receive him. "After what I've been through, it is quite difficult for me to set up the right goals at this particular time," Malkin said in that first interview after arriving in Los Angeles. "I keep thinking about the team, how they will accept me, and how I will fit in there. But I do know that I hope this season will be successful for me. I will do my best to become one of the best."

Malkin had little to worry about. Already his new teammates had started thinking about how his arrival in Pittsburgh might finally signal a change in their fortunes. "We're getting a world-class player," said Ryan Malone, the Penguins left wing.[8] "The Penguins are really setting us up for success. We're very lucky. He's so young, and Sidney (Crosby) and all of us will be a main group of guys who are planning to be here for a while. Now we get to start working to bring the (Stanley Cup) trophy back to the 'Burgh."

In his first game as a Penguin on October 18, 2006, Malkin scored a goal against New Jersey's Martin Brodeur – and then he went on to score goals in the next five games, a feat that had not been accomplished by an NHL rookie in 89 years. Malkin finished the season with 33 goals and 52 assists, and he was named the league's rookie of the year, becoming the first Penguins player since Lemieux to receive the honor.

---

[8] "Escape to L.A." By Karen Price, *Pittsburgh Tribune-Review*. August 23, 2006.

*Evgeni Malkin holds his hockey sweater with Mario Lemieux after signing his rookie contract with the Penguins. (*Pittsburgh Tribune-Review, *Chaz Palla)*

7

A Winner
December 20, 2006

The rear wall of the Forum Building auditorium in Harrisburg holds seven two-story maps and a timeline of civilization that traces Western history – from the beginning of the Egyptian calendar in 4241 B.C. – and early Asian history – starting with the construction of the Great Wall of China in 3000 B.C. The maps mark high points across time, recording the births of Jesus Christ and Buddha and the inventions of paper from rags, movable type from earthenware and the navigation compass. The two histories meet in the center at the first World War, with the words: "The great civilizations of the East and West, their religions, philosophies, politics, commerce, science, art and literatures achieved by the struggle of man throughout the centuries. The vast heritage from which the modern world draws rich and constant sustenance."

Across the ceiling, a celestial clock holds three historic interpretations of the heavens set against a backdrop of 365 illuminated crystal stars depicting the northern skies and constellations. The innermost rings show the Ptolemaic understanding of the universe, with the earth at the center and the sun and stars revolving around it. To the left, another diagram shows the planets moving in uneven circles around the sun. Finally, to the right, the solar system appears with the planets moving in elliptical orbits.

Designed to resemble an ancient Roman forum, the semicircular auditorium sits on the grounds of Pennsylvania's state capitol, and builders in 1929 hoped the setting would both humble and inspire at once. It would remind public officials of their insignificance on Earth as well as the possibility that at moments, leaders can emerge to change the course of history and time.

Pennsylvania lawmakers long believed the morning of December 20, 2006, would be one of those moments.

On the cold, clear morning with blue skies and thin wispy clouds, Pennsylvania gambling regulators had called a public hearing at the Forum to vote on awarding 11 casino licenses. For the first time, nearly all of the would-be kings of gambling were gathered in one place, along with the many characters of their various courts: Nineteen bidders were seeking licenses, each with an entourage of consultants, lawyers and spokesmen. The seven members of the state Gaming Control Board sat on a raised stage along one long side of a rectangular table so that no one had his back to the audience. Among the red velvet-covered seats of the auditorium, Philadelphia Mayor John Street stood behind a brass railing in the first row of risers toward the back of the room. Behind Street to his left and halfway up the raised seats, a lone protestor named Dianne Berlin wore a white CasinoFreePA t-shirt with a round anti-gambling button pinned to it. She led the charge against casinos everywhere in the state with rallies, homemade pamphlets and sound bites for reporters. Now she sat alone while other opponents had given up hope of stopping the tide of gambling. When lawmakers gave themselves pay raises the previous summer, citizens rose up and demanded that they return the money, and eventually they did, voting to rescind the increases. On gambling, however, many Pennsylvanians wanted slot machines, and even many of those who opposed them felt it would be all right to legalize casinos: If people are going to wager anyway, the argument went, then let them do it close to home so Pennsylvania can at least get some tax money.

On the far left side of the hall facing the stage stood two executives from Isle of Capri Casinos, general counsel Allan Solomon and Les McMackin, senior vice president of marketing. Neither Mario Lemieux nor Ron Burkle had come to hear the verdict on the casino-arena proposal. After months of trying to sell the Penguins franchise, the team owners still had their fortunes bound with Isle of Capri. Their hopes for a Pittsburgh arena rested on Isle winning the license and paying $290 million for the building. Eight hundred miles away in St. Louis, Isle's president Tim Hinkley sat in a boardroom, meeting with employees from the company's casino in Biloxi, Mississippi.

After Hurricane Katrina, company executives decided to move their headquarters back north. Company spokeswoman Jill Alexander waited in her office one flight above, watching the scene inside the Forum on her computer screen as other employees crowded around her desk to see the streaming video. Isle officials had bid on casinos and lost before. Hinkley and the others believed they had put together the strongest of the three Pittsburgh proposals, but they also knew that these types of decisions can hinge on other subjective factors and politics. No one from Isle had planned a party for that night. If they won, the executives planned to fly back home to start working on the casino.

Across the auditorium and farther back, executives from Forest City Enterprises sat in another cluster. They had worked for years on plans to put a casino at Pittsburgh's Station Square entertainment complex. The executives remained so confident of winning that they had arranged a lavish party for that night at the Sheraton Station Square Hotel back in Pittsburgh. Albert Ratner, the family patriarch, had flown in from Cleveland for the casino vote, and he sat next to his son Brian, who headed up the company's bid.

Closest to the front of the room, a third bidder for the Pittsburgh license sat at the end of a row of seats. Few experts thought Don Barden would survive even this long, making it through the board's background investigation and test of his financial wherewithal. Yet he had lasted all the way to the final vote. In theory, at least, he had as much chance to win the Pittsburgh license as anyone.

As he liked to tell the story, Barden grew up poor in the Detroit suburb of Inkster, one of 13 children, and from those humble roots, he built an empire touted as the nation's largest black-owned casino company. He had never built anything so massive as his proposed Pittsburgh casino, with 5,000 slot machines, restaurants overlooking the city skyline and an outdoor riverfront amphitheater, but that's the Barden way. From the start he had taken the proceeds from one project – his first business, a record shop – and tried to turn something bigger –

next, a real estate property leased to the United States government for a military recruiting station. If one of his plans failed, Barden moved on. If it succeeded, he used whatever money and connections he had gained to propel himself into the next project. That way he collected riches vaguely estimated by his assistants at some $300 million, but he also leveraged his wealth so that he owned dozens of companies in real estate, jukeboxes and even car production in the African nation of Namibia, as well as five casinos. Barden pressed every advantage, and in the weeks leading up to the gambling board's decision, he played up the coincidence that on the day when they would announce their decision, he would celebrate his 63rd birthday.

"I know how to fix a toilet," Barden once boasted as the keynote speaker at a formal dinner hosted by the Pennsylvania African-American Convention in Pittsburgh's Oakland neighborhood. "I know how to fix a furnace, right now." After one year at Ohio's Central State University, Barden dropped out of school and moved in with an older brother in Lorain, Ohio, a small industrial town about 30 miles west of Cleveland, along Lake Erie, that once housed both a U.S. Steel mill and a Ford auto plant. Barden worked at odd jobs as a furniture mover, a shipyard worker and a plumber. He got a taste for business by opening the record shop, and then he borrowed enough money to buy the building for the recruiting station. He started a weekly newspaper and ran for public office, serving on Lorain's city council in the mid-1970s. A decade later, when consumers started switching to cable television, Barden picked up the rights to help string the cable lines through small Ohio towns, and from there, he worked his way back toward Detroit, eventually winning the rights to provide cable throughout the city. In 1994, when Barden sold his cable interests to Comcast, he reportedly made more than $100 million on the deal.

By then, Barden already had started looking for the next big thing. Five years earlier, casino gambling had made its first push outside of Las Vegas and Atlantic City, as Iowa legalized slot machines to lift its river towns from economic failure. Soon, lots of places were looking at casinos for quick money. In 1994, the provincial government in Ontario, Canada, opened a temporary casino in Windsor on a site overlooking the river that separates the city from Detroit. Pretty soon the folks in Detroit started arguing that they should keep some of that money for themselves. In a referendum, voters agreed to allow three Detroit casinos, and Barden figured his hometown presence should give him an advantage for one of the licenses. Detroit Mayor Dennis Archer saw it another way, choosing instead bidders with more money and experience: MGM Grand and Mandalay Bay, along with the Sault Ste. Marie Tribe of Chippewa Indians. Barden fought back, demanding a public referendum that would force the city to give him one of the licenses after all. To build public support for the idea, he partnered with another hometown guy, pop singer Michael Jackson, on plans for a Thriller theme park with an aquarium, hotel and casino. Fans loved the idea, screaming for Jackson when he came back home to make the announcement, but voters rejected it. Barden later briefly ended up with a small share in the Chippewa's Greektown Casino.

While he was vying for the Detroit license, Barden also worked to get a riverboat casino for Gary, Indiana, another depressed U.S. Steel factory town. Sitting in the state's far northwest corner, Gary has a main advantage of being close to Chicago, and Barden figured gamblers might descend from the passing highway to stop at a casino even if they had no other reason to visit the city. He partnered with another bidder, developer Donald Trump, and together they built a dock for two floating casinos, Trump Casino Indiana and Barden's Majestic Star. From that success, Barden bought the Fitzgeralds Casino chain out of bankruptcy, instantly growing his company from one boat into a conglomerate. He now had a casino in a former Colorado gold-mining town, a Mississippi riverboat barge and his crown jewel, a 34-story casino hotel in downtown Las Vegas.

Barden's up-from-his-bootstraps story resonates with audiences, particularly African-Americans hungry to see one of their own succeed in a business with few black stakeholders. Whenever Barden recounted the tale, his biggest applause line came when he described how he beat Trump at his own game. To hear Barden tell the story, his Majestic Star boat in Gary performed so well that Trump was forced into selling his boat in 2005 to Barden, who renamed it Majestic Star II. The stump line makes audiences cheer. Critics, however, have wondered whether it wasn't the other way around, that Trump had known when to get out of the dying Indiana steel town. In the months after he purchased Trump's boat, Barden promised changes to his creditors as the two boats failed to do as well together as they had under separate owners. His excuse had been that customers had liked the competition from the two casinos. His proposed solution was to move the former Trump boat to another city, but Gary residents and Indiana lawmakers balked at that idea.

Part of Barden's appeal, too, was that he had the trappings of a mega-millionaire. Barden lived in a mansion at the Detroit Golf Club with neighbors that included the parents of retired Steelers running back Jerome Bettis. Barden traveled the world in private jets, vacationing in the Caribbean islands and visiting his companies in Namibia, where he served as an honorary consul to the United States. He palled around with celebrities ranging from Motown founder Smokey Robinson to presidential contender Dick Gephardt. Two months after Pennsylvania's casino bidding process started, the Steelers played against the Seattle Seahawks in Super Bowl XL, which happened to be played at Detroit's Ford Field as part of the NFL's effort to spread around its wealth. Barden bankrolled a three-day party of rhythm-and-blues artists before the game, and he hosted Pennsylvania lawmakers in his luxury box to watch the Steelers win 21-10.

Pennsylvania's casino bids were supposed to be complete by a deadline of December 28, 2005, and while the other bidders made lavish promises then about what they would deliver, Barden offered few specifics about his Majestic Star proposal. He waited four months to discuss his plans, until the morning before state gambling regulators were scheduled to open a series of meetings in Pittsburgh on the proposals. Barden called a surprise press conference to discuss a plan that seemed to borrow the best ideas from each of his competitors. Like them, he, too, promised a $1 billion development project larded with community givebacks. Just as he had done in Detroit when

he partnered with Jackson, Barden had looked for local partners in Pittsburgh that would give him a celebrity edge.
Robinson, the Motown singer, had married a Pittsburgh girl
named Frances, and this gave Barden a strong narrative when
the couple announced that day they would be buying a home
in a North Side neighborhood near the proposed casino. They
would be splitting their time between there and Los Angeles.
"I'm very happy to be back home," Frances said, calling
Barden's proposal a "life-altering" moment for her. Barden also
asked Bettis, the former football player, to join his team, but
after retiring from the Steelers, the running back had taken a
job as an NBC television analyst, and the network apparently
had no desire for one of its on-air talents to be tied so closely
with gambling. Instead, his parents, Gladys and Johnnie Bettis,
became investors. Mama Bettis already had gained a small bit
of fame as a doting football mother in a series of Campbell's
Chunky Soup television commercials. Barden seemed glad to
have any ties, no matter how indirect, to the Super Bowl-win-
ning Steelers franchise. The Majestic Star proposal included
more than a dozen other investors, but most were Barden's
business associates and many were from out of town. Barden
did not bother to announce their names at the press conference, and he declined to provide any information about how
much money any of the partners had invested.

To reach $1 billion in development projects for his proposal,
Barden promised a lot that he would not have to immediately
deliver. His plans called for a possible hotel connected to the
casino, money for sprucing up the North Side neighborhood
and, in a direct shot at the Isle of Capri bid, he offered seed
money for the Hill District neighborhood around the Civic
Arena. He counted the Hill District phase as a $350 million
neighborhood project with apartments, shops and parks. The
fine print called for Barden to invest just $1 million a year for
three years into the area. "Barden was purposely matching
whatever Isle of Capri was saying," said Ken McCabe, a former
FBI agent who had been appointed to serve on the Pennsylvania Gaming Control Board. "He felt he had to do that to stay
competitive."

Barden found a great location for his casino on an undeveloped warehouse site on the city's North Shore. The glass-walled casino would sit along the Ohio River, just feet from where it forms out of the Monongahela and Allegheny rivers, and the building would face Pittsburgh's skyline. A soaring glass drum would sit at the center of the casino with a martini bar in its crow's nest. The building would have 5,000 slot machines and room for table games such as blackjack and roulette, if the legislature ever legalized them. A parking garage with one space for every slot machine would be hidden partially underground and behind the main casino building. Even people who do not gamble, Barden said, would be drawn to the site for its outdoor concert amphitheater, its riverfront pathway for hikers and bikers and its restaurants. Unlike older casinos in Las Vegas and Atlantic City that famously guard out all light and any sense of time, Majestic Star would have daylight views to the outside world, even from its gaming floor.

While the state Gaming Control Board had the only real say in who would get the Pittsburgh casino license, its members agreed to hear from the public and arranged to hold a public hearing inside a conference room at the city's Omni William Penn Hotel. Because Barden had released his plans on the eve of the meeting, details of his proposal filled the front pages of the city's two daily newspapers on the morning of the hearings. Outside the hotel, the Penguins had called a campaign-style rally for their fans, handing out t-shirts with the Pittsburgh First logo. Inside, dozens of fans had signed up to testify to the gambling board that Isle of Capri should get the license so it could pay for the arena and keep the hockey team in Pittsburgh. With the fans sitting on the rows of stack chairs, wearing either black-and-gold hockey sweaters or the team's throwback powder blue jerseys, the hotel ballroom looked more like the scene of a pep rally than a hearing to determine which of three bidders would receive permission to open a casino.

Members of the public were allowed to testify on the second day of the hearings. Half of the 53 speakers favored Isle of Capri's plan to use slots money to pay for an arena. Michael Mooney, a Penguins fan who had created a Web site called SlotsforMario.com, delivered an electronic petition that had been signed by 36,000 people supporting the use of gambling

money for an arena. "It's now clear the Penguins' fate is directly tied to the issuance of a slots license," he said. Ten people backed Forest City's proposal for a Harrah's casino, noting that it projected to bring in a third more money than anyone else. No one directly endorsed Majestic Star. One representative from the North Side neighborhood said community groups had agreed they could tolerate a casino there but had decided not to endorse or oppose the idea. Group officials later explained that Barden had said he would give them $3 million for neighborhood projects if he won the license.

Members of the state's gambling board never talked to the public during the hearings, sitting quietly through the testimony and leaving through a back door without taking questions. Without a doubt, they had absorbed the message from Penguins fans. "We kept on hearing, 'Give it to the Pens, Give it to the Pens, Give it to the Pens,'" McCabe, who describes himself as a casual hockey fan, said after the bidding process ended. "Well, the Pens were not the applicant, for the first thing. We got tired of hearing 'Give it to the Pens.' It was Isle of Capri that wanted it, and Isle of Capri had committed to paying for an arena." Some gambling board members had started out seeing Isle's offer as a genuine opportunity to serve the Pittsburgh community and save taxpayers millions of dollars, but then they started to view the proposal more cynically – as just an attempt by one company to gain an advantage. "All of the applicants were looking at what would give them an edge over other applicants," McCabe said. "This was the Isle of Capri trying to single themselves out, to cut themselves out of the herd, so to speak." Getting money for an arena had never been the board's charge. Its members had been told to select the company with the best casino proposal, one that would raise the most money for the state and create the fewest negative impacts. An arena did not figure directly into those criteria.

The hearings served as proof to the gambling board, though, that Pittsburgh's hockey fans would not drop the issue of using slots money for an arena, preferably with Isle of Capri paying the full cost of the building. Lawmakers had never imagined when they legalized slot machines that the process of choosing a casino for Pittsburgh might depend on which company would pay for an arena. Once it became clear that the

Penguins and their fans had hijacked the selection process, however, Governor Ed Rendell sought to regain control of the discussion. During the Steelers victory parade after Super Bowl XL, fans booed the governor and local politicians while chanting demands for a new arena. A month before the public hearing in Pittsburgh, Rendell called a press conference in the top floor suite of the city's Regional Enterprise Tower, a 1960s-era building meant to evoke the supersonic age with an aluminum exterior and windows that looked like those on an airplane. Rendell called on all the bidders for the Pittsburgh license to help pay for an arena, figuring that would eliminate the issue. If Isle of Capri won the license, it still would pay the full $290 million for the arena, as promised. If either of the other bidders won, however, Rendell wanted them to put up $7.5 million a year for 30 years for an arena. That would raise less than half of the $290 million needed for an arena when interest on the debt was counted, and Rendell proposed that the team and public make up the difference. The state would dip into its take from casinos to pay $7 million a year. That still left a gap, and the Penguins would be asked to kick in $8.5 million up front and $3 million a year.

Local politicians, all Democrats like Rendell, declared a victory for this arena proposal. "It's a done deal," the county's top elected official, Executive Dan Onorato, told gambling board members at one point. "No matter who wins this, you have the arrangement now to build an arena with gaming money, and that's where you want to be." Board members figured the arena issue had been solved, too. If every one of the bidders was committed to helping pay for an arena, the board could ignore that issue and focus on the other factors. "We made (the arena) one of the conditions, and once it became one of the conditions, there was no getting out of it," said Sanford Rivers, the former football referee serving on the gambling board.

Naturally, the Penguins owners preferred the Isle of Capri deal, which would cost them nothing. But in another way, Lemieux and Burkle had won. Elected officials were now committing to help pay for a hockey rink, no matter what happened during the slots bidding process. Seventeen years after he had pulled the Penguins out of bankruptcy, Lemieux finally had won the support he felt had been promised all along. Some team insiders still worried, however, that Rendell's offer had arrived too late, provided too little help and did not include any solid details about just how the state would hold up its commitment. The governor's proposal also meant the Penguins could end up with one of two partners that Isle of Capri still was competing against.

From his perspective, Barden saw the immediate benefit of eliminating the arena talk from the casino bidding process. He readily agreed to Rendell's plan and added the arena promise to his proposal. On his own, he already had matched some of the best parts from the competitors' bids, and now he had taken away Isle's ace.

The Ratners had not been as eager to pay toward an arena. From the beginning, Forest City hadn't seen a need to partner with the Penguins. Now, Albert Ratner did not rush to answer Rendell's call for helping with the arena. The development company had too many ties to state politicians to completely ignore the proposal, and Ratner ultimately realized the advantage, too, of undercutting his biggest competition. Unlike Barden, however, Ratner left himself an out: He said Forest City would commit to the arena only if Lemieux and Burkle vowed to keep the team in Pittsburgh, no matter who won the casino license. Of course, the Penguins' owners could never make that promise with Isle of Capri still in the running.

In late November, a month before the gambling board would make its decision, each bidder was again required to come before the gambling regulators, this time at the Pennsylvania State Museum auditorium in Harrisburg. Isle of Capri and Forest City were chosen to present on the first day of testimony, and few secrets remained about either of their proposals. Barden, who would testify alone on the second day, quietly sat with his team of executives in the audience through the entire first day of hearings. They had the advantage of seeing the competition, and they took it, watching everything and saying little. That night, Barden's speech writer stayed up late reworking the entire Majestic Star presentation, learning from the other bidders' blunders and picking up on their promises. When Barden stood to introduce his plan on the morning of the second day, the auditorium sat more than half-empty. The hockey fans had gone back to Pittsburgh, along with most of the reporters who had come up to hear the frontrunners but had chosen not to stay in the capital any longer than necessary. Clearly, to many, it had not been necessary to hear what Barden would offer.

Those who left early missed the most entertaining moment in nearly a year of lobbying by the three bidders. Smokey Robinson, the Motown crooner who had partnered with Barden, arrived. After Barden gave his slideshow presentation, with one new wrinkle when he scuttled plans for a temporary riverboat casino, he turned to Robinson, who had been sitting next to him the entire time. The singer started talking, and for the first moment in two days of testimony, everyone in the auditorium stopped what they were doing and listened. The seven gambling board members looked up to see what he would say. Robinson started out talking not about Barden and casino gambling but about Motown records. As a teenager, Robinson had committed to his passion for music, and he had been lucky enough to meet other people who shared his vision. They had ignored the critics who said it couldn't be done. He talked about believing in a dream and getting caught up in a special moment.

"Many days I wish we had known we were making history – that we were not only making music, that we were making history – because I would have saved everything," Robinson said. "I would have saved every little scrap of paper I ever started a song on, every little piece of tape. ... But you just don't know because you are young and you're doing something that you love. So you are not thinking about what you are doing."

For Barden, building a Pittsburgh casino would be that kind of moment, Robinson said. He told the gambling regulators about his wife and called her a native "Pittsburghian," coining a new term. He talked about the millions of people around the world with a Motown record and the millions more who had heard of the company that started with a Detroit band made up of four boys and a girl. Robinson would not risk all that, he said, by partnering with someone who would embarrass him. No, Robinson came instead, he said, to testify about Barden's character.

"I believe in him," Robinson said. "I believe that he has what it takes to do all the things that he is promising will be done. … I have no doubt whatsoever that he will deliver on all these things because that is who he is."

When Robinson finished, one of the board members from Pittsburgh, Sanford Rivers, spoke up to correct the record. "Seeing how you are now one of us," he said, turning to the singer, "we are Pittsburghers. Those are Philadelphians."

The board took a quick break from the hearings, and Robinson stood up, pulled on his coat, and walked with Barden to the museum lobby. The men hugged, and then Robinson headed out to his waiting limousine. Quietly, in a hearing that few people attended, the Motown singer's passionate words had transformed Barden's bid from afterthought to underdog. Barden would remain the longest of long-shots among the three bidders, but suddenly it seemed he might have a shot at winning.

The biggest question about Barden's bid remained whether he actually could afford to build the new casino. A report surfaced in Las Vegas saying that he planned to borrow against his high-rise casino hotel there to come up with the down payment for the Pittsburgh property. He might even sell it if he needed the cash. As for the rest, Barden had produced a letter from a Wall Street investment firm saying it would provide the money to complete the project. The letter amounted to the equivalent of a mortgage pre-approval that could be voided for unspecified reasons, but in the eyes of the gambling regulators, the paper made Barden as viable as any other candidate. After that, they did not question again whether he would actually be able to pay the costs of construction if he won the license.

On the night before awarding the casino licenses, gambling board members met secretly inside their offices above a Harrisburg shopping mall called Strawberry Square. Some offices look out onto the capitol grounds, but the board members met inside a windowless conference room and did not allow even their staff members to sit in on the session. Rivers, a former NFL referee, started the discussion, saying that of all the applicants across the state, he had made up his mind first on who should get the Pittsburgh casino: Barden. Ken McCabe, the former head of the Pittsburgh FBI field office, went second: Barden. Jeffrey Coy, a former lawmaker who lived near Harrisburg, had been appointed by the Democratic House leader who happened to be from a rural community an hour south of Pittsburgh. That gave him sway in this argument, too, and he voted for Barden. The other four members from around the state offered their votes: Barden, Barden, Barden, Barden.

No one outside that room yet knew it – and the decision would not be final until the formal public vote the following morning – but Barden had won the license for a Pittsburgh casino with almost no discussion. Not a single board member had supported the supposed front-runners. Members felt Forest City had insurmountable traffic problems, sitting on a narrow site between the Monongahela River and Mt. Washington. Isle of Capri had a strong plan, but some board members were concerned about problems the casino might cause in the nearby Hill District neighborhood. They also did not want to feel coerced into choosing a gambling company based on the promise of an arena. Isle executives had realized this potential concern and actually had reached out to the SlotsforMario.com supporters more than once, asking them to tone down their demands. "In business, anytime you're forcing someone to make a decision, that doesn't necessarily mean you'll get the decision you want," one executive privately warned. Given a choice – and Rendell had ensured the board members had a choice when he asked all three bidders to put up some money for an arena – the board chose someone else.

The board's deliberations on all 11 licenses went so easily in their secret meeting that the members had nothing more than a few friendly disagreements that were easily resolved. In Philadelphia, the board chose Foxwoods, backed by Connecticut's Mashantucket Pequot Tribal Nation, and SugarHouse, backed by a Chicago billionaire named Neil Bluhm. It passed over Trump's bid. The group backed by Las Vegas Sands, which planned to turn a former steel mill in Bethlehem into a casino, won the board's support. Louis DeNaples, a businessman with close ties to Rendell, already had started construction on his Poconos casino, and he won approval, too. Each of the six open racetracks around the state would get a license.

When they finished, Thomas Decker, the chairman, staged a fight with some of the other board members so he wouldn't disappoint the anxious staff members standing outside the room. He stormed out of the secret meeting yelling over his shoulder, and then stopped to laugh at the worried looks on the workers' faces. In reality, the Gaming Control Board employees were out celebrating over beers before the night was over. Executive Director Anne Neeb, the board's spokesman and a few others retired to an Irish pub named Molly Brannigans, standing around the bar and drinking pints of Guinness. They told a reporter who happened to be standing there that the board members still were in deliberation. In reality, the process was all but over.

Members of all three groups vying for the Pittsburgh license had made reservations to stay at the Harrisburg Hilton, the capital's fanciest hotel. By the night before the official vote, their work had been done – and although none of them knew it, the decision already had been cast. Developers from Forest City sat at a round table in the first floor piano bar, drinking scotch and whiskey with Brian Ratner, the son of the company's co-chairman. A couple executives from Isle of Capri sat nearby at another table. In a back room of the hotel restaurant, Barden had thrown a private birthday party for himself. He felt like celebrating no matter how the vote turned out the following day. An unknown at the start of the process, he had somehow managed to keep up with the famous, well-funded competition. David Morehouse, the Penguins' consultant, stayed away from the capital the night before the vote, remaining in Pittsburgh to watch the Penguins drop a 4-1 game to the St. Louis Blues.

The close quarters inside the Harrisburg Hilton created a few awkward moments, especially given the billions of dollars and countless careers that rested on the outcome of the gambling board's decision. Early in the morning before the vote, two executives from Isle of Capri were in the hotel gym working out next to a reporter for a Pittsburgh newspaper who was running on the treadmill. Decker, the gambling board chairman, walked in a few minutes later for a run. All of the day's questions could have been answered in that room. Instead, everyone exchanged pleasantries, sweated in silence, and headed back to their rooms to get ready for the official vote later that morning.

Hundreds of people had gathered inside the Forum Building's auditorium for the 10 a.m. hearing. The board members and their staff knew who would get the licenses, but no one else could guess for certain just what had been decided. While the votes would be perfunctory for the board, they remained filled with suspense for everyone else. Board members treated the event as a normal, bureaucratic meeting, opening with the approval of minutes, the executive director's report and motions to pay for copying fees, among other things. With no fanfare, they moved to item D on their agenda, consideration of the casino licenses. First they awarded the Philadelphia licenses, and then they considered a motion by Coy to award the license to Barden's company. With no discussion, they started the roll call, leading with the Pittsburgh commissioners: McCabe, aye. Rivers, yes. Yes. Yes. Yes. Yes. Yes.

In his seat, Barden wept.

Moments later after the meeting ended, Barden stood in the entrance hall to the main auditorium near an oversized bronze door that clanged every time someone walked out of the building. He told reporters that he had been as surprised as anyone that the board had picked him.

"My heart skipped several beats," he said. "It was just an exhilarating and incredible feeling."

On the stage, Decker talked with another group of reporters and explained the board's thinking: No one could claim there had been a fix, and the arena still would get built, with Barden's promise to help pay for it. In the end, he explained later, board members had just liked Barden best. "You're watch-

ing him, and you're going, 'There's really substance here,'"
Decker said in the days that followed. "'This isn't some guy
taking a flyer at this thing. He's a small, meat-and-potato guy,
and he's against all these French restaurants.'"

More than a year after Lemieux and Burkle passed over
Barden because they didn't believe he had the money to win,
he won. They might have to work with him after all. His contribution would not be enough to pay for an arena, and Rendell
still had not fully explained how the state might make up the
difference. The deal to stay in Pittsburgh might be the best offer the team owners would hear, but it surely would not be the
only one. Already, officials from Kansas City, Houston, Las
Vegas and a few other cities had started making their own
pitches to lure away the hockey team.

Developers from Forest City figured that if they did not
receive the license for a Harrah's casino at Station Square, Isle
of Capri might win it on the strength of the arena offer, which
had garnered a lot of attention and support from fans and
public officials. No one from the group, however, expected for
a moment that the gambling board might choose Barden. After the vote, Albert Ratner, the patriarch, walked outside and
stood on a street corner in the subfreezing temperatures in
stunned disbelief. "We never, in all sincerity and honesty, gave
Majestic Star Casino very much consideration," said John
Verbanac, a public relations consultant hired by the Forest City
group. "We probably had more shock in Majestic Star Casino
being selected than we did in not being selected." After a few
moments on the street outside the Forum Building, the Ratners
and the others from their group realized nothing could be said
right then to change what had happened, and so they separated to head home. The whole group did not come together
again for several days, until the shock had eased.

Inside the Penguins' offices at Chatham Center in Pittsburgh, Morehouse had gotten together with Tom McMillan,
the team's vice president for communications, Ted Black, a team
lawyer, and some others to watch the results in the office of
Ken Sawyer, the team president. As the gambling board members voted for Barden to get the license, the Penguins executives felt stunned twice over – not only did Isle of Capri not
win, but neither did Forest City. The executives' reaction to

losing had been muted by the knowledge of all the work that remained. Black turned to leave without saying much. "I still had work on my desk," he recalled later. "I sort of shuffled my way back to my office."

Back at the Isle of Capri headquarters in St. Louis, Jill Alexander, the company spokeswoman, watched the board vote on her computer screen. It was her job to walk down a flight of stairs to give the news, one way or the other, to Hinkley, the company president. She stood up from her desk as the employees who had crowded around to watch the verdict on the streaming video quietly left. She followed them out and ran down the steps to the boardroom where Hinkley sat with employees from the Biloxi office. He looked up and tried to read her face.

"We didn't get it, did we?" he asked as she walked into the room.

"No."

"Who did?"

"Barden."

Alexander turned and walked out of the room before she could see the reaction on Hinkley's face.

He had known this might happen. It had happened before in other places. The company had bid on a casino license, spent millions of dollars on its proposal and lost for some uncertain reason. Often, decisions came down to subjective, personal reasons more than who had offered the most.

Still, Hinkley felt like he had been punched in the gut. He asked for a moment alone and stepped out of the boardroom. If the winner had been Forest City, he thought to himself, he could have understood why Isle lost. But it wasn't Forest City. It was Barden.

8

Moving Day
March 13, 2007

From inside the parole board hearing room on the 14th floor of Pittsburgh's State Office Building, Penguins owner Ron Burkle could see a sweeping view of Point State Park, the place where the Monongahela and Allegheny rivers form into the Ohio River. On the cold January night with temperatures well below freezing, the lights from Heinz Field, the city's football stadium, and PNC Park, its baseball field, glimmered along the city's North Shore. Burkle had flown in his jet back to Pittsburgh to talk with Governor Ed Rendell about state help for a new hockey arena now that the gambling board had not chosen Isle of Capri Casinos, the one company that had promised to pay the full price of construction. The governor arranged to hold the meeting inside the state office building, a 1950s-era rabbit's warren of bureaucracies.

The two sides already had met once in the month since gambling regulators gave the slots license to Detroit businessman Don Barden. Penguins officials felt that even if the board members had wanted to give the license to Cleveland developer Forest City for its proposed Harrah's casino at Station Square, they could not because of the hockey team's public lobbying – and then-Mayor Tom Murphy's infamous claim of a fix. If they didn't give the license to Forest City, they certainly wouldn't reward the Penguins, either. By giving the license to Barden, the board had fulfilled an unspoken commitment to ensure the state had at least one black-owned casino. That meant the members could give the two Philadelphia licenses to any of the bidders, rather than the only other black-owned company in the mix.

At the team's first meeting with Rendell two weeks earlier, the governor started out by telling the team owners that he knew they needed an arena and by offering up negotiating

Gov. Ed Rendell, center, with Allegheny County Executive Dan Onorato, left, and Pittsburgh Mayor Luke Ravenstahl walk out smiling from the first round of negotiations with the Penguins. (Pittsburgh Tribune-Review, Heidi Murrin)

terms that were surprisingly intriguing. The proposal had been better than anyone on the Penguins' side of the table had expected. Burkle and Mario Lemieux had agreed before the meeting that they would immediately start visiting other cities to come up with alternative plans for relocating their team if necessary. Neither of them had expected Rendell to be so eager and serious about setting terms for a Pittsburgh arena. As they left the state office building, Burkle turned to David Morehouse, the team's arena consultant, and said, "Let's make a deal. Let's not play any games." The owners changed their minds about threatening to relocate, deciding not to even look at any other cities.

Stepping onto the sidewalk outside, Lemieux smiled broadly as he walked toward reporters waiting there in the cold for any word about the negotiations. "I'm optimistic," he said.

Rendell and the local politicians had been "willing to step up and talk about some issues that were a big concern," he said. They had talked about problems that had gone unaddressed for more than seven years. Lemieux predicted the team would work out a deal in the coming weeks.

Local politicians started feeling surprisingly upbeat as well. "I remember leaving there thinking the same thing, just how encouraging it was that from our side of the table and their side of the table it seemed like there was a tremendous amount of good will and also common ground," Mayor Luke Ravenstahl recalled later. "I didn't know quite what to expect, but I didn't think we would be as close or have as productive a meeting as we did." That enthusiasm translated into the elected officials feeling like they had some leverage after all to limit how much the public would have to pay for the arena. The state's best offer after that night called for Barden's casino to pay $7.5 million a year and the public to pay $7 million from the state's tax on slots money. That meant the Penguins were still required to kick in millions of dollars, too. Rendell had vowed the team would not get an arena for free, and he remained committed to that promise.

Part of the elected officials' confidence seemed to come from a belief that the National Hockey League never would let a marquis franchise leave Pittsburgh, a city with a strong fan base, for some other uncertain market that had never been tested. When they started to hear this, Penguins executives sent a back-channel message to City Hall, telling the politicians to check the history books: Even the National Football League, which had become as powerful as any sports league in North America, had been unable to stop owners from moving teams out of Baltimore, Cleveland and Los Angeles. If the Penguins' owners were forced to relocate to get a better arena deal, the league would be unable to prevent such a move.

On the night of the second meeting between the team and politicians, Ravenstahl had high expectations. If the city's older leaders harkened back to the glory days of the Pirates and Steelers, the new mayor understood why the Penguins were important to a younger generation of fans. Ravenstahl had become mayor at age 26 because of an unfortunate twist of fate. Less than two years out of college, he ran for City Council and won a seat in the North Side neighborhood where his family had long been involved in local politics. When council members could not agree on someone to lead them, they had compromised on Ravenstahl with each side figuring their youngest member could be easily swayed to support their causes. Seven months later, Mayor Bob O'Connor, serving in his first term, was diagnosed with a brain tumor and died two months after that without ever leaving the hospital. On a rainy Friday night in September 2006, Ravenstahl became the youngest mayor in Pittsburgh history and among the youngest ever of any major United States city. For the Penguins, the sudden change in leadership brought in a mayor who already had backed Isle of Capri Casinos' arena plan and someone who enjoys hockey. Ravenstahl had grown up rooting for the Penguins when the team won championships in the early 1990s. If Pittsburgh could still be considered a city of champions in his youth, it was only because of Lemieux and hockey.

Heading into the state office building, Ravenstahl expected to build on the positive exchange from the first meeting. "We had high expectations and even thought we potentially could close a deal that night given the positives from the first meeting," he said later. Lemieux was in the Bahamas at a celebrity golfing tournament hosted by basketball legend Michael Jordan. Burkle and the governor would try to work out the details of an arena.

The two men already knew each other well from Democratic politics. After serving as mayor of Philadelphia, Rendell had chaired the Democratic National Committee and had proven again his ability to raise money for the party. Burkle had been one of the leading donors. He had given more than $1 million himself, and it had been reported that he had raised another $50 million from other donors. Rendell already had called Burkle the "real owner" of the team and said they did not need Lemieux for the negotiations because, while he had been a great player, Burkle was the businessman in the partnership. Rendell was having a tough time negotiating against a close political ally and one of his sports heroes. "It was hard sitting across the table from Mario because you knew how much

Mario had put into this," Rendell said later. "For him you wanted to make it work, but you also had the responsibilities to use the taxpayers' monies well."

Before the Penguins' arena bid with Isle of Capri collapsed, Burkle had been a mostly silent partner, a familiar face to team insiders but someone almost unknown to the general public. Many fans knew Lemieux, alone, as the team owner and could not place the California billionaire as the franchise's major cash investor. In a rare moment, Burkle had welcomed Sidney Crosby to the Mellon Arena for his first home game by flying in pop star Christina Aguilera to sing the national anthem. Otherwise, he watched quietly at games if he attended them at all, which was rare.

Born in 1952, Burkle had wavy brown hair and smooth tanned cheeks that made him seem eternally youthful. He often wore an untucked black Polo shirt over jeans, accentuating his carefree style. At play, he'd been best known as an ultimate FOB or friend of former President Bill Clinton. The two would fly around the world after Clinton left office, turning up in celebrity magazines and burnishing Clinton's legacy. Burkle had been a major backer of the Clinton Global Initiative, a nonprofit that helps poor developing countries, mainly in Africa, buy AIDS medicines and drugs. When he traveled, Clinton often flew on "Air Ron," his nickname for Burkle's luxuriously appointed 757 jet, and *Forbes* magazine once reported that Clinton kept a permanent guest room at Burkle's Beverly Hills mansion. The former president regularly stayed in that room on visits to Los Angeles — at least until around the time that Clinton's wife, Hillary, ran for president, and he stopped palling around so much.

Burkle made his fortune in the grocery business, starting out by stocking shelves in the store where his father worked as the manager and then getting fired when he failed in a takeover bid for the entire chain. Soon after, however, Burkle was using his savings to invest in real estate and looking for bargains that could be flipped for a quick profit. He eventually took on entire chains of grocery stores, often in poor inner-city neighborhoods that had value but that nobody wanted.

As decisions about running the team shifted from the ice to the board room while the Penguins negotiated for an arena, Burkle saw a need for his services. Even if he was not a hockey insider, Burkle had an investment to protect. Like Lemieux on the ice, Burkle could see several steps ahead in business and intuitively knew what others might do before they did it. This was his sport, and he would take a direct role in making sure his team won.

As Burkle sat in one of the black executive chairs around the long, dark-wood conference table, he might have expected the relationship with Rendell to pay a dividend. He knew, like everyone else, that the governor could make deals where others had failed, especially if it meant accomplishing one of his goals. A former Philadelphia prosecutor, Rendell played the role of power broker naturally. Not only had he won the legalization of slot machines, but his administration had ensured that the first casino opened within days of his re-election. In that race, Rendell faced off against former Steelers wide receiver Lynn Swann, a hall-of-fame player who made a second career as a naturally charming football sideline television reporter. Unfortunately for Swann, he had much more trouble talking about taxes, the state budget and pension funds than he did summing up football strategy or a player's twisted ankle. Rendell easily won the race.

The governor figured he could win back the Penguins' commitment to staying in Pittsburgh. The only question was how much it would cost. Barden's offer had never been as good as Isle's promise to pay $290 million immediately for an arena. Rendell's Plan B had been designed to remove the arena talk from the casino bidding promise, and he had acknowledged the plan had gaps. For one, he had never detailed exactly how the state would come up with the millions of dollars it would need for the agreement. Rendell had said the state would use the cash from its 55-percent tax on slot machines, but that money had been promised a half-dozen ways and none of them for a Pittsburgh arena.

As soon as Barden won the casino license, holes in his arena promise became obvious. During the bidding process, the Penguins' owners wanted detailed, written commitments of help from both Barden and Forest City, but each had signed only a vague statement of support. For Lemieux and Burkle, it seemed that history had been dialed back to when they brought the team out of bankruptcy, with local politicians saying only that they would endeavor to build an arena. When he was vying for the slots license, Barden said he would pay $7.5 million a year for 30 years – an amount equal to $225 million. With Barden stretching his payments over the life of a typical home mortgage, however, the Penguins could afford to borrow only about half as much to cover future interest payments. Under the Majestic Star deal, the team had just a little over $110 million for a building that might cost nearly three times as much.

Moreover, Barden said that he could not afford to start making payments for an arena until after his casino opened. Initially Barden had said he would open a temporary floating riverboat casino, allowing him to start making money immediately for the state, for his own permanent building and for the Penguins. However, he had backed out of that proposal when he realized that he did not have enough room on the North Shore to build a casino and run a riverboat from the same property. It would take him three years to open his facility and start generating money for the arena to be built. The Penguins would have to wait, he said.

A bigger question was whether Barden even could afford to build his casino. When the Penguins looked for a gambling partner early in the bidding process, they considered the Detroit businessman but did background research and ultimately decided he did not have a realistic chance of winning a license, largely because they believed he could not come up with the money to build a slots parlor. When he submitted his proposal, Barden had the backing of a Wall Street investment firm. After the bidding ended, the deal shifted and the company no longer was willing to put up the money.

Adding to the uncertainty of Barden's casino plan, both of the losing bidders remained in the process, having appealed the Gaming Control Board's decision directly to the state Supreme Court. Even with the slimmest of odds, Isle of Capri still had a chance to end up with the casino license. While the Penguins owners wanted to move forward with their plans, they could not completely ignore the fact that their initial partner still might end up with the license.

When Rendell arrived for the second night of negotiations at the state office building, he arrived late after an uncomfortable and turbulent flight, and he looked tired. The Penguins officials sat at one end of the long conference table with their backs to the window: Burkle sat between Chuck Greenberg, the team's lawyer, and Morehouse, the consultant; Ken Sawyer, the team president, sat next to Morehouse. The public officials walked in with a surprise guest: Barden had insisted on participating in the discussions if he was going to help pay for the arena. The Penguins executives had been caught off guard. They had no interest in dealing directly with the man whose casino proposal seemed to draw heavily from Isle of Capri's plan and who sank their chance of having the casino company pay the entire cost of the $290 million arena. If the state had chosen Isle, construction already could have started. Instead, they sat here still talking. "It didn't seem to make any sense to us," Greenberg said. "We were still smarting a little bit from Mr. Barden getting the license, and this seemed like it was supposed to be a private discussion. It just seemed odd that he was there."

As at the first meeting, the governor presented the terms of the deal that the state was prepared to offer – only the details had materially changed from what had been discussed earlier. As the Penguins' lawyer, Greenberg started pointing out the discrepancies and asking questions about why the proposal had changed so dramatically. One sticking point had been whether the team or Barden would get development rights to the Civic Arena parking lots. Rendell, who already seemed agitated, started turning angry. "At that point they were pushing the envelope and not understanding that we weren't free to use the public dollars any way we wanted to," Rendell said later. The state's offer, he said, would have done much more for the Penguins than the public had done for the Flyers hockey team in Philadelphia. The Penguins executives wanted to make comparisons with what the taxpayers had done to pay for new football and baseball stadiums in Pittsburgh and Philadelphia, but Rendell countered that that was not a fair comparison. On a minor point where Greenberg and the governor disagreed about what the Penguins legally could do under the proposed agreement, Rendell turned to Burkle and said, "You must have some lousy lawyer."

Unfazed, Greenberg continued to press his points about the changes in the state's offer as Rendell turned redder in the face with exasperation. Suddenly the governor snapped. He started slamming his hand over and over onto the long wooden table as his voice boomed with thunder at Greenberg. The Penguins owners had to deal with the state and work out an agreement to stay in Pittsburgh, he said. Pennsylvania could not make them a better offer, and they had to take it. He called Greenberg a liar and might have salted his language with an expletive or two, according to multiple witnesses. Rendell had never seemed so angry, one participant said.

Greenberg sat frozen in his seat, afraid that if he responded to the tirade by even moving his face, the governor might physically strike him. Dan Onorato, the Allegheny County executive, got up from his seat and stood near the governor and Greenberg in case he had to physically restrain Rendell to keep him away from the Penguins' lawyer. "I remember trying to sit there as stone-faced as possible," Greenberg recalled later. "I really thought that if I had given him any cause to be incited, a line might have been crossed that would be very difficult to undo."

Rendell said later that he was trying to send a message with his voice and intimidating presence, making it seem like he could attack. "I like to create that impression," he said. "Part of it is real, and part of it's acting." That night, Rendell said later, 60 percent was real and 40 percent, acting. "At that point, they were being absolutely unreasonable," he continued. "They were totally refusing to be cognizant of our responsibility to protect the public treasury."

Finally when Rendell ran out of invectives, the room stopped in silence as even the mayor and county executive looked on in slack-jawed disbelief at the governor's sudden explosion. Burkle, who stayed as cool as his trademark black polo shirt and jeans, was the first to speak up, calmly asking for a moment alone with his team. After the public officials and Barden left the room, Burkle turned to his aides and made a light joke to break the tension, saying that while he had a school named for him at the University of California, Los Angeles with experts on Middle East conflict, he had never seen anything like the governor's outburst. Greenberg spoke up next and said that the negotiating team did not need to leave the meeting on his account because he could take the heat of being yelled at by Rendell, even if it had been unlike any reaming he had ever experienced before.

"We've got to get out of here," Burkle responded. There was no way they could stay and continue negotiating after what had happened. The executives had come in hoping to iron out the final details of an arena deal, and instead the terms had shifted and the governor had crossed a line with his unprovoked anger. As the rest of the team packed up, Burkle and Morehouse went to tell the governor that the talks were over for the evening.

Moments later, as the Penguins group was leaving the conference room, Barden rushed after them. He stepped into the hallway, asking for a moment alone with Burkle – a multimillionaire chasing after a billionaire – to say they could still work out a deal. Burkle stopped for a moment and chatted with Barden. If they were going to come to terms, it would have to wait for another night. The Penguins group rode down in an elevator to a garage below the building. They drove away without talking to the reporters camped out by the exit.

Burkle headed to the airport while the Penguins executives drove back to Chatham Center where they met in a conference room to discuss strategy. Greenberg picked up his phone and left a voice mail message for Lemieux, saying, "The meeting was awful. I can't even put into words how terrible it was. I'm speechless. This is not at all good."

Then a short while later as he got ready to leave for home where his teenage sons were waiting, Greenberg heard his BlackBerry ring. It was Burkle. The two men had known each other for years, but they had never really worked closely. After Isle of Capri failed to win the slots license, the team's owners had assigned Morehouse and Greenberg to head up the negotiations over paying for a Pittsburgh arena. The two men spent so much time talking in the weeks after, that Morehouse's toddler-aged daughter first learned to answer the phone by saying "Hi, Chuck." While Morehouse had Burkle's total confidence, however, the California investor still had not entirely decided how much he could trust Lemieux's lawyer and close friend. As Greenberg went to answer his BlackBerry, he was not sure what to expect.

Burkle started talking right away. "Hey, Chuck, this is Ron. I just want you to know you didn't deserve that. You didn't do anything to provoke that. You shouldn't have been spoken to that way. I really appreciate that you took one for the team there. I've got your back. We're all going to stick together, and we'll figure out a way to get something done."

Inadvertently, Rendell brought the Penguins' negotiating team closer together than it ever had been.

Back inside the state office building, Rendell, the other public officials and Barden stayed another 90 minutes to talk strategy. An obvious opportunity had been lost, and the politicians were trying to gauge how much leverage the governor had just conceded and how serious the Penguins owners might feel about simply moving the team. "After the first meeting, (the Penguins) were so positive about everything, that they were putting themselves at a disadvantage from a negotiating standpoint, because hope started to trickle through the community, like, 'Hey, this is going to work,'" Ravenstahl recalled later. "From a negotiating standpoint, and they're very good at what they do, they felt leveraged. This meeting and the end result of the meeting allowed for continued negotiating. ... It was to the Penguins' benefit certainly that the meeting ended the way it did. We were in the driver's seat after the first meeting and after the second meeting it was equal, if not them now in the driver's seat. ... We knew what we had to do. That second meeting, from my perspective, allowed the Penguins to drive a harder bargain with us just because of the way it happened."

The mood inside the state office building was tense, with no one wanting to set off the frustrated governor again. The session finally broke up with the mayor and county executive quietly leaving on their own, and Rendell did not feel up to talking with reporters. He would have gladly stood before the television cameras if there had been good news, as he had hoped. There would be nothing but bad news tonight. Rendell sent an aide to deliver the message instead: "We hope to be able to work out a deal at some point in the near future."

The local officials had become so unsettled by the outcome of the second meeting that they felt they had to do something to try to set things right again with Burkle. He had seemed stunned by the governor's outburst, and no one knew whether he would come back to negotiate again. The following Monday, Ravenstahl and Onorato boarded a commercial flight to meet Burkle and Morehouse in Manhattan. They did not tell Rendell about the trip, figuring the meeting might be more fruitful if they simply went on their own to try to smooth over any hard feelings that had come out of the previous negotiating session. The politicians met with the billionaire investor at a loft apartment in the city's SoHo neighborhood, and they told him how they hoped he and Lemieux would not move the team without at least giving Pittsburgh another shot at coming up with an arena proposal. Without the governor, and more importantly, the state's slots money, the two local politicians could not offer up anything more definitive. "We had no authority to make a deal," Ravenstahl said later. "We're there without the ability really to negotiate anything. ... We had no intention of doing a deal that night. It was more an expression of our interest to continue the dialogue." The two officials flew home that night feeling that they at least had re-established communications with the Penguins owners.

Rendell blew up again when he found out the mayor and county executive had gone to meet Burkle on their own. First he uninvited the two officials to a major press conference the following morning to announce $12 million in state grants and tax credits for a downtown housing development. Then in a conference call with the politicians later that day, Rendell demanded to know what they had given away. "The conference call was the governor basically asking me and Dan, 'What kind of deal did you guys put together?'" Ravenstahl said later. "'Well, how could you do a deal if you're not using city and county money? So what city money are you putting in, Mayor, and Dan, what are you putting in from the county?' We pushed back and said, 'Governor, we can't afford to do that. We've communicated that to you. There's just no appetite for local dollars in the deal. It's just not going to work.' He said, 'Well, then what were you doing in New York? What were you negotiating, my money?' The governor kind of put us in our place."

Later that night, Rendell reached out to Burkle himself, and they spoke by phone. The governor told reporters the next day that it had been a friendly conversation, and that, in his opinion, all the drama was just the Penguins owners trying to get the best possible arena deal. "He's trying to get every advantage," Rendell said that day. "He'll keep trying. We just want to make sure the resources we devote to this are not too much and not too little."

Threats by the Penguins owners to relocate had some credibility because more than a half-dozen cities already had eyed the franchise. Plus, the team knew it could not operate financially in the old arena. Modern arena negotiations often require team owners to flirt with other cities. The courtship frightens the team's hometown fans, and they put pressure on politicians to ante up the most tax money possible to keep the franchise from leaving. Cities without a franchise, meanwhile, act as willing participants. The flirtation, no matter how contrived, allows local leaders in the potential new city to argue that their burg or hamlet has a lot to offer a major league investor: "See, we're just as good as those other cities that already have teams." If they seriously want a team, city leaders also know that being mentioned as a relocation destination will put them on the short list of new markets when leagues look to expand or another owner really does intend to move.

In the Penguins' case, Lemieux and the team's top executives wanted to keep the franchise in Pittsburgh, but they also needed to know that the team would have a future somewhere else if Pennsylvania's political leaders pulled out of the negotiations or could not come up with favorable terms. Sawyer had been one of the stalwarts among the executive group who saw Rendell as a champion for the Penguins' arena and believed a deal to keep the team in the city eventually would get done. Yet even he saw the need for negotiations with other cities, as well. "If the governor ever pulled the deal off the table in Pennsylvania, the team was not going to be in Pittsburgh," Sawyer said later. "Whether it was going to Kansas City or not, I don't know, but there was no future. You had to lay the groundwork for eventualities." In a perverse way, too, the team owners' talks with other cities might have helped Rendell make a better case for spending millions of dollars on an arena. When the Penguins had a longterm lease at the Civic Arena, few elected officials could justify taking a political hit to build a new hockey rink. But as long as Lemieux and Burkle were actively engaged in negotiations to relocate, the sense of crisis those negotiations created made it easier for the governor and lawmakers to tell their constituents why the state needed to chip in for a new building.

Other Penguins executives and employees could not believe that the negotiations had turned so acrimonious that Lemieux and Burkle would even have to consider relocating. When the team won the rights to draft Crosby, it seemed to some that the arena problem would be resolved quickly and politicians would certainly do whatever was needed to keep the franchise in Pittsburgh. Now that no longer seemed to be the case, and some team insiders could hardly believe what was happening. "Why would you let this team leave?" one executive wondered, recalling his tormented feelings years later. "They're going to win a championship. You don't know when, but they are going to win a championship."

Some suitors had been more serious than others, and the hockey team owners had batted their eyes at more than one in return. By the Monday morning after the second meeting, Rendell said he had heard Lemieux and Burkle would be going to Houston to check out the Toyota Center – and local leaders throughout North America said they would meet with the owners, too. Morehouse and the other Penguins executives said little about what was going on with the Pittsburgh negotiations or whether they had a serious interest in any of these other cities.

The two sides in Pittsburgh had gotten as close as $500,000, when Morehouse joined representatives from the state and local governments for a Saturday conference call. The difference was so small that the team should just agree to the terms, one of the public officials said. Morehouse replied that the sticking point was no longer just the money. "It's more about trust at this point," he said. "We're going to be working together for 30 years. It's not about the money anymore. We've had this adversarial relationship. You've treated us like an adversary. You need to show us that you're going to be more collaborative."

Without pausing, the state official shot back by saying, "But you are our adversary." Morehouse said, "OK," signed off and hung up.

Later that afternoon, Morehouse called a conference call with Burkle, Lemieux, Sawyer and Chuck Greenberg. "Listen, this is where they are," Morehouse said. "They're not getting the message. We've tried everything. We're going to have to explore a move." After that, he and Tom McMillan, the team's vice president for communications, came into the Chatham Center offices to write a letter explaining what had happened and why the owners would be looking at other cities. Writing the first version of the letter had been a catharsis, allowing the executives to vent all of their frustrations from the previous months. Sending it out, however, would have been like burning the ships, one insider later admitted. There would be no way to ever go back to negotiating for a Pittsburgh arena. As good as it had felt to pour out all that vitriol, the executives wrote up a cleaner but still tough-worded version for public distribution.

Dated March 5, 2007, the letter signed by Lemieux and Burkle opened by saying, "We can do no more." For eight years, the letter continued, since bringing the team out of bankruptcy, they had been working to get an arena. Under the latest compromise, the team would pay $3.6 million a year in rent and another $400,000 a year for capital costs. That would raise $120 million over 30 years for the arena. "Unfortunately, we still don't have a deal and are faced with mounting uncertainty," the owners wrote. The letter talked about the lack of collaboration from elected leaders, especially compared to the warm reception waiting for the franchise in Kansas City. In an effort to keep the team in Pittsburgh, the owners had not talked with the media or seriously courted other cities since early January, they said. "Our good-faith efforts have not produced a deal, however, and have only added more anxiety to what we thought at best was a risky proposition for us moving forward. Those risks and the fact that our lease expires in less than four months leave us with no choice but to explore every option to ensure the longterm future of the Penguins organization." The owners had declared an impasse and would notify the league that they would "aggressively explore relocation."

Kansas City had offered the most serious bid for the Penguins so far. As in many cities, officials had fallen under the spell of a movie line that had become a cliché in professional sports relocations: if you build it, they will come. A leading national economic development group had even been holding an annual conference with that title – albeit with a question mark, rather than an exclamation point, after the phrase.

Kansas City had spent $276 million on the arena, and two-term Mayor Kay Barnes was on the hook to deliver on her theory that if taxpayers built a state-of-the-art building, they could attract big-league interest to the small-market city. Under a naming rights deal, the arena already was named the Sprint Center. To help sell the building to sports teams, the city hired entertainment promoter and stadium manager Anschutz Entertainment Group, which operates more than three dozen arenas and stadiums from the United Kingdom to China, and in major cities across the United States. More significantly for Kansas City's bid to lure the Penguins, AEG's top executive Timothy Leiweke lived in the same Beverly Hills suburb as Burkle, and they're friends.

Burkle used his connections to take a serious look at the Sprint Center. Already, he and Lemieux had visited Kansas City in January – before their first meeting with Rendell and local politicians in Pittsburgh. At that time, they had toured the Sprint Center arena and met with officials from AEG. "I remember being impressed," Morehouse said years later about the trip. Given a day's notice, the Kansas City officials had put together a full itinerary for the team owners. "We got there at night and we had dinner with some people. The next morning at 6:00, we met with all the CEOs of all the top companies in Kansas City. They had them all there. They had this huge room, all full of them." The Penguins executives had been left to wonder why they could not generate this same sort of enthusiasm at home. "There is no one in Pittsburgh who is giving us that kind of support to keep us from leaving," Morehouse said later, recalling the moment. "The amazing thing is how badly they want us in Kansas City. We want to stay here in Pittsburgh, but there's no one here showing that kind of support for us, in the corporate or political community, at least."

It was now two months later, and the Penguins were talking with officials in Kansas City again about a serious arena deal. The team owners were running out of time to find a new home before their lease expired in June. Kansas City offered a logical solution, with its ready-made arena. No matter what they offered, local leaders felt like spectators in an event that only the Penguins could control. "I can't read other people's minds," Mayor Barnes said later, but the Penguins' owners seemed serious. "You take every potential opportunity seriously. You explore it and see where it goes."

Kansas City's offer was sweeter than any of the executives expected: Even without knowing whether they would get a new team, local companies already had purchased all 72 luxury boxes in the city's new sports complex, a cool-looking circular building encased in 224 enormous glass panels and filled with the latest high-tech gadgets. They also guaranteed that any team coming in would sell every club seat, and they promised sponsorship contracts, as well. The Penguins would get to use the arena rent-free, and the team would collect money from seat licenses, luxury boxes and ticket sales. It would take half of the profit from concessions and parking, even at non-hockey events. The city already had a fledgling fan base, too, with a group dedicated to bringing the NHL to town. Paul McGannon, the head of a local group called NHL21, even had invited team executives to try out the city for an exhibition game against the

St. Louis Blues. "We want them to sample the barbecue, the hospitality and the good crowds," he said. "Then they have a decision to make."

Since Rendell's blowup at the state office building, other cities had lined up for the Penguins, too. Even if Jim Balsillie, the founder of BlackBerry manufacturer Research in Motion, no longer planned to purchase the hockey team, officials in Hamilton, Ontario, remained interested in drawing the club there. Although the city sits close enough to Toronto to make up part of the Maple Leafs' home fan base, local officials have long argued that southern Ontario can support its own franchise. "Always the bridesmaid and never the bride," said Terry Whitehead, a city councilman and chairman of the local NHL steering committee. "That's certainly the experience of Hamilton. But, again, if you don't buy a ticket, you don't win the lottery. We persevere."

Hartford remained in play, with the old Whalers boosters club pressuring developer Larry Gottesdiener to somehow make a play for the Penguins. Houston's mayor made an offer for the Penguins to stop in his city. And officials in Oklahoma City, which had a taste of professional sports when the New Orleans Hornets played two seasons there after Hurricane Katrina, also showed some interest in getting the hockey team.

Las Vegas presented an interesting option. The desert gambling mecca has wanted the legitimacy of a major league sports franchise to bolster its status among America's fastest-growing cities. Sports leagues have stayed away from the city because of Nevada's legalized sports books. A fan could potentially walk into a casino, place a wager on a game, and then go next door to watch it taking place. Worse, according to the thinking, players, managers, referees and even owners might be more tempted to place bets on games they could influence. Each of the major leagues has been tarred by a gambling scandal at some point, and as a consequence, the leagues are extra vigilant against even the appearance of impropriety.

Now that they seriously started to explore alternatives in the event a deal could not be reached in Pittsburgh, Morehouse and Greenberg flew out to Las Vegas and met with Burkle, who had come in from California. The three of them sat down in the office of Mayor Oscar Goodman, a Philadelphia lawyer who had gone to the desert and ended up defending men accused of organized crime. He had even appeared briefly in the movie *Casino*, playing himself as a lawyer to the mob. Goodman told the Penguins owners and executives what a great destination Las Vegas would be for a hockey team, and then he had an assistant take them on a tour of the local arena that would be the Penguins' temporary home until a new rink could be built. The lack of a new arena confirmed what the team officials always felt, that Las Vegas seemed a stretch to land the franchise. It would have meant trading a strong market in a wintry climate for an uncertain Sun Belt destination. No matter. Goodman told reporters afterward he had a "very pleasant chat" with team officials for about a half-hour. Las Vegas had been in the running for a major league sports franchise.

One other scenario had been discussed at the time. Under the proposal, Philip Anschutz, the founder of Anschutz Entertainment Group, would have moved the Los Angeles Kings to Kansas City so the Penguins could relocate to Los Angeles. The idea had been that Sidney Crosby, Evgeni Malkin and the team's other young stars would make a bigger splash in the nation's second-largest media market, which also happens to be Burkle's hometown, than in Kansas City. While intriguing, the idea apparently was considered impractical by all involved and never moved off the draft board for real consideration.

Before the Penguins entourage headed back to California to figure out their next moves, Morehouse made one last check with a friend in the Houston mayor's office to see whether the lukewarm interest there had solidified at all. The Rockets basketball team had quietly raised some concerns about whether it made sense for the city to court a hockey franchise. Houston could not match the lucrative terms being offered by Kansas City, anyway. Even if the Texas officials could not present a viable alternative, they could still help the Penguins make a case with Rendell and the politicians back home. They called an impromptu press conference. "It sounds like Kansas City has offered them a much more favorable deal," said Tad Brown, CEO of Rockets Clutch City Entertainment, the operator of Houston's Toyota Center.

Just as Burkle, Morehouse and Greenberg arrived in Los Angeles, Bill Daly, the league's deputy commissioner, called to say a meeting with Rendell and the other public officials had been arranged. It would take place on the East Coast, but he wouldn't say where.

Back home, Rendell had grown tired of watching the negative news reports every time the Penguins owners traveled to a potential new hometown. The governor finally called for a secret meeting that would bring Burkle and Lemieux back to the bargaining table for the first time in two months. The two sides had not faced each other since the governor's angry tirade inside the parole board hearing room had sent Burkle out into a freezing January night. Rendell had hoped for good news at that meeting, but it had not happened when he lost his temper. This time, he wanted to make sure no one left without at least something positive to share with the public, if not a handshake agreement. All the major players would be on hand. For the Penguins, both Burkle and Lemieux would come, while Rendell would lead a delegation that included the mayor and the county executive. Just to make sure everyone got along, NHL Commissioner Gary Bettman would serve as referee.

The governor's aides wanted the public to know that a meeting was taking place, but they did not want any reporters interfering with the discussion. They gave word that the session would occur near Philadelphia but refused to say where. Pittsburgh reporters who had traveled out for the meeting were told to congregate inside Philadelphia's City Hall, beneath its rooftop statue of William Penn, a Quaker who founded the commonwealth. Reporters, being reporters, spread out to find the meeting, heading to local government buildings and high-priced hotels. Two reporters were sure they had discovered the secret location after going to the high-rise building housing Ballard Spahr Andrews & Ingersoll, the law firm where Rendell remained on the payroll. Saying they were in the building for the meeting among the governor and the Penguins, the reporters were escorted to the penthouse offices, expecting to find the participants engaged in hushed negotiations. Instead, the law firm's secretaries were as interested to find out from the reporters what they knew, or at least thought they knew.

Not even the participants knew where the meeting would take place. Ravenstahl checked into a Center City hotel, figuring the meeting would be nearby. During a conference call that afternoon, the governor said he had another location in mind. "He said something like, 'The car will be there to get you guys.' We said, 'Where are we going?' and he said, 'Don't worry about it. We'll take you where you need to go.'"

Even as Burkle and his small entourage flew back across the country, they still did not know where the meeting would occur. Throughout the flight, Greenberg stayed in touch with Daly, the NHL deputy commissioner, about the logistics of the session. The setup for the meeting would be important, the Penguins lawyer said, for setting the right tone. Everyone in the room would want to reach a deal, and the NHL executives needed to work with the team to make sure they sent a unified message. Bettman had said he planned to sit in the neutral space between the team owners and the public officials, but Greenberg argued that would be the wrong move. The commissioner needed to make it unambiguously clear that he sided with his franchise. The public officials had gotten the idea that the league would never let the Penguins leave Pittsburgh, Greenberg said, so Bettman needed to sit between Lemieux and Burkle so no one could mistake his allegiance.

As the plane neared the East Coast, Daly sent a text to Greenberg letting him know that the meeting would take place in New Jersey, at the Crowne Plaza in Cherry Hill, just off the Garden State Parkway. Greenberg could not help himself from making a reference to *The Godfather*. He texted back a paraphrased line from the movie: "Should we leave the gun and take the cannoli?"

Onorato described a similar experience, saying he gave little thought to where the meeting might take place until he was almost there. He was sitting in the back seat of a chauffeured car, reading over papers and preparing what he would say for the negotiations, when he looked up suddenly. The car was passing over a long bridge above the Delaware River, and he saw a sign: Welcome to New Jersey.

Rendell knew no one would look for his meeting beyond the Pennsylvania borders. "We just wanted to be somewhere where there weren't reporters standing outside," he said later. "We wouldn't have to face reporters until we wanted to."

The Penguins' ownership group arrived first, with Lemieux, Sawyer and Tom Grealish, a close friend of Lemieux and a minor investor in the team, coming from Pittsburgh in a chartered plane. The team owners and executives met up inside a restaurant near the hotel lobby, where they could watch the other participants arriving. The goal of that night's meeting, Burkle told the group, would be to see whether they could re-establish trust with the public officials. No one believed the session might actually lead to an agreement to build an arena. While the Penguins officials sat there, they watched as Rendell, Ravenstahl and Onorato arrived with their entourage and headed straight upstairs to the meeting room. Bettman, who was running late because he had gotten caught in midtown Manhattan traffic, came in and spotted Burkle and Lemieux. He was as aware as anyone that feelings had been hurt in the previous few weeks, and he made a point of telling the team owners that he hoped that could change when everyone finally sat down together again.

Bettman seemed to have nearly as much riding on the night's negotiations as the team owners and public officials. The league's owners and players had finally reached an agreement on resuming play, and its biggest star, Crosby, was playing in Pittsburgh. The Penguins also had the best-known ownership group with Lemieux, a hall-of-fame player who had returned to the ice, saying he wanted to stay in the city. If the team could not find a way to remain there, it would be another embarrassment for a league that had experienced too many. As he arrived at the New Jersey hotel, Bettman could not afford to trade another snowbound, Northeastern city for sunny, glitzy Las Vegas or even another small market like Kansas City. And while Balsillie might have dreamed about getting a team for Hamilton, Ontario, the league seemed to have no desire to split up the lucrative Toronto market.

As the Penguins group walked into the meeting room with Bettman and Daly, Rendell and the public officials already had set up along one side of the long tables arranged in an open square. The governor gestured for Lemieux and Burkle to sit down on the opposite side. The owners would sit together, and the rest of their staff would be off to a corner of the table. For much of the night, the big decisions would have to be made by Lemieux and Burkle, anyway. They would be the ones who would have to feel comfortable enough with the progress of the talks to determine whether they could work out a longterm relationship with the city, county and state. Rendell then suggested the league officials take a place between the two groups on a third side. Bettman shook him off. He walked over between the team owners and said, "I'm going to sit with my friends Ron and Mario." The message had been clear, and from the looks on the faces of the public officials, it had been received as intended. Rendell saw the seating choice as symbolic. "I didn't think much of it. I knew Bettman was there to argue their case. I didn't think for a minute he was going to be a neutral arbiter."

Bettman took charge of the meeting, with Rendell and the owners each realizing they had become too emotionally involved to work out a deal on their own. The commissioner started with the easy negotiations. Again, the commissioner noted that emotions had been running high in recent weeks and said he hoped the session would help the team and public officials see that they could work together on the common goal of keeping the Penguins in Pittsburgh. Rendell spoke up and said he shared the same ambition for the evening. The two sides already had worked out most of the deal, so Bettman asked them to begin by formally agreeing that each wanted to keep the team in Pittsburgh. They did. By now, it seemed everyone had grown tired of the gamesmanship.

Next Bettman handed out two-page term sheets with about a dozen discussion points. Suddenly the mood in the room had shifted from people on each side wondering whether they could trust the others, to one in which it seemed they might actually be able to work out the terms of the arena deal that night. The two sides already had agreed on some of the positions, such as the team getting revenue from concessions and other events at the arena. The Penguins and public officials also had agreed that Barden's casino would contribute $7.5 million a year for the arena and the state would contribute from its slots money. The deal seemed to be coming together. During one break, Lemieux turned to his friend Grealish and said in almost disbelief, "Are we getting this done?" Yes, it seemed they would be getting it done, finally, after all these years. That it would come down to a meeting in the ballroom of a New Jersey hotel only added to the sense of destiny for a team that had been through so many odd turns since the day two decades earlier when General Manager Eddie Johnson had called Lemieux's name on draft day and he had sat motionless in the stands over a contract that had been worth less than $250,000 a year. Now Lemieux was the team's owner, and he was on the precipice of reaching terms on an arena deal worth more than $300 million.

Even then, when it seemed everyone had finally come together, the talks nearly broke off again. Rendell joked at one point, saying with a laugh to Burkle something about the team getting a sweet deal and bleeding money from the city, county and state. Burkle didn't laugh along. He took offense. "I sit here and listen to you say that when this guy here sitting next to me, my partner," he said as he pointed toward Lemieux, according to one participant, "spent all of his time and all of his effort trying to keep this team in Pittsburgh. With everything he's done for Pittsburgh, and everything I've done in business, and the integrity I've had and the way I've approached this, you're gonna say something like that? We're done." All of the negotiators on the Penguins' side of the table stood up and walked out of the room.

"In all good negotiations, there's posturing and there's acting," Rendell said later. "It was absolutely true what I was saying: They were trying to take the city to the cleaners. Did I regret it? Sure. But I knew they weren't going to blow up the deal over that."

Bettman stayed for a moment to talk with Rendell and the public delegation, and then he went into the side room where the Penguins had been gathering to discuss strategy throughout the evening. The governor had used a poor choice of words and did not mean any offense, Bettman said. The terms of the deal would remain, if the Penguins owners would agree to come back to the table. Burkle said that was fine with him if it was all right with Lemieux. He said that it was.

When Bettman returned alone into the negotiating room, the public officials thought for a moment he was coming to announce that Lemieux and Burkle had left the building. Ravenstahl said it crossed his mind that the night might end like the second meeting in Pittsburgh when the Penguins group never came back to the discussion.

Instead, after a few moments, Lemieux and Burkle returned to the room. Everyone made up, and they finally worked out the major terms of the deal.

In the end, the Penguins had won the last great arena deal before the Great Recession at the end of the decade. Terms of the $310 million agreement had been so narrow that they turned on the cost of interest. The state committed to a higher starting price for the arena, at $290 million, and the two sides agreed to split up to another $20 million in overruns. Rendell had said taxpayers would cover an extra $500,000 a year, bringing the public's portion to $7.5 million annually, with the money coming out of the state's take from slot machines. Barden's Majestic Star Casino remained on the hook for its $7.5 million a year, and the two sides agreed that he could not be expected to pay any more. In the final negotiations, the Penguins also insisted the state guarantee the Majestic Star contribution, so that if Barden's project failed for any reason, it would not delay construction of the arena. Burkle and Lemieux agreed to kick in another $200,000 a year – bringing the team's annual contribution to $3.8 million – but only if the city and county agreed to tear down the Civic Arena so the Penguins could develop the 28 acres on the site.

The two sides remained $500,000-a-year short of what they needed to pay for an arena. Burkle suggested checking whether falling interest rates had lowered the amount needed to make payments. The rates had fallen, and the numbers worked.

The actual terms of the deal had not really changed all that much from early January, two months earlier, when the owners and elected officials first met to talk about using casino money to pay for an arena. Instead, strong sentiments among both groups – anger, frustration, jealousy – had nearly caused the deal to implode. For the previous 72 hours, it had seemed not only possible, but probable that the hockey team would leave. Lemieux and Burkle proved they had other options. The fear that kept one team insider awake at night was that neither side would realize what had happened until the Penguins already were gone.

Before 11:30, in time for the end of the local evening news back in Pittsburgh, the two sides had reached a handshake deal – the closest Lemieux ever had come to getting his wish for a new arena in his adopted hometown. Rendell wondered whether the group should make a definitive announcement that night, but Burkle and Morehouse suggested that both sides should take several days to go over the terms. If everyone still agreed, they would make a formal announcement the following Tuesday in Pittsburgh. Inside Philadelphia's City Hall, reporters had entertained themselves through the evening with parlor-game discussions about where the meeting might be taking place. Most of these reporters had spent the past 24 months together, competing with each other one day and cooperating the next. The governor's spokesman, Chuck Ardo, arrived just before the start of the evening news to feed the group a few morsels of information. Ardo appeared to be the most unlikely mouthpiece of any administration, with ruffled black hair and bottle-thick glasses. As the TV cameramen were setting up for the impromptu press conference, local reporter Andy Gastmeyer stood before the microphone so the cameras could be focused. In the punch-drunk, campy spirit of the night, he gave a rapid-fire narration of the NBC studio tour that he

had learned as a page for the network in New York City decades earlier. For reporters who had spent more time traveling than actually working on that particular night, Gastmeyer's quick rendition encapsulated the mood of relief at the end of hours – and really months – of chasing a story that seemed to be reaching a climax. A moment later, Ardo stood at the microphone and gave the reporters another small tidbit, just enough so each newspaper and station could justify having sent reporters across the state for a meeting they never saw. The news that night was not only that the two sides had met, but also that they seemed very close to an agreement.

Back at the Crowne Plaza hotel after the negotiations ended, the Penguins group that was heading back to Pittsburgh started packing up to leave for their chartered jet, when someone realized that Ravenstahl and Onorato would be stuck in New Jersey for the night. Both elected officials were supposed to be on hand back home the next morning for a press conference about a minor collapse at the city's convention center. Lemieux walked over to the politicians and offered them a lift back to Pittsburgh with him and the team executives. The mayor, the county executive and one staff member accepted, realizing the only other option would be to find a hotel room and then get up early and try to catch one of the first commercial flights.

Once the plane was in the air, Grealish, Lemieux's close friend, reached into his bag where he had stuffed a bottle of red wine from 1999. As he proposed sharing a drink, someone asked whether that had been a particularly good year for wine. Nothing was special about the vintage, Grealish answered. He had chosen a bottle from that year because that was when the Lemieux group started working to get an arena. He opened the bottle and poured out the contents as everyone – both the team officials and the politicians – toasted the good fortune of finally reaching a deal that would keep the team in Pittsburgh. The transformation from only hours earlier, when Lemieux and Burkle had wondered whether they would ever be able to trust the elected officials, had been complete.

Five days later, Rendell was finally ready to face reporters with good news. He had called a late-afternoon press conference inside the Senator John Heinz History Center, a former ice house that has been turned into an interactive museum about Pittsburgh. Inside the building's main hall, with exposed red bricks and steel beams painted green, Rendell stood among pieces of the city's past, a retired trolley car and a World War II Jeep. Lemieux stood with him at the podium, beaming, along with NHL Commissioner Bettman. Asked whether he would still try to sell the team as he had twice before, Lemieux looked incredulous. "The team is not on the market," he said, "and we don't plan to put the team on the market anytime soon."

Burkle, in polo shirt and jeans, stood away from the cameras, in the shadows, watching the official scene taking place. Kansas City probably had made the better offer, he said. Officials there had been waiting for him to come back and finalize the relocation over the weekend, after the meeting broke off in

Mario Lemieux talks about the Penguins arena deal as Gov. Ed Rendell stands behind him looking on with other public leaders and team officials. (Pittsburgh Tribune-Review, *Philip G. Pavely*)

Cherry Hill. He never made the trip. If the decision had been only about the best offer on paper, the Penguins might have gone. Talk about moving to Kansas City had been real. "Things started dragging out" on the Pittsburgh negotiations, Burkle said. "Then we kinda lost faith that we were going to get a deal done, because we didn't feel like there was any motivation to get something done. So we had to face reality. ... We had to go out and get busy and figure out what our alternatives were."

After Pittsburgh came up with a competitive offer – and showed an open willingness to work with the hockey team – the decision had been easy. "At the end of the day," Burkle said, "if you have a good deal and a fair deal, we would rather stay here and be here where the fans are."

9

The Trade
February 26, 2008

With less than five minutes until a 3 p.m. deadline, Penguins General Manager Ray Shero still had not decided whether to pull off the biggest trade of his career.

The son of a legendary coach for the Flyers and Rangers, Shero had participated in some major transactions as an assistant, first in Ottawa, and then in Nashville, joining the Predators when the franchise entered the league in 1998. That had been different, however, than having the final say on a player exchange worth millions of dollars, and one with the potential to forge a champion if it worked – or to cost the franchise and its owners dearly if it did not. To that point, the Penguins had followed a strict five-year plan that included finalizing an arena deal to keep the team in Pittsburgh, which had happened the previous March; drafting talented players, which management had done repeatedly after finishing near the bottom of the standings and getting high draft choices in return; and nurturing talent with the goal of having a winning team in place when the new arena opened in 2010. According to the plan, the Penguins still had more than two years left until the franchise started spending up to the league's salary cap on player payroll. Shero had a choice to make about whether to accelerate that plan.

The talk had started a month earlier at the National Hockey League's all-star game in Atlanta. Executives with the Thrashers, the host team, wanted to see what they could get for their star Marian Hossa. He would be appearing as an all-star for the fourth time, but he would become a free agent after the season. The Thrashers approached the Penguins, among others, to see how much the team might be willing to give up in young talent for a player who could help them make a playoff run – but who might be around only a few months. Already

Hossa had let it be known that he wanted to test the free agency market to have some say, at least, in where he would play and for how much money. Originally drafted by the Ottawa Senators, Hossa had been traded to Atlanta after the lockout, and this time he hoped to play for a contender.

To get Hossa, the Penguins would have to sacrifice part of their future. The trade also could create some chaos for the Penguins to lock down their star players for the future. Center Sidney Crosby already had signed a long-term contract, but it had not yet started to count against the salary cap. After the season, goaltender Marc-Andre Fleury's contract would be up, and the Penguins had not decided yet whether the team could afford to keep him. Evgeni Malkin, the second-line center who had joined the team 17 months earlier, would be entering the last year of his contract. Left wing Ryan Malone, a Pittsburgh native who had attended Upper St. Clair High School before the Penguins drafted him in 1999, would be a free agent, along with defenseman Brooks Orpik. If the team traded future players to get Hossa in the final months of his contract, it would likely make a bid to try to keep him, too. At the same time, Shero was working on another deal to acquire established defenseman Hal Gill from Toronto.

When Shero met with his hockey staff the day before the trading deadline weeks later, he told them, "We've got nothing going." The Penguins had inquired about Hossa and some other players, but the team did not seem to be in a position to attract attention from anyone looking to deal. By the next morning, however, the mood had shifted. The Penguins were suddenly under consideration for Hossa, Gill and at least one other forward.

Chuck Fletcher, the Penguins' assistant general manager, took over the negotiations with Toronto, where his father, Cliff Fletcher, recently had returned as general manager. The talks went back and forth until Shero agreed to give up a second-round pick that year and a fifth rounder the following year to get Gill.

By then, Atlanta's interest in the Penguins' offer for Hossa seemed to have cooled. It was believed that Ottawa had made a strong offer. Shero had been an assistant with the Senators when the team had drafted Hossa 12th overall in the 1997 NHL

draft held at Pittsburgh's Civic Arena. Now Ottawa's executives seemed to believe that getting him back might give their
team a chance to win the Stanley Cup a year after advancing
to the final round and losing. Montreal also desperately wanted
Hossa. Word leaked out early that afternoon that Montreal's
team Web site had been set up with a page that could go live to
start selling Hossa sweaters the moment a deal was announced.

Then suddenly, around 2:20 p.m. – just 40 minutes before
the trading deadline, when it seemed no deal would happen
with the Penguins – Atlanta called to say Pittsburgh might
have the best offer after all. Pittsburgh would be giving up some
young prospects, so Shero insisted that the Thrashers include
another forward on the left side. Atlanta offered Pascal Dupuis,
a left wing who would become a free agent after the season.
Talks continued until 2:55. Shero sat at a desk inside the Civic
Arena with three phones in front of him: He had Atlanta's
general manager on one line; an executive from another team,
who was willing to accept a fourth-round pick in a softer deal
for another forward, on another line; and Mario Lemieux on a
cell phone. The Thrashers wanted to make a deal with Pittsburgh, and the team needed an answer. Shero asked for a
moment, and he put the Atlanta executive on hold.

Shero picked up the cell phone to talk with Lemieux. This
would not be like the Gill trade or any other deal Shero had
made so far. With millions of dollars and young prospects on
the line, this was not the sort of decision any general manager
could make and then tell the owners about only afterward.
Shero needed to make sure the team's owners supported taking a chance on Hossa. He had already laid out the potential
risks to Lemieux and Ron Burkle. "Here's the money, but also
here are the assets I'm giving up," Shero recounted later. "These
are assets that might set us back a little bit if it doesn't work
out. In the worst case situation, you do this and you get knocked
out in the first round? It's a disaster. I mean, it is."

As he talked into the cell phone, Shero said to Lemieux,
"Here's where we are." The general manager explained that
the Atlanta executive was on hold and needed an answer. If
Lemieux did not want to pursue Hossa, Shero could work out

the trade for the other forward by giving up the fourth-round pick. After weeks of considering a trade for a marquis player, the moment finally had arrived.

Lemieux listened to the details of the two options, and he said, "What do you want to do?"

Shero knew what he wanted to do. "Hossa's the impact player," he said. Then he laid out the ways Hossa could help the Penguins and where he would fit with Gill and Dupuis, the Atlanta left wing who would be part of the deal.

Again Lemieux asked his general manager, "What do you want to do?"

"This is a risk," Shero responded. "We're giving up lots of assets."

"Ray, I'm a risk-taker," Lemieux responded. "I bought this team out of bankruptcy. If you think this is going to help our team, you've got my support."

Shero said, "I've gotta go."

He hung up the cell phone and picked up the line where the Atlanta executive had been waiting on hold. They finalized the agreement with about a minute to spare before the 3 p.m. deadline.

When he hung up from that call, Shero sat at his desk with his hands shaking. "What did I just do?" he thought to himself.

A moment later, news of the trade flashed across the television screen in his office. Shero's phone rang, and he answered it to hear the voice of the other general manager who had been on hold. In the excitement of the Hossa trade, Shero had forgotten about the softer deal for the fourth-round draft pick. Instead of being mad, the other executive seemed impressed at what had transpired while he was waiting. He congratulated Shero on making the trade.

Two nights later in Boston, Shero's last-minute trade hardly seemed worth celebrating. The Penguins lost 5-to-1 to the Bruins, Gill had a terrible night, and Hossa injured a knee that had been a nagging problem for him before. Shero sat in the press box toward the end of the game, feeling like he was about to throw up. He turned to Fletcher and said, "Man, I just gave up a lot for Pascal Dupuis." Luckily, it turned out that Gill was just having a bad night and Hossa was out for only three weeks, meaning he would be back before the end of the regular season.

The hockey philosophy of the Penguins really had started to change two years earlier, at the end of Sidney Crosby's rookie season when the team did not renew the contract of General Manager Craig Patrick. Unusual for a front-office guy, Patrick had become a Pittsburgh icon to even casual hockey fans, because he not only had a rich personal history with the game, but he also led the Penguins to two Stanley Cup championships with Lemieux. Patrick had played hockey, and he had grown up around the game. His grandfather, Lester, had been a founding father of the league, and his father and brother had played for the NHL as well. The family's influence on the league had been so great that the Atlantic Division had been named the Patrick Division for 19 years until a massive reorganization in 1993. Two times in the 1990s, the Penguins under Patrick had won the regular season title in the division named for his grandfather. The general manager obviously had a close personal connection to the game.

But just as the division name had changed as the league modernized, the game had grown, too. In many ways, the Penguins had remained an old-style franchise – run the way professional hockey teams had been run for decades, drawing on the camaraderie of a league where everyone seemed to know everyone else. General managers knew other general managers, and even agents typically came up through the system so that they often seemed closer with the guys they were negotiating against than with the players they represented. Teams in that era paid little attention to niceties, figuring players had to be grateful enough just to be in the league and fearing that small acts of kindness might somehow translate into softness on the ice. Players could take care of themselves without the team providing too many comforts. Rubber mats on the floor in a small room with bare hooks hanging on the wall would be enough for a locker room, and travel arrangements could be handled by one of the girls in the front office rather than a high-priced travel coordinator. If players needed tickets in a visiting arena when the team was on the road, they could tell one of the hockey staff guys who would make a note on the back of a napkin and write down the player's credit card information to pay for the seats. Patrick had grown up in that system, and he had become a leading architect within it, building a championship franchise while playing by those rules.

As the game changed, the Penguins failed to adapt as quickly as some of the other franchises, remaining a pencil-and-paper organization in an age of laptop computers. In Patrick's defense, people within the Penguins organization acknowledged that money had become so tight at the time that the team rarely invested in anything that would not immediately bring a return. By the first year after the lockout, insiders believed the difference between their organization and the league's other teams had become obvious. On the ice, the Penguins were losing night after night. At the end of that first season back, the Penguins did not renew Patrick's contract.

The transition to the future had been abrupt, then, when the team hired Shero as general manager. From the moment he arrived in Pittsburgh, Shero knew he was taking over from a legend and coming into a good opportunity. "Craig had been here 17 years, had twice won the Stanley Cup, and was one of the best general managers in the game for a long period of time," Shero said years later. What he found in Pittsburgh was that Patrick and his assistants had loaded the Penguins with young talent that still needed to be formed into a championship-caliber team. "This was a great situation to walk into," Shero said. "The pieces were in place to eventually, hopefully, have a good team."

Shero started out by computerizing the team's player evaluation and development processes. Just as Sabermetrics had redefined baseball, with general managers using statistics and mathematics to identify players who had been overlooked, science transformed hockey, too. Almost anyone reading *The Hockey News* could have picked out big-name stars like Crosby, Malkin and Fleury, but it took real study to find the supporting players who would fill out the rest of the roster. Shero hired guys such as Fletcher, who had backed up his hockey credentials by graduating from Harvard University. Fletcher had been a candidate for the Penguins' top job, but rather than Shero feeling threatened by that, he saw an opportunity to hire someone who could be trusted to work just as hard as himself. Now on trading days, the Penguins had a war room with computers and dry-erase boards so they could quickly evaluate players and look for trends that others had missed.

Other changes by Shero had more to do with style than substance. One of his first transactions had been to sign free agent defenseman Mark Eaton in 2006. After working out the details of Eaton's contract, Shero walked into the Penguins' offices with a directive for the staff: Send flowers to Eaton's wife, along with an infant-sized Penguins jersey for their baby. The staff was stunned. Under the old rules, the franchise never would have shown such a soft-hearted gesture to one of its hockey warriors. Shero saw things differently, realizing that the Penguins had signed not just Eaton, but his entire family. Players have a built-in support system when they move to a new city and link up with a roster full of new buddies, but their wives and children often end up in a new place without knowing anyone. Every franchise talked about being family-friendly, but Shero intended to ensure the Penguins made good on that promise. He started an annual tradition of having the players invite their fathers along for a long road trip each year, bringing them on the chartered flights and hosting banquet-style dinners along the way. The Penguins also set up a family room during games where the players' wives, girlfriends, children and parents could hang out between periods at home games, and the team started offering baby-sitting services, too. Small gestures like that cost little compared to million-dollar salaries, and the acts would live forever in the memories of players who would, no doubt, tell others around the league about how the Penguins welcomed them. More than anything, Shero believed treating the players well was the right thing to do.

"It does get around, for sure, but I don't think that's why you do it," Shero said. "I think it's the right thing to do, and that's how I run the team. Whether you're dealing with players, dealing with trainers – I know what's right and wrong, and I know how I want to treat people."

Next, Shero focused on adding leaders to the Penguins locker room. At the trading deadline the next winter, in 2007, he gave up a young defenseman named Noah Welch, a second-rounder from the 2001 draft, to obtain Gary Roberts, a veteran grinder playing in Florida. Shero wanted his young stars to see a fierce competitor up close, so they could study how he plays, what he eats, how he trains during the day, and then they could start to emulate that tenacity themselves. Roberts had a no-trade clause in his contract and wanted to play near his Ontario home, but Shero reached out to him, anyway. In Pittsburgh, with a team of young stars, Roberts had an opportunity to leave an enduring legacy in the NHL by showing these players what it would take to stand up for themselves against the best players in the world. Whenever those young Penguins stars won a championship – whether Roberts was still playing with them or not – he could take pride in knowing that he had been the one who had forged them in greatness at a time when they were still trying to find their way. No matter what happened to that franchise, Roberts would always be part of its maturation. Roberts accepted the opportunity as it was presented, waiving his contract restriction so Florida could send him to Pittsburgh.

The same day he landed Roberts, Shero traded for another NHL bruiser, Georges Laraque, an enforcer who was known not so much for being a goon in the hockey tradition of playing only so they could pick fights, but as a heavyweight champion on skates. Laraque would not only protect the Penguins' young stars but show them how to fight for themselves when other teams tried to knock them off their skates in an effort to derail what was becoming a fast-moving, high-scoring team. To get him from the Phoenix Coyotes, the Penguins gave up another prospect and a draft pick. A bottom-feeder for so long, the Penguins had stockpiled talented young players, but Shero had seen that he would need to give up some of that future talent to make sure he had the right chemistry to mold the nucleus players of his franchise.

That same spring, as Shero was building the physical backbone of his team, Penguins owners Burkle and Lemieux had agreed to terms with state and local leaders on building a Pittsburgh arena. The general manager's mandate, then, had been to make sure the franchise had a Stanley Cup contender ready to play in the new building by the time it was scheduled to open in three years. On the night the arena deal was announced, Lemieux went to the ice at the Civic Arena and talked directly with his team's fans: "Tonight, I'm proud to announce that *your* Pittsburgh Penguins will remain right here in Pittsburgh, right where they belong. Thank you, Pittsburgh. Have a great night." The line drew thunderous applause from the crowd of spectators who wondered for years whether their team that seemed destined for greatness might achieve it in some other city. That night, the Penguins won a 5-to-4 shootout against the Buffalo Sabres.

The arena deal – and the commitment from Lemieux and Burkle to keep the franchise – helped ease the minds of the Penguins' players and hockey executives, too. They would have been happy for any opportunity in the NHL, but knowing the team would be in Pittsburgh for decades brought some comfort. When Shero came to Pittsburgh in May 2006 while Isle of Capri Casinos was still vying for the city's slots license, the general manager warned his wife they might be moving again soon if the Penguins' owners decided to relocate. The couple bought a home in Pittsburgh's suburbs, but they did not put up new curtains until the team's long-term future was settled, Shero said with a laugh.

Over the rest of the season after the arena deal was reached, the Penguins won 10 of the final 14 games down the stretch, finishing in second place in the Atlantic Division, two points behind the New Jersey Devils. For the first time in five seasons, the Penguins had qualified for the post-season. A fever descended on the city and its fans, unlike anything Pittsburgh had seen in years. It was not only that the Penguins had been losers for so many hockey seasons but also that the team could have been going to the playoffs somewhere else, for some other fans. But it wasn't.

Before a first-round series against the Ottawa Senators, more than 1,000 fans crammed into the inner courtyard of Allegheny County's historic courthouse for a mid-Wednesday Penguins rally. One 50-year-old fan had dug into the basement of her Crafton Heights home in the Pittsburgh suburbs to retrieve a homemade Stanley Cup she made more than 15 years earlier, when Lemieux had been seeking his first championship as a player. Mayor Luke Ravenstahl, who participated in the negotiations to keep the Penguins in the city, appeared and announced that he planned to grow a playoff beard in solidarity with the players. Allegheny County Executive Dan Onorato spoke for many of the fans when he took the podium and talked about the relief he felt, looking out at the crowd with many people wearing Penguins sweaters and hats. The arena negotiation process, he said, "might have been ugly — not pretty — but the end result is that the Penguins will be right where they belong for at least the next 30 years."

The Penguins lost the first game in the series with Ottawa, on their way to dropping out of the playoffs in just five games. Even in losing that series, the Penguins players learned something about themselves and what it would take to become champions. When Michel Therrien had arrived as the team's new coach a year earlier, he sought to change the players' mindset from what he believed was a "country club mentality." His predecessor, Ed Olczyk, had a different, more nurturing style that emulated the coaches he respected as a player. "There are a lot of different ways to get from Point A to Point B," Olczyk said later. Therrien had been the coach of the Penguin's minor-league affiliate in Wilkes-Barre/Scranton, and he came to the NHL demanding that players have more discipline and put in more effort and sacrifice. "When I came to Pittsburgh, I wanted to change the culture, change the mentality, the commitment, the style of play, the conditioning, the atmosphere," he said years later. "There's always a reason when you lose."

Success the following year came quicker than anyone expected. When the Ottawa Senators went on to win the Eastern Conference championship, the Penguins' young players wondered just had far they had come. They had not lasted longer than a single round, but they had played against the team that went to the Stanley Cup final. A seed had been planted. Nervous before their first playoff game, the Penguins players came away from the series knowing how to act if they earned a chance to come back to the post-season. "We surprised a lot of people that year," Therrien said. "We faced a team that was better than us, but it was a great experience for us to get ready for the next season."

The owners had gotten a taste for winning, too. Lemieux, of course, could remember what it had been like to hoist the Cup. Burkle, who had been a casual hockey fan, suddenly took a deep personal interest in the sport. He started showing up at games, often with his son. If he had looked at the team before as only an investment, he now had a rooting stake in whether the Penguins won or lost. Burkle quickly realized he could have a lot more fun when they won.

Still, few people around the Penguins organization were thinking seriously about the team competing for the Stanley Cup the following season. The first breakout moment seemed to happen on the night of Thanksgiving in the United States – again in Ottawa, against the Senators. The Pens had lost seven of 10 games that month and seemed headed toward dropping another. Going up against the team that had bounced them from the playoffs, the Penguins quickly fell behind by two goals. Fleury had been pulled from the net after stopping just two of the first four shots he saw, adding to concerns about what

---

[1] For these game notes and other insights about the Penguins, the author relied on interviews with Rob Rossi, Penguins beat writer for the *Pittsburgh Tribune-Review*, and the articles he wrote. The author is grateful for Rossi's enthusiastic cooperation on this project.

Coach Michel Therrien had referred to earlier that month as his "fragile" psyche.[1] Then the Penguins responded with three consecutive goals – by Malkin, Malone and Tyler Kennedy, a right wing – to take a lead. Ottawa came back again, scoring three goals of its own to go up 5-to-3. The Penguins rallied again, seeming to realize their season was on the line, responding with two goals – by Malone and Sergei Gonchar, a defenseman – to tie the game. Then in a 2-to-1 shootout, the Penguins won the game. It had seemed to be a defining moment. In the press box, members of the media had felt the momentum shift, too. "We were talking about it the next day, saying, 'That might be the win that we look back and go, OK, this is where they righted their ship,'" said Rob Rossi, Penguins beat writer for the *Pittsburgh Tribune-Review*.

For a team that still had a losing record, winning a championship seemed a stretch, and that did not change in the following weeks, even as the team started taking more games. The breakthrough started with the sort of game-changing moment that can destroy a season. As the Penguins took home ice at the Civic Arena against Tampa Bay, Crosby stood as the top vote recipient for the NHL's all-star game. He had missed only four games since joining the league two-and-a-half years earlier – one with the flu and then three with a groin injury. Crosby possessed not only finesse but durability. Heading toward the Lightning goal at 7:37 of the first period, however, he fell to the ice as he was slashed by a defender. Crosby slid on his backside with his feet headed toward the boards. He expected his legs to go up when they hit the wall, as they typically do. However, as he made contact, Crosby felt his left foot hit and his leg went up, but his right skate turned outward and stuck in the boards. The Penguins star had to be helped off the ice, and team doctors later diagnosed him with a high ankle sprain, an injury that can linger for weeks if not months. Doctors predicted Crosby would be out for six to eight weeks. Already that season, Fleury, the goaltender, had a similar injury that kept him off the ice for six weeks, and forward Maxime Talbot lost a month to a high ankle sprain.

Crosby did not talk to the media the night he was injured. When he did speak out three days later, he acknowledged that it would be up to his teammates, and Malkin in particular, to figure out how to keep winning without him. It might take a different person every night, and no one player – not even the Russian star – would have to win by himself. That couldn't be done.

At first, Malkin played like he needed to carry the franchise. The team had beaten Montreal the next night on the road and lost a shootout to the Capitals at home two nights later. Then as days turned into weeks, Malkin started to adapt. Therrien, the coach, had reiterated Crosby's words, telling the reserved Russian that he needed to give his all but that others would play next to him, giving their best as well. Malkin seemed to understand his new role, and he emerged as a different type of player, going from someone who had been an intriguing second-line center to a legitimate star. In the 28 games Crosby missed, Malkin scored 20 goals and 24 assists. He began to chase down fellow Russian Alexander Ovechkin of Washington for the league scoring title. At the all-star game, Malkin took Crosby's roster slot, and he had two assists when the Eastern Conference team scored five goals in the first period.

Malkin's personal transformation also changed the way the Penguins owners and management saw the team: If they played this well without Crosby in the lineup, what could they do when he returned? And what would it take to put the team over the top? "If you're talking about turning points, I honestly think the best thing that happened to the Penguins that year was Crosby getting hurt, because Malkin elevating his game is what turned them into a great team," Rossi, the beat writer, said. "There was nothing to suggest Malkin was going to go up like he did. But when he did, that's when it started to make hockey sense: Geno is playing like this, we're getting Sid back. You add Marian Hossa to that mix, who in the East is going to stop this team?"

As Malkin started to emerge as a star, Burkle talked among the team's hockey staff through a series of phone calls. At the all-star game, he wanted to know whether the Penguins had a chance to win right away if they made a play for Hossa. The team had made about $5 million more than expected that year, largely because of the fans' excitement over the team staying in Pittsburgh. If the Penguins did not have a legitimate shot at advancing in the playoffs, Burkle would not spend the money to add players and risk the long-term health of the franchise. But if Lemieux and Shero thought the Penguins had a shot to win right away, Burkle wanted them to take it.

The team's owners and executives – Lemieux, Burkle, Shero, CEO Ken Sawyer and President David Morehouse, among them – gathered inside a conference room at the hotel where many of them were staying for the midseason festivities. At least one other minority owner was present in the room, and others listened on a conference call through the phone at the center of the table.

Shero spoke up, raising the possibility of trading for Hossa or a player like him. Spending extra money on trades or free agents did not fit with the team's five-year plan, Sawyer said. The team was not supposed to start spending the maximum on players' salaries – about $10 million more a year – until the new arena was ready to open. That would not be for at least another two years.

"The Soviet Union had five-year plans," Burkle said, according to people who were present. "It didn't work well for them." He turned to Shero. "The question is, do we have a shot if we make this move?"

"Well, we have a five-year plan," Shero started saying again.

"I understand, and I like planning," Burkle said. "But are you saying that if we go get Marian Hossa today, we can win now?"

"Yes," came the reply.

Burkle turned and looked at Morehouse, his confidant who had been hired to win public money for a Pittsburgh arena. The five-year plan called for the Penguins to win the Stanley Cup after the team moved into the new building in 2010. Making an earlier run at a championship would only build excitement and increase the team's chances of success when it moved across the street. "If we're going to be arrogant enough to say when we're going to win the Cup," Morehouse said, "let's do it this year."

Burkle did not know enough about hockey to say what the team should do to win a championship. He wouldn't have been able to pick Hossa out of a lineup. Lemieux, his co-owner, understood the game and what acquiring a top free agent could mean for a team on the verge of post-season success. "Once you're in the playoffs," Lemieux said, "anything can happen, and he'll help us go deeper."

Burkle was sold. "Then I think we ought to go get him now. Don't we owe it to our fans to try and win every single year?"

There, in a hotel board room far from any playing surface, the fortunes of the hockey franchise changed again, insiders said. Acquiring Hossa would have an impact on the team's ability to win games for certain, but the decision to pursue him would alter the mindset of the team's top executives, too.

Burkle did something in that meeting that he hadn't done much of before: he spoke up about a hockey decision. He had started out as a mostly silent investor, and then he had become the point man for finding a business plan that allowed the team to make enough money to stay in Pittsburgh. Now he was talking about whether the hockey staff should turn aggressive on the ice, as well. As a businessman, Burkle sensed that opportunities for success come only at certain moments. The question would have been the same in any boardroom: do we have a chance to win? If the answer was yes, and the organization had the ability to make the change, Burkle would want to pursue it.

Having a five-year plan has become a staple of sports franchises, constantly planning for the future. "I don't even know if I had a five-year plan," Shero said years later. "Everybody says they have a five-year plan. ... Part of this whole management thing is flexibility. You've got to be able to make decisions and change." Winning a championship – feeling that rare moment when a special mix of players comes together with a chance to win it all – cannot be planned. It has to be felt. Team executives cannot often answer yes to a question about whether they can win a championship. When it happens, they have to recognize the opportunity and then take the risks to give players the best chance at victory. "There are times in sports when you have to seize the moment or you can find yourself building forever," said one Penguins executive. "Burkle brought a business-world mentality to this. In sports, the windows are very short. You can't say 'We'll be fine. We can win next year.' There are only so many years you have a legitimate chance to win a championship. You've got to maximize this."

Financially, a trade for Hossa seemed to make no sense. If the Penguins traded for him and then failed to make the play-offs or last very long in the post-season, the owners could lose millions of dollars. But Burkle and Lemieux were all about trying to win. Put another way, the Penguins owners decided once again to take a measured risk, with the odds playing in their favor.

Given that directive to build a winner without waiting, Shero still had to figure out how to do it. Lemieux stayed back and allowed the people running the team to make decisions about what should happen. Rather than meddling in the day-to-day operations – saying "Bench this guy," "Play Crosby more," or "Hire my buddy" – the owners demanded excellence from people they trusted. Then, they applied pressure to insist that the executives took chances when they made sense. On the Hossa trade, Shero had looked at other players before identifying the one he wanted. To get a wing player for Crosby, especially when it looked like Hossa would go to Montreal or Ottawa, Shero upped the ante late in the negotiations by agreeing to give up a first-round pick the following year. That had been enough to swing the deal.

Looking back, team executives said the Hossa trade transformed the Penguins organization – not just because of the quality of the player, but for the message it sent. The Penguins were ready to start winning now, even if that required bold moves. "It was a huge decision on (the owners') part, because the arena was not built yet and the revenue was not coming through," said Jason Botterill, who became the team's assistant general manager. After years of losing, the owners wanted to build an elite team for a championship run that year – and for the years ahead. They had asked the question, and they decided that, yes, the Penguins did have a chance to win right away. It had been risky, but all trades are somewhat dangerous. Conventional thinking said the Penguins should have stayed with their five-year plan. It had been working, and from an accounting standpoint it made the most sense: Slowly build the team from the draft and minor leagues, saving money to sign existing players, until the franchise could get a new arena that would allow it to generate the additional cash needed to afford high-priced free agents. Instead, the Penguins could afford to keep Hossa along with the team's other stars only if they made the playoffs, and even then the franchise would need a deep run to break even financially. No accountant would certify a business plan based on such an uncertain proposal. Yet to win now would transform the franchise, carrying it to the top of the league and placing it among the most successful teams in North American sport. To win, to seize that moment, the Penguins owners would have to take a chance that defied convention. "You compare yourself with competitors in the Eastern Conference, and you know, you're not missing a lot to be the best team in the East," said Michel Therrien, the Penguins coach at the time.

The players understood what the risk meant to them, too. The message they took away from the Hossa trade was that they had an opportunity to do something special, and the team's owners and general manager believed in them.

That night after acquiring Hossa, the Penguins beat the New York Islanders on the road. Down the stretch, the team finished with 12 wins and seven losses, ending the regular season with 102 points atop the Atlantic Division, and second in the East to the Canadiens by two points.

In the playoffs, the Penguins started out where they had finished the year before, going up against Ottawa in the first round again. The previous year, the Penguins had won just one game in the series. The players had been nervous about the playoffs then – realizing that the post-season brings a new level of intensity and different pressures, Therrien said. This time would be different. "We were ready mentally," the coach said later. "Those kids knew what to expect." The Senators never had a chance as Pittsburgh swept the series in four games.

Through the entire Eastern Conference playoffs, the Penguins lost only two games: They beat the Rangers in five games, and then the Flyers in five. After years of losing, not making the playoffs or getting bounced early from the post-season, the Penguins made it look easy, practically walking into the Stanley Cup Final. They seemed to have figured out what it took to win and to do it consistently.

After taking the Eastern Conference championship on home ice, Crosby and his teammates skated away from their prize, the Prince of Wales trophy. The league has been handing out the 40-pound hardware, donated by the prince and bearing his coat of arms, since the 1920s. The Penguins didn't want it, or more appropriately, they didn't want just the Prince of Wales trophy. Thinking of superstition, the players had convinced themselves that it might somehow bring bad luck if they celebrated winning the conference championship, when the league title and the Stanley Cup remained their ultimate goal.

Crosby stood near the trophy for a photo but would not place his hands on it. When a white-gloved league official asked if he could bring the prince's gift trophy into the Penguins locker room after the game, the players turned him away. The players refused even to wear the Eastern Conference hats and t-shirts handed out by the league to the winners. At a post-game press conference, the hats sat in front of Crosby, Fleury and Malone as they talked to reporters. None of the three picked them up on the way out.

When the Penguins reached the Stanley Cup Final, however, it seemed almost like the previous year, when many of the players had reached the playoffs for the first time – and did not know what to expect. As his team arrived in Detroit for the first two games, Therrien looked around at his players and realized they seemed tense and uncertain again. "They were nervous, nervous as hell," Therrien said. "Their focus was not quite there. It was big for them. I could see the tension before the game."

Part of the calculation in trading for Hossa had been that the other teams in the Eastern Conference that year had seemed beatable. Detroit was a different story. The Western Conference champion Red Wings already had lifted the Stanley Cup 10 times through their franchise history. This year, the difference in maturity levels between the teams seemed as obvious as the hair on their faces: Henrik Zetterberg, Detroit's star center, came into the game with a thick northwoods beard after weeks of not shaving in the tradition of the hockey playoffs; by comparison, Crosby and Malkin had little to show for weeks of avoiding a razor other than wisps of dark hair. Facial hair alone does not offer a fair comparison of athletic ability, of course, but the Red Wings played with experience. The first two games at Detroit's Joe Louis Arena did not go well for the Penguins, with the Red Wings scoring seven goals over six periods compared to none for Pittsburgh.

After coming home to the Civic Arena, the players seemed to become more comfortable with playing in the championship series, but they already were down so far. When the Penguins split the next two games at home, the Red Wings needed only one more win to clinch the series.

Before Game 5 in Detroit, Lemieux and Burkle met privately that evening to talk about the future of their franchise. The gamble to accelerate the five-year plan and try to win right away had paid off, even if the playoffs run ended with the Penguins losing that night. Burkle's question – Do we have a chance to win? – had been answered not only by Shero and the team executives who traded for Hossa, but also by the players themselves, who had risen to the challenge and taken the franchise to the brink of winning the Stanley Cup. Before that magical run ended, the owners wanted to decide on a strategy for the off-season. Keeping together the team that had reached the Stanley Cup Final would not be easy or inexpensive. If the Penguins were going to continue to give themselves a chance to win, the owners would now have to back up their gusto with the cash to keep Hossa and the other young players who had been drafted and were going to be looking for new contracts. After reaching the final round, almost every Penguins player could expect to command more free agency value than before the playoffs started. To keep them, the owners would have to spend up to the level of the NHL's new cap on player salaries. Team executives had not expected under their long-term plan to make that kind of investment until the new arena opened in 2010, or maybe the season before. This new gambit would require paying out top cash two seasons earlier, and it could leave the ownership group on the hook for millions of dollars if the Penguins failed to run deep into the playoffs again the following year. The league's salary cap that season was $50.3 million, and the Penguins' payroll was about $10 million below that.

Coming up to the luxury box where he would watch the game, Lemieux was greeted by one of the team's minority owners, who wanted to know how much money the team – and by extension all the investors – could be losing the next season. Lemieux smiled, put his hand on the man's shoulder, and said, "It'll be all right." He and Burkle had just decided that no matter what happened in that night's game or how the series ended, they would spend up to the cap that summer and make a play to keep as many of their stars as they could.

After not scoring at Joe Louis Arena at all in the first two games, the Penguins came out in Game 5 with two goals to take the lead and to try forcing the series back to Pittsburgh. Hossa scored the first goal of the game, stunning Detroit's home fans. Minutes later, the Penguins scored again for a two-goal lead in the first period.

Knowing the series would be over if they lost the game, Penguins players fought for every moment. Already playing with a broken nose, left wing Ryan Malone stood on the ice in front of the Detroit goalie with 1:22 left in the second period. Detroit had scored its first goal earlier in the period. Now with the Penguins on a power play, a shot by the team's defenseman Hal Gill sailed toward the net between Red Wings players. Malone saw the puck coming and ducked to his left to avoid the shot, but no one could have moved fast enough to get out of the way. The puck slammed into Malone's already broken nose like a hard rubber mallet at 100 miles per hour. He collapsed across the ice as if he had been shot. Team trainers helped him up and took him inside the locker room to stop the bleeding and examine the fresh fracture. As they worked on Malone's face, an equipment manager attached a clear shield to the front of his helmet to protect him from any more hits. When he was handed the headgear, Malone looked at the shield and threw the helmet across the room.

When he returned to the ice in the third period, Malone had pieces of rolled-up gauze sticking out of his nostrils like cigarettes – and he did not wear any kind of guard across his face. When Detroit scored two goals to take a 3-to-2 lead with 9:23 left in the game, Malone's return served as inspiration for a Penguins comeback.

With less than a minute left in regulation, the Penguins pulled Fleury from the goal in the desperation move of hockey to put a sixth player on attack while leaving an empty net behind them. As Penguins players crashed toward Red Wings' goalie Chris Osgood, Hossa took another shot on goal but he was denied this time. As the puck bounced back toward the ice, Talbot trailed behind. He whacked once at the puck and whiffed. He swung again, and the puck slipped past Osgood for a tying goal with 34.5 seconds left in the third period.

Inside the Red Wings locker room, workers quickly put the champagne back on ice and tucked the championship t-shirts and hats back into their boxes.

Two hundred miles away inside Wayne Gretzky's, the Toronto bar owned by the hockey legend, it seemed everyone had a rooting interest for one team or the other. Even those who did not wear a team's colors seemed to find a reason to root for Pittsburgh or Detroit, whether they recalled seeing Lemieux score some spectacular goal years earlier or had grown up cheering for the Red Wings with their deep history and tradition of winning. At the end of regulation, Red Wings fans walked out the door of 99 Blue Jays Way for a smoke or breath of fresh air before the start of sudden-death overtime. No one knew how long the game would last or how it might end: with a Detroit goal giving the Red Wings their 11th team championship or the Penguins sending the series back to Pittsburgh.

Through three overtimes, the pattern lasted, with fans stepping outside between periods and then coming back into the bar to watch every moment weighted with anticipation. Fleury stopped 24 shots in overtime, while Osgood stopped 13 – all but the final goal by Petr Sykora. The Penguins right wing had not played a great game, but he had predicted before the final period that he would get the game winner and finally send everyone home. When he scored after 109 minutes, 57 seconds – the fifth-longest game in Stanley Cup Final history – the Pittsburgh players redeemed themselves. After starting the series slowly, they fought down to the final seconds of elimination for the chance to play at least another game.

Inside the luxury box where Penguins executives watched the game, jubilation over Sykora's goal turned immediately to the concern of a medical emergency. Food and drink had run out before the overtime periods as the executives and their wives watched the game, hanging on every shot and turnover to see whether the series might end. When Sykora scored finally, everyone jumped up from their seats. As Morehouse looked over toward his wife, Vanessa, who was sitting in the front row, he saw her bent over and looking down. Fear gripped him that someone had fallen over the balcony in the excitement. Instead, Shero's wife had become light-headed and fainted. Morehouse darted outside looking for a paramedic or an arena worker who could call for help. Inside the suite, Sawyer's son, a doctor, went to help. Shero's wife turned out to be fine, just overcome by heat and the stress of watching the game with so much depending on the outcome.

Cinderella does not always get her slipper back in real life. Despite the excitement of Game 5 in Detroit, the Penguins could not will themselves to yet another narrow victory. Therrien believed that Game 6 was probably his team's best of the series, and yet the Penguins still lost. They battled with the Red Wings again to the final seconds of a 2-to-1 loss.

In the end, the Red Wings lifted Lord Stanley of Preston's Cup on the Civic Arena ice. Hossa, who had a chance to tie the game but came up short, leaned against the boards as the Detroit players celebrated. Four months earlier, Shero had gambled when he traded for the Atlanta player. Hossa had contributed off the ice by confirming to the other Penguins players that they were good enough to take a shot at winning it all that season. Twelve of his 15 goals and more than half of his assists had come through the playoffs, as he finished second to Crosby in points. Hossa had contributed to the Penguins' season in ways that had been expected and in others that no one had imagined.

As he left the arena on his way home that night, Morehouse walked past Detroit's two chartered buses. Red Wings' executives were giddy with celebration. Morehouse let his mind dwell on the loss. "I don't want to have this feeling again," he thought, "them beating us on our ice, clinching the Cup and celebrating … on our ice."

Even though the team had come up short, the deep run through the playoffs had been good for the Penguins owners and management. Conservatively at $1 million per home game, the team brought in an extra $11 million through the playoffs, although not all of that could be considered profit, because expenses had to come out of it. The playoff run, combined with the deal for a new arena, started to transform the value of the Penguins franchise, lifting it from among the least valuable of the league's 30 franchises.

More significantly, the playoff run had convinced the Penguins – from the players through the top management and on up to the owners – that they had a championship-caliber team. Even in the final series, the team had discovered, after going scoreless in the first two games, how to come back and win. Each of the last four games was decided by one goal. In the dramatic Game 5 that went into triple overtime, the Penguins had found a way to win, and they had proven that they belonged in the championship series. Hossa had been a key part of that discovery. Now that the team had a winning formula, management and owners wanted to find a way to keep it going, to replicate the success – but to come away with a Cup win the next time.

10

Shooting Star
December 11, 2007

A dozen orange-and-black earthmovers – bulldozers on tracks, backhoes with shovels that scoop dirt toward them, and empty dump trucks – sat silently on a stretch of pavement lined with parking spaces near the Ohio River. The lot has a clear view of downtown Pittsburgh stretching out behind The Point, where waters from the Monongahela and Allegheny rivers come together on their way toward the Mississippi and ultimately the Gulf of Mexico. Owners of the land considered the site such prime real estate that they never built anything on it, using the 17 acres for surface parking instead, while they waited for a worthy project. Finally, they believed, that day had come.

Don Barden stood nearby, inside a heated, white party tent with the side flaps rolled down against the chilly gray morning and a misty rain. He wore a dark suit, white shirt, and a blue striped tie with a matching handkerchief in the breast pocket. He also wore a white construction hat. Within minutes, after all, this fallow land would become an active construction site.

Nearly a year earlier, almost everyone except the seven members of the state Gaming Control Board had been surprised by the decision to award the Pittsburgh casino license to Barden. Now it seemed that maybe the Detroit casino owner should have been given the best odds all along. In the months after Barden won the license, city officials finalized plans to use $435 million in federal money to extend the city's one subway line under the Allegheny River to the North Shore, around Heinz Field where the Steelers football team plays, and ultimately to within feet of the front door of the Majestic Star Casino.

Barden had only to hold up his end of the bargain by building the casino. That work would start today – but only after another lavish party to celebrate this longest of long shots. Image had been an important part of Barden's bid, as he projected a vision of himself as someone with the means to pull off such a massive project. The groundbreaking ceremony had been designed to extend that narrative by suggesting the inevitability of the casino and deep public support for its owner.

More than 250 people had turned out for this invitation-only moment, sitting on rows of folding chairs facing a raised stage with a clear acrylic podium in front of a backdrop printed with the Majestic Star logo. Mayor Luke Ravenstahl, who had sided with the Penguins' gambling partner, Isle of Capri Casinos, and Allegheny County's top elected official, Executive Dan Onorato, sat facing the audience. When it became his turn to speak, Onorato vowed his support for Barden. "Whatever it takes, we are with you," he said. "We are going to get this done, and we – I say, we – are all going to benefit when this casino opens."

Smokey Robinson, the singer and Motown founder who had agreed to invest in the casino, sat on the stage, too. His wife, Frances, had grown up in Pittsburgh's tony Shadyside neighborhood, and they had decided to purchase a home on the city's north side, near the casino. Robinson had mistakenly referred to the city's residents as Pittsburghians during the bidding process, but for the groundbreaking ceremony he had taken the first step toward becoming an authentic Pittsburgher by wearing a black suit with a gold tie and pocket handkerchief. "Thank you to all the people who are here this morning, all you wonderful Pittsburghers," Robinson said. "I made the mistake of calling you Pittsburghians when we were trying to get the license. I'm surprised we got it." Again, he vouched for Barden's character, just as he had done in a pivotal moment before the gambling board. "He is a man of the highest integrity. He's a great person and a brilliant businessman. I'm very, very proud to be associated with him, despite the grabbing of straws and the last-ditch efforts of a mighty few factions who have their clandestine or hidden agendas for trying to delay us – and I feel like it's almost a shame that they as citizens of the great city of Pittsburgh will benefit by what's going to happen once we're up and running, because they have been so 'protesty.' ... I guarantee that you put your trust in a man who is a wonderful person, just a wonderful human being, who has the best interests of the city of Pittsburgh at heart."

Jerome Bettis, the retired Steelers running back, had wanted to partner with Barden on the casino, too, but he could not get involved in gambling. In the weeks after Barden submitted his casino proposal to the state, the Steelers had barely qualified for the playoffs and then they had won three games to reach Super Bowl XL. The National Football League typically plays its championship in a warm-weather city, but for this game, it had chosen Detroit's Ford Field. Bettis had grown up in Detroit, and his parents now lived in the same golf-course community as Barden. After the Steelers won the game, Bettis immediately announced his retirement, but he went to work as a commentator for NBC Sunday night football broadcasts and still could not invest in a casino. Instead, Bettis persuaded his parents to put money into the project, and now he sat in the front row of the audience for the groundbreaking. Johnnie Bettis, the running back's father, had died suddenly from a heart attack during the slots bidding process, and Barden asked everyone to stop for a moment of silence to remember the man.

Don Barden, chairman and CEO of Majestic Star Casino, tells construction crews to start their engines, as the singer Smokey Robinson looks on. (Pittsburgh Tribune-Review, *Keith Hodan*)

"John was the first person who convinced me we were going to win," Barden said. "In the old Steelers tradition, he pulled me to the side and said, 'Don, we're gonna win this thing.'"

Three members of the Gaming Control Board had come along too – Sanford Rivers, the former NFL referee, Kenneth McCabe, a former FBI agent, and Mary DiGiacomo Colins, a former Philadelphia judge who had become chairman of the gambling board. She informed Barden again that the gambling board's staff would be on hand throughout the months ahead as construction progressed. "Our job," she said, "is to ensure the interests of the public are protected at all times in the commonwealth."

After the short ceremony, Barden stood with the politicians, state regulators and his celebrity guests behind a symbolic pile of dirt. With gold-painted shovels, each of them picked up a shovelful of dirt, lifted it in the air for the television cameras, and threw it back down. Barden then turned around to the former parking lot behind him where construction workers had climbed into the operator's seats of the heavy equipment. "Gentlemen," Barden said into a microphone with the enthusiasm of a carnival barker, "start... your... engines."

As carefully as Barden had worked to craft the moment, he could not stop rumors. People had whispered for months that even though he had won the casino license, Barden did not have the money to build it. If he could not find the money to open the casino, Barden risked upsetting the plans for the arena, too – having agreed his casino would pay $7.5 million a year for the hockey rink. That morning, he answered one set of questions: Clearly, he had the money to break ground and start the construction. But he still had to answer another round of them about whether he could finish. More than a dozen reporters gathered around Barden with tape recorders and microphones near his face. Someone asked him how it felt to finally get this far. Then someone else asked whether the groundbreaking meant that Barden finally had all the cash he needed.

"Why would you ask a ridiculous question like that?" Barden said, turning with anger in his greenish-blue eyes. "I'm sick and tired of it."

Behind him, the backhoe had started the real work of digging up the blacktop of the former parking lot.

"What do you think that's out there going on now? We've always had the money."

It became obvious seven months later that Barden did not have the money.[1] The gentlemen – and women – who started their engines on his command in December turned them off in July because they had not been paid in weeks. The hulking steel frame of the half-built understructure stood empty and silent on a prime piece of Pittsburgh real estate, visible from the scenic overlooks on Mt. Washington, the bluff overlooking the city, and from the office buildings downtown that look westward toward the Ohio River.

The entire groundbreaking ceremony, it seemed, had been essentially a $107 million bluff: Barden apparently figured that if he could start the project and make it seem like a sure thing, he could convince investors to put enough money into the casino so he could finish the work. If Barden had told politicians and the gambling board from the start that he did not have enough financing to finish the casino, they could have simply taken the slots license from him and given it to someone else. Barden would have been out. Now he was invested. If they took the license from him now, they would have to abandon the steel carcass of his casino sitting along the river. Public officials could no longer simply give the license to one of the other bidders without leaving behind a mess. Besides, by breaking ground, Barden had won the support of people like Onorato, who had pledged to stand by him and get the building open. Ravenstahl, the mayor, personally had stepped in to block groups of designers and architects who challenged Barden's plans.

Later in hindsight, Barden's supporters claimed he had been among the first developers in the country to face the Great Recession, starting in March 2008 when the Wall Street investment firm Bear Stearns collapsed. Gambling regulators supported this narrative by claiming that they had never consid-

---

[1] Pennsylvania Gaming Control Board, Adjudication Docket #42028.

ered the specifics of Barden's financial situation once they saw that another Wall Street firm had agreed to back the Majestic Star Casino. "I'm going to go back to those bankers," Sanford Rivers said later. "If they think you're a risk, you know you're not going to get (the money)."[2] The board members apparently gave little thought to whether that commitment was binding or what would happen if the backers did not put their money into the project.

Unlike the public, however, the state gambling board had an opportunity to know everything about Barden's finances and to determine whether he could pull off paying for the casino. The board could demand any financial records it wanted, and it had hired financial investigators to evaluate each of the bidders. The investigators determined that all three Pittsburgh bidders were at least "high risk." Barden's Majestic Star Casino – a separate company from the one behind the Pittsburgh project – had a "history of operating with a very high risk financial profile," the investigators warned. Then in the weeks before the gambling board's vote to award the license, Wall Street bond ratings agencies sounded an alarm, too. All three bidders had been deemed speculative-grade investments by the agencies, but now both Standard & Poor's and Moody's Investor Services issued new negative outlooks for Majestic Star. S&P said the company had "weaker-than-expected operating results," citing the casino company's "substantial debt levels, its limited market position ... and moderate-size cash flow base." In June 2007, as Barden had been desperately seeking investors for the Pittsburgh project, his company had reported debts of more than $600 million to the U.S. Securities and Exchange Commission. To illustrate the depth of his problem, that debt was about $100 million more than Barden said he needed to build the Pittsburgh casino.

None of that mattered, the gambling board later explained in a filing to the Pennsylvania Supreme Court: Risk comes with the gambling industry, because many companies are highly leveraged with debts. The board members knew the details of

---

2 "Casino hopefuls were all financial risks, documents show." By Brad Bumsted, Andrew Conte, and Richard Byrne Reilly. *Pittsburgh Tribune-Review.* Sunday, October 28, 2007.

Barden's finances, but they were convinced he would have the money to build the casino because of the backing from the Wall Street lenders, McCabe said. Besides, every bidder presented unique liabilities. "Gambling is gambling," McCabe said later, "but gambling is a risk."

Claims that Barden was a victim of the economy have merit. "The only reason Barden ran into financial troubles was the recession," Governor Ed Rendell said years later on his way out of office. Had the casino owner been able to start construction in December 2006 when he won the slots license, he might have been able to get in under the wire before Wall Street investors started calling in outstanding loans and stopped making new ones. Until then, Pennsylvania's casinos had seemed like a sure thing, with each of the Pittsburgh bidders planning sprawling projects that they said would be funded with almost unimaginable amounts of money from gamblers: Barden boldly predicted that after five years, his casino would rake in $1.4 million a day after paying out to winners.

Instead of starting construction right away, however, Barden had to play out the rest of the state's bidding process. The state gambling board had chosen Majestic Star, but the losing bidders still could appeal that decision to the state Supreme Court. After spending more than a year and millions of dollars (some estimated that Isle of Capri alone might have spent as much as $10 million on its bid), firms had an easy choice to make about appealing the gambling board's vote. Because each losing bidder believed it had the best proposal – and had been wronged in some way – executives had every reason to believe they might actually convince the judges to overturn the gambling board's decision.

Two months after awarding the license to Barden's PITG Gaming, the company that would own the Majestic Star Casino, the board issued an order explaining its decision.[3] In denying the license to Cleveland-based developer Forest City

---

[3]   Commonwealth of Pennsylvania Gaming Control Board, Order, February 1, 2007.

Enterprises, the board cited concerns about the proposed location, saying it had the potential for "severe traffic congestion" in an already popular and busy area of the city. Members said they did not entirely believe that Harrah's plans for an international player rewards program would bring in as much money as projected, either.

Isle of Capri, meanwhile, had focused too much on its offer to pay for an arena and not enough on how it would build a casino, the board members wrote. Confusion over Canadian businessman Jim Balsillie's last-minute decision not to purchase the Penguins before the vote added to the board's "uncertainty" about whether giving the license to Isle of Capri would keep the hockey team in Pittsburgh. "While the board is not unsympathetic to Pittsburgh's hockey fans, who fear the Penguins moving to another locale, or to the local businesses which benefit from the Penguins' presence, the board is not beholden to award a license upon that basis," the order stated. More than anything, board members seemed to resent that Isle of Capri and the Penguins had so successfully changed the casino discussion into one that also focused on paying for an arena. "Isle of Capri, their only hook was, 'Save the Penguins, save the Penguins, save the Penguins,'" Sanford Rivers said months after the vote. "The animosity that I had is that the city of Pittsburgh is more than just the Penguins. Pittsburgh was in dire need of a variety of help, and that's what I was looking at."

By early March, both Isle of Capri and Forest City had appealed the board's ruling to the state Supreme Court. State lawmakers already had streamlined the appeals process by requiring losing bidders to go directly to the state's highest court, and justices moved quickly on the appeals. Still, that process lasted more than four months – until mid-July, when the court upheld the Gaming Control Board's original decision.

By then, Barden's company had encountered other problems. In late June, the Pirates baseball club and the Steelers football team had filed lawsuits against PITG Gaming over impacts the casino could have on fans trying to reach their stadiums on the North Shore, near the proposed development. Barden negotiated with the team owners until November to reach a deal that addressed their concerns.

Even on the day of his groundbreaking, Barden still was fending off critics concerned about his plans. Hours after public officials and celebrities stood next to each other to throw symbolic dirt with the gold-painted shovels, Barden's architect went before the city Planning Commission with last-minute changes designed to make the building and its mammoth parking garage look more appealing – and to silence a growing number of people who said the building now looked little like the one that had been planned. In the renderings he had used to win the casino license, Barden had displayed a magnificent building with a glass cylinder rising at its center and a martini bar sitting in its crows' nest, high above the entire structure. In the months after he won the license, the 110-foot glass drum shrank to 87 feet. A parking garage that had been tucked behind the casino building suddenly loomed over it from behind, as the casino got shorter and the garage grew higher rather than having spaces underground. In a concession to groups opposed to the designs, the architect agreed to install metal screening on each level to block the view of cars parked there, and to paint the exterior a "warm tan" rather than keeping the gray concrete. The Planning Commission approved the proposal in January – a month after the groundbreaking ceremony – and still Barden ran into trouble when a local nonprofit which was focused on developing the city's rivers filed another appeal to the state Supreme Court over how the building would look.

By July 1, Barden had burned through more than $107 million on construction costs and could not afford to keep going. The prime contractor was owed $44 million by the end of June, money that was supposed to pay for subcontractors and construction workers.[4] They walked off the job because they had not been paid. Credit Suisse, which had given Barden a short-term $200 million loan, meanwhile, wanted to be repaid and threatened to sell off Majestic Star's assets if Barden didn't come up with the money. The gambling regulators and politicians who had vouched for Barden and vowed to help his com-

---

[4] Commonwealth of Pennsylvania Gaming Control Board, transcript of public hearing on August 14, 2008.

pany complete the project now had to step in with a plan to keep the casino out of bankruptcy court. A legal case like that could be tied up for months, if not years, while the half-built steel understructure sat along the Ohio River rusting. Barden had played his hand, perhaps the only one he could, and now he would have to salvage what was left.

To finish the casino, Barden needed to come up with at least a half-billion dollars – at a time when the nation's housing bubble was starting to burst in what would quickly unfold as the worst economic slump since the Great Depression. By now, lenders were waking up to the fact that they either had many bad loans on their books or were invested in companies that had unknown numbers of defaults waiting to happen. From the time that Barden broke ground in December until he needed to repay the bridge loan the following May, the crisis had started to unfold. Wall Street investment firm Bear Stearns had collapsed in March after its stock had fallen from $172 a share to less than $2. The Pittsburgh casino had seemed like a sure thing, but suddenly most of the biggest players had lost their appetite for any risk at all. Worse for Barden, few of those who might have considered such a gamble had the money available to get into the game. A month after construction stopped, Barden went back before the state gambling board: "I'm convinced that on December 20, 2006, you made the correct decision. What has changed are the circumstances and the credit markets and the world. That made it difficult for us, individually, and the company that you selected, to get this toward the goal line."

The gambling board members were sympathetic to Barden's plight. They had given him the license at a time when it seemed that money would be no problem, but then the economy had shifted. "It never crossed my mind that he was not funded," Rivers said. "I don't know what fully funded means to you, but what it meant to me was that with the project that he was presenting, they were guaranteeing the financing was in place to complete the project as presented. That was the one thing we looked for in all of them: who was financially backing this project? And it was there. It was right there. It's on the record." Even if the commitment was on the record, the actual money was not there when Barden needed it to complete the project.

Too much had changed. "It was the economic downturn," McCabe said. "Loans tightened up. It was no longer easy to get the money, the millions of dollars from the bank."

About the only ones who could afford such a massive pay-out were pension funds and institutional investors with billions of dollars. For someone with money, the Pittsburgh casino represented a good long-term investment. Walton Street Capital, a Chicago-based investment firm, had the money. Barden and the lead contractor flew to Chicago in late-June to meet with Neil Bluhm, one of five shareholders in Walton Street, to see whether they would invest in the Pittsburgh casino. Already Bluhm was affiliated with gambling through investment funds with stakes in the Fallsview Casino and Resort in Niagara Falls, Ontario, and the Riverwalk Casino in Vicksburg, Mississippi. He had also been on the Penguins' short list of potential gambling partners, but he had ended up instead as an investor in the Sugarhouse Casino, one of two groups that won a license for a Philadelphia slots parlor. Now he was being given the opportunity to take a major stake in the state's next biggest market, the only other one large enough to be guaranteed to get its own casino. Bluhm and his partners were willing to take a look at helping Barden. "These are not easy times," Bluhm said weeks later. "But we thought it was a terrific project and wanted to see if we could put something together, make a good investment, and do something that we thought would be beneficial to the city of Pittsburgh and the commonwealth."

Still, money had to be found. Bluhm told gambling regulators in mid-August of that year that he had been involved in more than $50 billion worth of projects around the United States and had never seen money so tight before. In 2006, when Barden and the other bidders were vying for the licenses, Bluhm said, "Credit was so available that it was unbelievable. ... You could borrow, in business, money more cheaply and more money than I had ever seen. And what often happens is the pendulum swings too far in each direction. So at that point two years ago credit was too available, there was too much money being borrowed, too much leverage, and starting with the subprime residential issue, that credit condition has spread from residential for-sale housing to commercial real estate, casino, new auto loans, virtually every type of credit, not only in the United States but throughout Europe." As the pendulum swung back in the other direction to correct the overextension in one way, money dried up so much that lenders were calling in loans, and businesses that needed cash to get started no longer could find any.

Bluhm, however, ranked among the few who still had access to money. His Walton Street funds purchased the largest stake in the Pittsburgh casino, with investments from public pension funds, insurance companies, university endowments and charitable organizations. More money for the casino came from the pension funds for police, firefighters and city workers in Barden's hometown of Detroit. A family trust created for Bluhm's grandchildren purchased a stake, and Bluhm's partners made personal investments. In all, the investors pulled together $205 million in direct investments and credit enhancements large enough for lenders to put up an additional $595 million. The total cost of the project had now ballooned to $800 million, and Bluhm's group touted it as the single most-expensive real estate project in Pittsburgh's 250-year history. "It's a miracle in these economic times that this could happen," John Donnelly, a lawyer for Bluhm, told gambling regulators when he unveiled the terms of the new agreement. "It is a miracle."

The miracle that saved the Pittsburgh casino, however, meant Barden would get a smaller share. Rendell had no trouble convincing Bluhm to invest in the Pittsburgh casino, but it had been a challenge getting Barden to concede his majority stake. The project always had been his, from the beginning when he formed his Pennsylvania subsidiary in 2003, even before lawmakers legalized slot machines. He had picked out the site along the waterfront with its scenic views of the city and surrounding bluffs. He had sought out the celebrity partners, Robinson and Bettis' parents. In the beginning, Barden even had answered his own phone when reporters called with their endless questions. When members of the state Gaming Control Board did not know whom to choose for the Pittsburgh slots license, Barden had shown up at their meetings and quietly persuaded them that he offered the best option – not the group that had offered to pay for a brand new arena nor the one with a brand, Harrah's, recognized around the world. When the terms for the Majestic Star bailout were finalized, Barden was left with a 16.66 percent interest. That would not be enough for him to maintain control of the project or even the name. The other partners chose a new brand, calling it Rivers Casino.

"I have to ask the question, what do I get out of this? Not much," Barden told the gambling board, saying he would not see any profits until all the loans were repaid. "I don't get anything out of this for years to come. There probably won't be any money for my children or my grandchildren's trust out of this, because all the money that's being invested has to be returned to the investors before I get a dime. I'm getting no money at closing. So I am doing this at great personal sacrifice."

Perhaps no one would have been more embarrassed by the Pittsburgh casino failing than the people who had chosen Majestic Star. As the new investment group came forward, gambling board members heaped praise on Bluhm. "Thank you for removing the doom and gloom that hovers over the Pittsburgh casino," Rivers said. Not only had the investors saved the riverfront casino, but they had prevented the taxpayers from having to bail out the rest of the arena project, too. If Barden had taken the case to bankruptcy court, a federal judge easily could have reduced or eliminated the casino's commitment to pay toward the arena.

"The people of Pittsburgh owe the Bluhm group a tremendous thank you," Rivers said. "You talk about saving the Penguins. That saved the Penguins."

Just as they had done 20 months earlier, the members of the gambling board took a vote on the Pittsburgh casino. This time they would decide whether to allow Bluhm and the institutional investors to take over the majority control of the project. Again the members voiced unanimous support: Yes, yes, yes. Seven times, yes.

11
Getting Back
June 2009

No one person – no matter how strong, fast or talented – can lift the Stanley Cup by himself. It takes a team to win a championship in the National Hockey League.

Victory starts with years of preparation. Your childhood hours are spent on outdoor rinks across dark winters, playing the game for fun until the point of exhaustion, warming up inside and then going out for more. Next, you endure early-morning practices, riding in a minivan with an overstuffed bag filled with pads, skates and tape to reach the local indoor rink whenever time comes available, even long before the sun rises and the first school bell rings. At age 15 comes the moment of leaving home to attend school in another country to find enough talented competition that will constantly challenge your skills and forge you into a stronger player. Finally, you find the courage to leave your family and closest friends to reach a place you have dreamed about your entire life but have rarely seen even on television, and where you do not speak the language or really know many people.

Just because you put in all those hours and take all those risks, hockey does not guarantee you will become a champion either. Players must wait for opportunity and recognize their shot at winning the Cup when they have the ability to make a run at winning it. Despite his greatness and the promise that comes with being heralded as a once-in-a-generation player, Mario Lemieux did not win an NHL championship until his seventh season in the league. He got there only after the franchise owners surrounded him with other talented stars – some from free agency and trades, and others, like Jaromir Jagr, through the luck of the draft. After finally lifting the Cup, Lemieux sat at his locker in front of newspaper reporters and television cameras and wept, with joy, of course, but also with the relief of having lived up to the expectations of a lifetime of hype that comes with being a prodigy.

Halfway through the Stanley Cup Final against Detroit in 2008, the Pittsburgh Penguins' new generation of young players realized they had done enough work and put together enough talent to win a championship, too. The awakening had come late, after the first two games in which the players felt awed just to have reached the foot of the summit. While the Detroit Red Wings ran ahead to a familiar place at the very apex, the Penguins had fallen behind just enough that they did not reach the top themselves – even after taking Detroit to triple overtime in Game 5 on a last-minute tying goal to stave off elimination for just a little longer. When the Penguins eventually lost in Game 6 at the Civic Arena, with the Red Wings players throwing their gloves in the air and skating around the ice with the Cup lifted over their heads, the Penguins – despite coming so close – fell back to Earth with 28 other teams that did not win the championship. If Pittsburgh wanted to have another chance to reach the summit, if the players really believed that destiny called them to finish that journey, the path started in the quiet solace of defeat.

Just days after the Penguins' season ended with a Game 6 loss to the Detroit Red Wings in the 2008 Stanley Cup Final, General Manager Ray Shero picked up the phone and called Marian Hossa's agent with an offer. Pittsburgh would pay Hossa up to $50 million, with at least $7 million a year for his choice of five, six or seven years. For the first time in years, the Penguins had made an aggressive play the previous February to get a talented, high-priced free agent, and now they wanted to keep him. Hossa had completed the Pittsburgh Penguins, elevating their game by giving star center Sidney Crosby a reliable linemate. With his help, the Penguins had reached the championship round. In Game 5, when the Penguins finally figured out how to win against the Red Wings, Hossa had scored the first goal, with assists from Crosby and Pascal Dupuis, the other player who had come to Pittsburgh from Atlanta. Hossa had been on the ice getting an assist, too, when Maxime Talbot scored the tying goal with less than a minute left. Even in the end, Hossa nearly helped the Penguins pull off another miracle in Game 6 to force a decisive final game. Keeping Hossa meant the franchise would have a harder time paying the salaries of Crosby, Evgeni Malkin and another young star center, Jordan Staal, but team managers were willing to take that long-term risk with the immediate reward of keeping those players together for another run at the Cup.

By July 1, weeks later when the free agency period started, Hossa still had not accepted the Penguins' offer. He had said even before Pittsburgh traded for him that he wanted to test the free agency market, to see how much money he could make and – apparently more importantly – to give himself the best chance of adding his name to the Stanley Cup. In a rare moment for any professional athlete, Hossa had a pick of several teams: At the trading deadline the year before, Montreal and Ottawa had competed for Hossa right down to the final minutes when Shero had closed the deal. Now other teams entered the mix. Edmonton was rumored to have offered Hossa more than $9 million a year, topping the Penguins offer but giving him less of a chance for a championship. Hossa could be a difference-maker for any team, but he hoped the difference would be winning a title and not merely qualifying for the playoffs.

By July 2, Hossa had made up his mind. He called Shero on the phone. Hossa said he was going to Detroit, not because it had offered him more money or long-term stability – because it hadn't. Hossa went with the Red Wings because he had just watched them win a championship, and he had seen how hard it had been for the young Penguins to keep up with an older, more experienced team. "I want to have the best chance to win the Stanley Cup," Hossa told reporters later that day.[1]

---

[1] "Hossa spurns Penguins, signs with Red Wings." By Rob Rossi, *Pittsburgh Tribune-Review*. July 3, 2008.

"When you look at all the teams I could choose from, at the top there were two teams. ... At the end of the day, I felt like I would have a better chance to win the Cup with Detroit."

The words stung the Penguins players and management more than any of them would admit. Evgeni Malkin, the Penguins' Russian center, was still reeling from losing the Stanley Cup Final when he learned that Hossa had decided to leave. Coming so close to holding the Cup had only made the players hungrier to go back and get it the following season. "When we lost in the Cup Final, it was very tough because I had never won a big trophy with any team," Malkin recalled later. "Every time, I'm second or third. I never won in Russia or with the national team. Every time, second, and to lose again in the final was tough for me." Now, as he found out that Hossa had decided to leave – and not for just any team but for Malkin's childhood favorite – the departure added to the sense of gloom. "He's a good player, and I thought he would try to help the team win again," Malkin said.

Since taking the bold move to acquire Hossa six months earlier, the team had decided it could win now without waiting for a new arena. The players had blown through the Eastern Conference and in the final days of the Stanley Cup Final, they felt like they had a shot to win it all. Given another chance, they could take the championship. Hossa had been part of that process, giving the Penguins his all down the stretch when they needed it. Now, just days after Detroit won, Hossa decided that given a choice, he would side with the Red Wings over his former teammates in Pittsburgh.

"It wasn't disappointing that he left," Shero said later. "It was more disappointing that he said he had a better chance to win there."

Even around the league, the move was seen as an insult. One NHL employee summed up the reaction in a text to Rob Rossi, the Penguins beat writer for the *Pittsburgh Tribune-Review*: "How can this be viewed as anything other than Hossa slapping Mario Lemieux, Ray Shero and Sidney Crosby in the face?"

Rossi texted back: "I don't know, but he better hope they don't see him in the final, because it's not going to end well."

None of the Penguins really wanted to talk about Hossa's decision, but people close to the team could tell that it had bothered them. Perhaps that was unfair – to Hossa and to themselves. He had never said he was going to stay, and in fact, he had been adamant with anyone who asked that he did not want to talk about his contract until after the season when he would become a free agent. But there had been a presumption that he would stay. Why would anybody leave this situation? The Penguins – to a man – were thinking this guy would never leave. Why would you leave Crosby? Why would you leave Lemieux? And he did.

"It was just a splash of cold water for an organization that had really felt like, 'OK, we had figured this out,'" Rossi recalled later. "By him not signing, it was basically him telling them, 'The money's not important here. I don't think you can win. I think this other team is better than you still.' And that was the most insulting thing. After years of having not been able to spend money, the Penguins were willing to spend money to keep this guy. They were going to give him money to play for the best center in the world, for an owner who had been the best player maybe in the history of the game, and for a GM who had really shown that he's one of the bright young GMs of this game. It would be one thing if he had left for more money. He didn't leave for more money. He didn't leave for more security. He left for one year."

No longer worried about having to pay Hossa's contract, Shero refocused on building his team. Even as he overhauled the Penguins' hockey operations, the one thing Shero had not changed when he took over as general manager was the coach. Michel Therrien had come up to Pittsburgh from Wilkes-Barre after management had fired his predecessor, Ed Olczyk, when the team failed to improve in the first months after the lockout, despite acquiring Crosby. Keeping Therrien had been a condition of taking over as general manager. Together they had found success, qualifying for the playoffs in their first season and then making a run all the way to the finals the next. A month after the 2008 playoffs ended, Shero signed Therrien to a contract extension.

The Penguins opened the 2008-09 season in Sweden as part of the NHL's attempt to build interest in its games beyond North America. With 10 days in Europe, the team split a two-game series against the Senators, winning the first game in overtime and then losing the second. After returning home, the Penguins started stronger than anyone might have guessed, surprising even their coach by winning 14 of their first 23 games through November. The long NHL season does not reward sprinters, however, and by December, the Penguins had lost momentum. The team posted a losing record that month and headed into January with five straight losses and no goals on 33 power play attempts. Worse, they had fallen from second to ninth place, out of a playoff spot.

Burkle called Morehouse and wanted to know what was going wrong. After the Penguins reached the arena deal, Morehouse figured he would go back to life as a consultant, and he started looking forward to making another list for the next transition in his life. But as Morehouse prepared to leave the Penguins, Lemieux appealed to Burkle for help keeping him in Pittsburgh. Morehouse had proven so valuable during the arena process that the owners wanted him to remain in his hometown – if he wanted to stay there. After growing up on Pittsburgh's streets and finding his way to 1600 Pennsylvania Avenue in Washington, D.C., Morehouse had remembered his roots and staked his future back in the place where he had started out. He had discovered his own destiny in the very place where he had sneaked into games as a boy, riding into Pittsburgh with older neighborhood kids and climbing over the low walls of the Civic Arena to get into games when he could not afford to buy a ticket. Morehouse gladly accepted the offer to stay in Pittsburgh, becoming the team's president. He and Vanessa moved with their growing family from their rented house into a suburban home, not far from Lemieux's own. By luck and wit, Morehouse had joined a small group of people who would set the course of a franchise he had cheered for all his life.

When Burkle called Morehouse that winter, he wanted answers. Not only was the team losing games, but no one in the front office had called a meeting among the executives to talk about what changes needed to be made. A year earlier, Burkle had looked into the eyes of these same men and asked them one question: Do we have a chance to win? He already knew the answer to that question now. The team had responded that season by playing its way into the Stanley Cup Final. Of course the team could win. It just had stopped winning and playing well. Everything that had coalesced the season before seemed to be gone. Management could make excuses: Hossa had gone to Detroit; Sergei Gonchar, a top defenseman, had dislocated his shoulder during the pre-season and not returned; Crosby and Malkin felt tired after the short off-season the previous summer.

With the team scheduled to play the Rangers in New York on January 5, Burkle called a meeting with Lemieux, team CEO Ken Sawyer, Morehouse and Shero. The five men sat at a corner table inside Gemma, an Italian restaurant styled to look like a French brasserie inside the Lower East Side's Bowery Hotel. In the early evening before the hockey game at Madison Square Garden, they essentially had the restaurant to themselves. Burkle turned to his top executives in a way that was not angry but firm. It would not be acceptable, he told them, for the Penguins to miss the playoffs a year after nearly winning the Cup. The team was too good to fail that miserably in less than a year.

Once again, Burkle was not going to say what moves the team should make. "Ron's got that business savvy," Shero said years later. Burkle did not know enough about hockey to suggest what the Penguins should do to regain momentum, but he wanted to know why his team was failing. "Ron, like Mario, has never ordered me to do anything – 'Do this' or 'Do that,'" Shero said. Sawyer, Shero and Morehouse would have to come up with the specific plan. But when it came to winning and losing, the team owners had put their own wallets on the line by deciding to spend up to the NHL cap before the new arena opened. If the Penguins failed to make the playoffs, Burkle and Lemieux would have to open their own checkbooks to cover the team's expenses. Losses could amount to $10 million or more. Even more than concerns about the money, Burkle feared the team would fail to meet its potential. By being aggressive the year before to acquire Hossa, the team also had scuttled its long-term building plan. That move had signaled to the players, the fans and rest of the league that the Penguins were ready to move up among the league's elite franchises. Failing to make the playoffs now would send another message: that the Penguins' playoff success had been a fluke and the franchise was not building a dynasty that would consistently vie for the Cup.

Burkle looked around the table and asked one question again. "How long are you going to put up with this?"

No one had an easy answer. As always, Shero had been looking for other trades that would spark the team, but no one like Hossa was available, and the Penguins did not have the salary cap space for a major acquisition, anyway. Shero would make changes but none that would be a blockbuster. If the coach was to blame, the Penguins had just signed Therrien to a contract extension, and firing him now would mean losing the money they had spent to keep him. Besides, Therrien had proven he could win with the team. Burkle made it clear Shero should do something. Again the owners told the general manager they would support him. If he needed to fire Therrien, he should do it – and not worry about the cost.

The owners sent one other message, too, that they were not about to give up. Given the team's spot out of the playoffs, they could have made the decision to cut their losses by dumping salary. Trade away high-priced players and tell the fans they would build for the future. Other teams do that all the time, giving away star players that cost millions of dollars in salary for prospects that cost little. Management makes the argument to fans that this will help build a winning franchise for some distant day in the future, when they want to save money without taking the risk of trying to win right away. Businesses make that kind of decision all the time, too, although with an audience of shareholders rather than fans. Rather than setting a winning course and making adjustments to stay focused on that goal as problems arise, executives often feel more comfortable retreating to a safe position. Already Burkle and Lemieux had changed the culture of the Penguins by demanding excellence and hiring people like Shero, who made the small decisions that added up to a long-term philosophy for winning. That sort of thinking could be contagious. The owners also had re-educated their staff to think about winning and to take appropriate chances when it would give the franchise an opportunity to get ahead: Yes, we can – if it makes sense. Now they were telling Sawyer, Shero and Morehouse again to do whatever they needed to win. The owners did not want to give up. They wanted to regroup and figure out what changes were needed, even if that meant firing Therrien. "The difference was that you could have cut costs," one team executive said. "They moved not to cut costs but to ask, 'How do we turn this around?'"

Team executives left the dinner with Burkle not knowing what they would do, but confident that they would do something – and that they had the support of team owners to make whatever changes were necessary to get back to winning. That night, the Penguins went out and lost to the Rangers 4-to-0. They had not gained a point in the standings for five straight games, the longest streak in three years.

Facing his first long stretch of losing after finding so much early success, Shero was learning on the job. "Going through that is part of my growth, because the team was not doing well," Shero said years later. "Coaching, managing and playing is pretty easy when you win 15 in a row. It's when you go through hard times that you become a better manager, better player, better coach. It's part of the experience, and if you don't experience that then you haven't lasted very long as a manager, for sure."

By Valentine's Day, the Penguins still did not rank among the playoff contenders. At the all-star break in late January, Lemieux had decided to take a more active role in setting the team's direction. Shero would have responsibility for the daily operations, but now he would report more directly to the team's co-owner on those decisions. With the Penguins continuing to lose, none of the moves would be easy.

Through the weeks of losing, Therrien felt the pressure more than anyone. Yet when he looked at his team before its February 14th game in Toronto, he believed the worst moments were in the past. He recalled the team's surprisingly strong start and how it had been hobbled by injuries to key players. Gonchar, the team's leading defenseman, would be coming back for his first game of the season that night. At first, when the game started inside the Air Canada Centre, Therrien's hopes for a miraculous recovery felt possible. The Penguins jumped out with two goals in the first period. Then in a monumental letdown, the team gave up six goals to the Maple Leafs over the rest of the game.

The next day, Shero called team owners and told them he had decided on a change: Therrien had to go. Shero talked that afternoon with Dan Bylsma, the coach of the Penguins' minor league affiliate in Wilkes-Barre/Scranton, about filling in on an interim basis. Then Shero talked with Therrien and abruptly let him know that he had been fired.

In Wilkes-Barre, Bylsma coached an afternoon game – a win against the Worcester Sharks – and then talked with his minor-league players to let them know he would be leaving. He got in his car and drove to Long Island that night, where Penguins staffers were waiting for him in the hotel lobby. The interim coach met with players the next morning.

What Bylsma found was a team that had transformed itself at almost every level. Lemieux, the former player, and Burkle, the once silent investor, had formed a new kind of ownership by combining their skills to create a partnership that could adapt intuitively both as a hockey team and a business. Shero had changed the way the front office was run, putting a renewed emphasis on professionalism and investing in advanced analysis of not only players but also salary cap implications. Morehouse had joined Sawyer in the front office, bringing an outsider's perspective to decisions about how the team would interact with its fans and local business leaders. Now, Bylsma came in with a polished smile and an open office door. While Therrien had instilled discipline among the players to transform a losing franchise into a Stanley Cup contender, Bylsma would attempt to inspire the players to lift their game again.

The Penguins went out the next day and lost a 3-to-2 shootout against the Islanders. After that, however, they lost only six times in their final 24 regular-season games, finishing second in the division and fourth in the Eastern Conference. Malkin won the Art Ross Trophy for scoring the most points of any player in the league. It had been an unbelievable turn-around for a team that had not even been in a position to make the post-season.

Given the freedom to be more aggressive about addressing the Penguins' weaknesses, Shero made two other moves that spring to improve the team. After the 2004-05 lockout, the NHL had started to become more like the National Football League with its salary cap on payroll. Before the lockout, the Penguins were spending about $20 million a year on players' salaries, while some other teams were paying $80 million or more. In the first year of the cap, no team could spend more than $39 million. The new contract also set a minimum amount teams had to spend on salaries, at 55 percent of the maximum, or $21 million that first year. As league revenues increased, the cap would grow, too.

Shero already had overhauled the Penguins front office, with a focus on organized analysis and attention to the players that made the franchise a class act. With the talent Shero had collected around him in the executive suite, the Penguins started to break down the salary cap implications like few other teams in the league. To succeed, teams suddenly needed executives who could not only evaluate talent but also figure out how to make the most of a limited budget. In football, teams often hire mathematicians who know more about accounting than X's and O's.

The Penguins could easily have been forced into a similar decision, but Shero lucked out by finding a former NHL player, Jason Botterill, who had been a step too slow as a player but who had gone back to the University of Michigan, where he had played four seasons, to get an MBA degree. A first-round draft pick in 1994, Botterill played eight years with four different NHL teams, often bouncing back to the minors. He finally retired in October 2004 after a concussion left him with symptoms that lingered for more than two years – seeing a spinning room and black spots any time he elevated his heart rate. As a former player with a master's degree in business, however, Botterill had a unique perspective on managing the sport. After graduate school, he spent the first year after the lockout working in the NHL's central registry office, fielding questions about the new salary cap and working on a record number of player arbitration cases. Shero did not have any openings in his front office but agreed to interview Botterill as a favor to another friend. For the tryout, Botterill had to break down the contract possibilities and cap implications for the team's ongoing negotiations with defenseman Ryan Whitney over his free agency contract. Shero immediately realized the advantage of having an assistant who understands the intricacies of the cap and players' salaries – for not only the Penguins but other teams in the league as well. Shero created a position for Botterill, giving him the freedom to move between the executive suite and the playing ice where he could remain involved in light workouts with the players.

Because of the narrow cap limitations and with the unique understanding they had developed, the Penguins were able to take steps that other teams did not always see. When Shero wanted to trade with the Islanders for veteran right wing Bill Guerin at the March 4, 2009, trading deadline, the team needed to make a salary adjustment. Already Guerin had nearly gone to other teams – the Rangers and Capitals were believed to be interested in the veteran player – and he had been pulled out of a pre-game skate at one point when he was almost dealt to one of those other franchises. Shero, however, had been willing to accept an unusual request from the Islanders when the other general managers had not: If the Penguins traded for Guerin, they would give up a higher draft pick the further into the playoffs the team traveled. The conditional pick terms called for the Penguins to give up at least a fifth-round pick to obtain Guerin, but if the team qualified for the playoffs it would give the Islanders a fourth-round pick. If the Penguins won that first playoff series, the team would give up a third-round draft slot. The trade required a little imagination, but Shero realized that Guerin could complete Crosby's line, and he knew that if the team made a run deep into the playoffs, that would be worth giving up a higher pick in the subsequent draft.

To obtain Guerin, the Penguins also had to get creative about their own salary situation. The team did not have enough salary room under the limits of its current roster to add the Islanders right wing. Realizing that players' salaries count against the cap only during the regular season and not the playoffs, Shero talked with another veteran already on the team about temporarily going back to the minors. He reached out to Miroslav Satan, a right wing with 17 years in the NHL and a pregnant wife at home, to see whether he would be willing to spend a couple months with the Penguins' minor league affiliate in Wilkes-Barre/Scranton. He would continue to receive an NHL salary, but he would be back to playing before smaller crowds and riding buses to games rather than chartered jets. Penguins executives knew the risk was that Satan might simply return home to Slovakia, figuring he would rather leave than take even a temporary step back to the minors toward the end of a successful career. "You just never know how the players are going to react," Botterill said later. Satan wanted to know whether the Penguins would call him back to Pittsburgh before the end of the season. Shero told him honestly that was unlikely because of the salary cap limitations. He said it might be possible, however, for the team to call up Satan for the playoffs – but only on the condition that he acted as a good teammate in the minors.

Satan agreed to those terms, and he embraced his role as a veteran leader in Wilkes-Barre/Scranton. The Slovak star helped develop younger players by staying late after practices to work on skills and by setting a professional tone. Almost every day that Satan stayed in the minors, Shero called him to make sure he was doing all right. The general manager said he knew Satan had made a sacrifice for the team, especially with his wife due to deliver their baby at any moment. Shero wanted the player to know that he had not forgotten about him.

Shero's savvy paid off again that season when he added another wing to Crosby's line. He wanted to get Chris Kunitz from the Anaheim Ducks, but that meant giving up Ryan Whitney, one of the first young players who made up the core of the Penguins' talent from the draft. The team had taken Whitney fifth overall in the 2002 draft, and he had helped comprise the solid foundation of the franchise. But to give Crosby more opportunities at the goal, Shero was willing to give up a little defensive talent. At the same time, Shero wanted to get as much out of the trade as possible – especially if he planned to give up a promising talent who had proven his worth many times. Shero knew the Ducks also had a left wing prospect, Eric Tangradi, who had been taken 42nd overall in the 2007 draft but who had yet to play in the league. From his research, Shero believed Tangradi could grow into a solid NHL player, so he asked the Ducks to make the prospect part of the deal. Ultimately, Anaheim agreed to the terms, and Shero picked up a promising young talent to replace some of the youth the team had traded away. Holding out for Tangradi, however, could have cost Shero the entire trade.

The Penguins walked through the Eastern Conference in 2008 with just two losses in 14 games. However, they would face more opposition the second time around. The playoffs this time started against the Philadelphia Flyers, a cross-state rival that meant more from the perspective of history than perhaps any of the Penguins' young players were prepared to acknowledge. The Penguins and Flyers both entered the NHL during the league's 1967 "Next Six" expansion, but the Flyers won the first game in which they faced each other and held a definitive 129-76-31 lifetime advantage of victories over Pittsburgh by the start of the playoffs. Worse, for a period of 42 games over 15 years, from 1974 to 1989, the Penguins did not win even a single game in Philadelphia. In the modern age of North American professional sports in which leagues strive for parity, the tilted ice across Pennsylvania had been as unusual as it had been humiliating for the Penguins players and fans. Even when the Penguins drafted Lemieux in 1984, the streak continued, not ending until February 2, 1989.

This time around, the Penguins were not weighted down by the history of the rivalry, and they took the opening series in six games. After the series, Shero rewarded Bylsma with a contract to stay on as the permanent, rather than interim, coach.

The Washington Capitals presented a bigger challenge. In 2004, the Penguins should have had the rights to draft Alexander Ovechkin, the Russian star who had been the unquestioned number one overall pick that year. The Penguins had finished in last place, a game below the Capitals, but under the NHL's reformed rules for the draft, futility no longer guaranteed the top pick. In the draft lottery that year, Washington won the pingpong ball to get the first slot, and the Penguins fell to second place, where they took another young Russian star, Malkin, considered by most to be nearly as good as the top pick that year. Because the Penguins did not win that lottery, the franchise had a better shot at getting the top pick the year following the lockout, when every team had a chance to pick Crosby first overall. If the Penguins had won the rights to Ovechkin, the team would have had just two balls in the Crosby lottery, instead of three. "Who knows which ball was picked?" Sawyer recalled years later. "I like to think it was the extra one. I firmly believe that there's bad luck and there's good luck. The goal in business is to be able to hang in there long enough for the good luck to arrive, to weather the storms, because we had plenty of adversity to deal with. We were able to weather them, and then lucky us when we won the lottery the year that Sidney Crosby was available."

Because of the lockout, Crosby and Ovechkin came into the NHL at the same time, two number one picks competing to be the league's best rookie. Ovechkin won the Calder Memorial Trophy as the rookie of the year with 106 points, while Crosby surpassed Lemieux for first-year franchise records with 63 assists and 102 points. Two years behind Ovechkin in age,

Crosby also became the youngest player in league history to score 100 points in a season. The rivalry of their rookie seasons has lingered, so that whenever the two players take the ice at the same time, their teammates, like fans, watch to see what will happen.

Now in the playoffs against each other, Crosby and Ovechkin determined to see which one of them could not only win the round but also score the most points. Crosby scored the first goal of the series off a pass from Guerin just 4:09 minutes into the game. Ovechkin answered with his first goal of the series toward the end of the first period, with the Capitals holding a 5-on-3 advantage. Malkin picked up an assist, as Washington went on to win the game 3-to-2.

The real drama between the two stars started in Game 2, with the Penguins looking to even the series before heading home. Crosby scored the first goal six minutes into the game, and then Ovechkin scored two minutes into the second period to tie the game. Crosby had another goal eight minutes later, while Ovechkin picked up two more in the third period to give his team the lead. The home crowd littered the ice with ball caps in celebration of Ovechkin's hat trick, as Crosby watched. With barely 30 seconds left in the game, Crosby scored his own hat trick. In the battle of NHL stars, Crosby had kept pace with Ovechkin – but it had not been enough to win the game. The Capitals had picked up one more goal halfway through the game, winning the first two games of the series.

Returning home, the Penguins reversed the momentum by winning Game 3 in overtime and then tied the series by winning Game 4. They took a 3-2 series lead with another overtime victory in Washington in game 5, but the Caps came back to win Game 6, also in overtime, at the Civic Arena. The competition was fierce — the stakes were high, and the two superstars were the best players on the ice.

Sixty minutes remained to determine who would go to the conference finals and who would go home, as the series returned to Washington's Verizon Center for a winner-take-all Game 7. Three minutes into the game, Ovechkin broke free against Pittsburgh goalie Marc-Andre Fleury, firing a shot on goal that the perfectly positioned Fleury caught in his glove. Momentum turned on that one play: The Capitals had been intent on scoring the first goal by moving quickly around the Penguins and taking four shots on goal in the game's first minutes, but none of the shots hit the back of the net. In the 12th minute, Crosby took his turn to change the game again, setting up to the left side of the goal, taking a pass from Sergei Gonchar and putting it into the net. Eight seconds later, the Penguins' next line took the faceoff, moved into the Capitals' end, and Craig Adams scored a wrist-shot goal to give Pittsburgh a quick two-goal lead. The score was 5-to-0 by the time Ovechkin scored Washington's first goal of the game late in the second period. Crosby scored his second goal in the final period, and the Capitals never recovered.

In the contest of the superstars, Ovechin had 14 points on eight goals and six assists – one more than Crosby, with eight goals and five assists. But the Penguins had won the right to advance. Crosby would move on to the Eastern Conference finals versus Carolina, while Ovechkin went home.

If the series against Washington showcased Crosby's talents, the conference final would be Malkin's turn in the spotlight. Since sneaking away from his team in the Ural Mountains nearly three years earlier, Malkin had proven the scouts correct that he had been worthy of the second pick in 2005 – 1A to Ovechkin, the first pick overall. Still, critics whispered that he had not been a major factor for the Penguins in either of his first two trips to the playoffs with the team. In his first season with Pittsburgh, he played in five games against Ottawa that year with four assists but no goals. The Penguins lost, and the Senators advanced all the way to the conference finals. The next season, Malkin had 10 goals and 12 assists over 20 games when the Penguins advanced to the Stanley Cup Final and lost. It had been a strong showing, but still critics said he had not had a dominating performance worthy of his skills. Malkin, too, worried about whether he had the ability to play like a champion. At every step in his career, Malkin had played for talented teams and had reached soaring heights – but his teams always finished as a runner-up in second or third place. In the Olympics at Turin, the Russian team had finished in fourth place. In the 2004 Russian Superleague, the Metallurg with Malkin had finished in second place. In the Stanley Cup Final the year before, the Penguins had lost to Detroit. Malkin wondered whether he would ever live up to the expectations that surrounded him and the ones in his own mind that told him he should be a champion despite the history of falling short.

Those doubts dissipated at 12:25 in the third period in Game 2 of the conference finals against Carolina. Fans had filled the stands at the Civic Arena with white shirts. Malkin won a faceoff to the right of the Hurricanes' goal. He kept the puck, following it into the corner and then bringing it around behind the net. Malkin circled around the front of the goal, turned away from the net and without looking over his shoulder, fired the puck behind him – placing it neatly over the shoulder of goalie Cam Ward. It was Malkin's third goal of the game, and it gave the Penguins a two-goal lead on the way to a 7-to-4 victory. It seemed at the moment of Malkin's goal, one Penguins official said later, that the Hurricanes players decided they could not keep pace with the faster, more creative Penguins.

Pittsburgh swept the series to get another shot at the Stanley Cup. Getting through the Eastern Conference had been more difficult the second time around, and it had taken a team effort. Satan, the Slovak player who had gone down to the minors to make salary cap room for Pittsburgh to acquire Guerin, came back to the Penguins for the playoffs, and he scored the first goal of the Eastern Conference finals.

After the series-clinching game at the RBC Center in Raleigh, North Carolina, Crosby skated over to the Prince of Wales trophy. This time, he picked it up, paused for a moment with Malkin for a photograph, and skated around the ice holding the trophy in his hands. Superstition be damned.

A year earlier, the Penguins' players had been nervous when they entered the Stanley Cup Final, but now they knew what to expect. For nearly 12 months, they had wondered what might have been against the Red Wings. Now they would get a chance to rewrite history with a second-straight championship series against Detroit.

This time, they would face Hossa as well. No team wins a championship by trying to spite a single player from the other team, but no one could deny either that Hossa's decision to sign with Detroit – because he felt the Red Wings had a better chance to win the Cup – had given the Penguins organization additional motivation. "Hossa became a really interesting figure in Pittsburgh history," Rossi said. "He was only here five months. He left. And he was a guy who really sort of cemented their status as a true Stanley Cup contender, and he served as a galvanizing force when he left."

No team since the Edmonton Oilers in 1984 had lost in the Stanley Cup Final one year and come back to win it the following year. According to the history books, it would be easier to repeat as a champion than to somehow win the Cup after coming as close as the final round and not picking it up. The Penguins had repeated as champions in 1991 and 1992. Detroit had done it in 1997 and 1998. Some teams made winning more than once seem easy: The Islanders and Canadiens each won the Cup four years in a row, in the 1980s and 1970s, respectively. Before that in a smaller league, Montreal had won the Cup five straight times in the 1950s. By those odds, the Red Wings had a better shot of winning a second championship than the Penguins did of finding a way to victory that had eluded them a year earlier. No one who was connected with the Penguins – not the young stars who had been drafted by a perennial loser, not the coach who had spent only two-thirds of a year coaching in the minors before coming to Pittsburgh late in the season, not the team owners who had pushed for greatness on the ice as soon as they had guaranteed their franchise would have a long-term home in the city – cared about those odds. A Penguins team that had been out of playoff contention at midseason would get another chance at the Cup, and that was all that mattered.

215

A year earlier in Detroit, the Penguins had been half-asleep through the first two games at Joe Louis Arena, almost as if they were in awe just to have reached the Final against a team that had been there many times before. This time would be different, the Penguins players told themselves. Yet as they headed back to Pittsburgh for Game 3, the results had been the same. The Penguins had dropped the first two games and needed a win at the Civic Arena just to stay in the series. Getting that win, however, would not be enough. They had won Game 3 the previous year, too, but then had dropped the next game at home and had to fight to keep the series alive after that. The Penguins won Game 3 at the Civic Arena again. The players knew the decisive moment, however, would come in Game 4 – when the Penguins either would tie the series for a real chance to win the Cup or cede the advantage back to the Red Wings, who would be able to clinch a second-straight championship with only another victory.

Less than a minute into the start of the second period of Game 4 with the score tied at 1-to-1, the Red Wings prepared again to take control of the series away from the Penguins. It was the sort of moment the Detroit team perfected, putting its skate on the back of its opponent to seize momentum on the way to another championship. The slap shot from Brad Stuart moved so quickly toward the goal that the puck passed through Fleury's legs before he could get down, and it sailed into the back of the net as the arena fell silent. When the Penguins' Brooks Orpik was called for tripping minutes later and the Red Wings started a two-minute power play, this seemed to be the moment when Detroit would break the hearts of Penguins fans. With the Penguins on penalty kill, Jordan Staal – a center taken second overall in the 2006 draft – took a pass from Maxime Talbot near center ice. Instead of dumping the puck into the Red Wings' end, Staal made a move toward the net. Shifting the puck from his backhand to the forehand in front of goalie Chris Osgood, Staal slipped the puck past him on the stick side for a short-handed goal. Fans inside the arena jumped to their feet, bringing life back to the funereal place. At a crucial moment – the place where they had broken down a year before – the Penguins stood up to the Red Wings this time and refused to go away quietly.

Two minutes later, with momentum on the Penguins' side, Malkin blocked a shot near the blue line in the Penguins' end and kept the puck in front of him as he quickly shifted direction and moved toward Osgood with one defender ahead and Crosby streaking down the ice to his left. As Malkin stopped inside the faceoff circle on Osgood's glove side, the goalie had a decision to make: move toward Malkin with the possibility that he could make a quick slapshot on goal or drift the other way to guard against a quick pass to Crosby, who was moving toward the net. Osgood made the only move he could, going toward Malkin. Just as quickly, Malkin passed across to Crosby. The Red Wings goalie had no chance of getting back to cover up, and Crosby whipped the puck quickly over Osgood's stick. Pittsburgh had regained the lead, and after getting another goal in the third period, the Penguins won the game, knotting up the series as it headed back to Detroit for Game 5.

Again, as in 2008, the Red Wings brought the Penguins to the brink of elimination. Detroit responded to losing two games in Pittsburgh by scoring five goals and preventing the Penguins from scoring in Game 5 when the series returned to Joe Louis Arena. Malkin engaged in a fight, Crosby was penalized, and the team lost its composure. Any advantage the Penguins captured in the previous game was gone in the 5-to-0 loss, as the odds of history returned to Detroit's side. Champions are meant to repeat as champions, while losers are destined to go away.

Lemieux wanted no part of that history. In retirement, he had never been one to show up unannounced in the locker room to talk with the team or to tell the coaches what they could be doing better. He kept his distance, respectful of the jobs that others had been hired to do. But in the final minute of the Game 5 loss, the hall-of-fame player stood in the hallway outside the locker room as the players came off the ice, and he followed them inside for a closed-door meeting. Because he so rarely showed up to talk with the players like that, his very presence made a powerful impact. His words encouraged the team to move past the loss.

Later that night, Shero sent a text message to Lemieux and thanked him for coming into the locker room. A lot of people show up when the team wins, but Lemieux came at the players' lowest moment. No one who was in that room could forget what it had been like to have Lemieux appear in person to voice his support.

Lemieux wrote back:

"See you Monday …

"We are a family and in this together …

"We don't need anyone that is only with us WIN OR TIE.

"I really think this is our year. Let's forget about tonight. … It happens.

"We will win Tuesday and win the Cup Friday."

Shero asked whether he could forward the message to the players, and Lemieux agreed. The next morning, every Penguins player woke up to read that message in his inbox.

A year earlier, Game 6 had been when the Penguins lost the series, when Detroit had raised the Cup on the Civic Arena ice before thousands of fans stunned into silence. Hossa had been on the Penguins side that night, watching Detroit's celebration, and he had decided to switch sides. The Penguins who remained with the team had resolved to get back to the brink of a championship again – to give themselves another chance. Facing elimination again, the Penguins had given themselves that opportunity. Now it would be up to the players to determine what they might do differently this time to keep their hopes alive of going farther than they had been able to go before.

Through the first 20 minutes of Game 6, no one scored. Then in the first minute of the second period, Jordan Staal again came through. Quickly converting a turnover in the Penguins' end, Staal banged the puck off the side boards and started moving quickly toward the Detroit goal. It looked almost like a repeat of the short-handed goal two games earlier when Staal scored, except that the teams this time were at even strength. As he neared the faceoff circle on Osgood's glove side, Staal fired a shot toward the goal and kept moving forward toward the net. Osgood deflected the puck so that it rebounded to Staal as he closed on the goal. Staal put the puck past the goalie as he dove forward toward his left in a desperate attempt to cover it up.

With everything on the line, the Penguins were determined to write a different ending this time around. After one more goal by each team in the third period, the Penguins won the game and earned a chance to redeem themselves with a winner-take-all Game 7 for the Stanley Cup in Detroit.

Game 7 rarely goes well for the away team. Among all four of North America's major league sports, no visitor had won a championship in the ultimate game since 1979, when the Pittsburgh Pirates won the World Series at Baltimore's Memorial Stadium. If the Penguins were going to lift the Cup, they would have to defy the history books one more time.

Already the Penguins had abandoned convention. When Shero had come to Pittsburgh three years earlier, he had taken over a team built with high draft picks and molded it through free agency and well-timed moves at the trading deadline to give them a chance at becoming champions. Midway through the 2007-08 season, when Burkle had insisted on knowing whether the Penguins had a chance to win right away, Shero abandoned the long-term playbook to get Hossa, a legitimate star, and to send a signal to the Penguins players that they were primed for a run at the Cup. And when Hossa left at the end of that season for Detroit, saying he felt the Red Wings had the best shot of winning the Cup again, the Penguins players had been galvanized in their desire to prove him wrong.

Even then, getting back had not been easy. The Penguins had fallen out of playoff contention by the darkest months of the winter, and Burkle again called the hockey staff together and urged them to figure out what had gone wrong. The team's co-owner did not know enough about hockey to say exactly what steps the executives should take, but he understood business and opportunity as if he could see into the future. It did not matter whether this was a hockey team or a grocery store: If the operation had been in first place a year earlier, Burkle wanted to know, how could it have fallen so far and so quickly? Given a nudge once more, Shero took the steps to give the Penguins another chance. He fired the coach after a bleak road trip to Toronto, and then he was creative enough to add two players – Guerin and Kunitz – on the line with Crosby. Taken together, the Penguins owners, top hockey staff and players had accomplished more than any of them could have done on their own. They had gotten back to the edge of the summit just one year after falling short.

The night before the final game, Lemieux sent another text message for the coaches to share with players:

"This is a chance of a lifetime to realize your childhood dream to win a Stanley Cup.

"Play without fear and you will be successful!!!

"See you at center ice."

By that, he meant that they would be at center ice to celebrate the Stanley Cup victory after Game 7. Just as Burkle had known when to nudge the team executives to be more aggressive about trying to win, Lemieux had innately realized he had one chance to inspire his players with his words. He no longer could lace up skates and go onto the ice to score goals. Yet he could speak to the players from the perspective of having been in their position. When he spoke, his words carried the unique weight of experience.

In a private exchange that night before Game 7, Tom McMillan, the team's vice president of communications, wrote a text message to Lemieux to let him know the coaches were going to share his words with the players in a text message the following morning and post them in the locker room. Lemieux wrote back: "Go for it. We are going to win tomorrow."

McMillan sent him some more details, and Lemieux responded again:

"You got it. I'm not a novelist but I speak from the heart, and I think that might give the boys a little boost before they step on the ice. Hope so anyway. See you at center ice."

Game 7 would be on the road, but it would not be in front of an entirely hostile crowd. It takes less than five hours to drive from Pittsburgh to Detroit, and when the Red Wings started selling tickets for the last game of the series, legions of Penguins fans committed to being on hand in Joe Louis Arena to support their team. When the Steelers won Super Bowl XL at Detroit's Ford Field in 2006, the building looked like a home field, with thousands of Pittsburghers filling the stands and waving gold Terrible Towels. Now as the Penguins took the ice in Detroit, they could look out in the audience and see almost 5,000 people wearing their sweaters and cheering. The Pittsburgh fans had even timed their chants to be heard in hostile territory: In the brief quiet pause after the home fans chanted the words, "Lets go Wings," Pittsburgh fans shouted out, "Lets go Pens." Anything can happen in a Game 7, and the Penguins supporters were prepared to show their players how much they believed that destiny had shifted sides.

Back home in Pittsburgh, Game 7 on an early summer evening had become a reason for impromptu block parties throughout the city. In the crowded South Side and on quiet cul-de-sacs and suburban streets across the region, friends gathered around televisions set outside in anticipation of a party. On Shadowlawn Avenue in Mt. Lebanon, the suburb that had once been Lemieux's home, a contractor named Terry Lynch nailed together two pieces of sheetrock to make an oversized screen at the end of his driveway. As he ran the televised game through a projector he had scavenged from a secondhand store, neighbors showed up with beer and snacks to watch the game.

Through the opening period, with each team eager to get out to an early lead, no one scored. Then two minutes into the second period, Maxime Talbot skated behind the net and came out on Osgood's glove side just as the puck deflected off Malkin's skate. Talbot picked up the puck on his stick, turned toward the goal, waited a moment and took his shot. Osgood lifted his stick off the ice at that very moment, and the puck slipped through his legs. Penguins fans inside Joe Louis Arena erupted in a roar.

Nine minutes later, Talbot took another shot on the net. With a two-on-one breakaway starting out of the Penguins' end, the wing moved down the center of the ice toward

Osgood's stick side of the net. Near the center of the faceoff circle, Talbot flicked his stick from his left side and lifted the puck over Osgood's glove and into the net. Penguins fans roared once more, making the road trip seem like a game at home.

Champions do not go down easily, and Detroit would not give up. Through the entire third period, the Penguins had only one shot on goal, while Detroit drove repeatedly to the net. The Red Wings scored for the first time with just over six minutes left in the game. With one more goal, the home team could tie the game. Then, with just five seconds left in the game and Osgood on the bench to give Detroit another attacker, the Red Wings' Henrik Zetterberg took a shot on goal, and his teammate Nicklas Lidstrom prepared to drive the rebound into an open net as Fleury shifted across the crease. The Penguins goaltender blocked the shot.

In the moments of celebration after the game, many of the key figures who had contributed their unique talents over the previous years to create that one moment gathered on the ice for a team photo with the Cup. Lemieux, with a playoff beard and a dark-colored suit, stood to one side of the team next to Sawyer, while Morehouse, the one-time consultant who had figured out how to get an arena in Pittsburgh, leaned in from the other, wearing a white championship hat.

Hossa had become an afterthought amid the Penguins' victory, but even then his betrayal – at least to the players left behind – was never completely forgotten. Beating him had not been the top motivation for the Penguins to win the Cup, of course, but team insiders had to admit that it felt good afterward to be on the right side.

From his home in Hartford, Sam Fingold, the developer who nearly purchased the Penguins three years earlier, watched the Stanley Cup celebration unfolding on his television. Before Lemieux or any of the team's top executives walked on the ice to celebrate, Fingold picked up his phone and sent a text to Sawyer, saying, "Congratulations. You guys deserve it." Instead of hard feelings about not being the owner that would have his name engraved in sterling, Fingold felt a small sense of ownership for helping Lemieux and Burkle make the case for keeping the franchise in Pittsburgh. Within 30 seconds, Sawyer wrote back with a quick thank you. "I look at it like it worked out for everybody," Fingold said later. "Would I have liked to have owned them and won the Stanley Cup? Yeah, that would have been great. But on the other hand, I'm not so sure the Penguins would have gotten everything they got if it wasn't for us."

Michel Therrien, the coach who took the Penguins to the Stanley Cup Final and lost a year earlier, watched Game 7 on television from his home in Pittsburgh. Penguins insiders knew the former coach had been an integral part of the Stanley Cup victory. Therrien had set championship expectations for the players, teaching them the importance of details and focusing on hard-nosed defensive hockey. "Our success and why we won the Stanley Cup was a combination of Michel Therrien and Dan Bylsma," said Botterill, the assistant general manager. "There's no way we win the Stanley Cup the second year if we don't get to the Stanley Cup Final the year before." Still, while the players and hockey executives celebrated on the ice at Joe Louis Arena, Therrien turned off the lights at his Pittsburgh home and went to bed. The next morning, he headed to Punta Cana, a resort in the Dominican Republic, for a long-planned vacation away from the city.

When it was time to leave Detroit and head home, Burkle did not board his private jet for the flight. He sent the plane on its own, with only the crew on board. Burkle and his son, Andrew, decided to fly back with the Cup instead. They boarded the team's chartered plane and rode with the champions.

"You can have $3.5 billion and buy a team," one Penguins executive said afterward. "But you can't buy that feeling. He was genuinely excited and wanted to be on the plane with Andrew."

*Penguins owners Mario Lemieux and Ron Burkle ride in a victory parade through Pittsburgh. (*Pittsburgh Tribune-Review, *Christopher Horner)*

Burkle, who rarely appears in public, rode in the championship parade along Pittsburgh's Boulevard of the Allies four days later. Fans lined the wide street 20-people deep just to catch a glimpse of the sterling trophy and the players who had brought it back to the city after 17 years. Police estimated 375,000 people had turned out for the event – a crowd that was slightly larger than the one that had come just four months earlier to celebrate the Steelers' Super Bowl XLIII victory. When the Steelers players had celebrated with their fans that day, the Penguins had been in 10th place – two slots away from making the playoffs. Now, in a football town, hockey had come out on top.

At a stage near the western edge of the boulevard, fans who had packed in two hours before the ceremony started chanting "Let's go Pens" and bouncing a beach ball under a sky as blue as the throwback sweaters the Penguins had worn at the Winter Classic the year before. People lined railings inside parking garages, and office workers wearing neck ties stood next to fans in black-and-gold t-shirts.

Lemieux and Burkle rode in a convertible to lead the parade. Crosby carried the Cup and lifted it over his head. Malkin rode with the Conn Smythe Trophy, which he won as the playoffs' most valuable player. He had become the first NHL player since Lemieux to win the playoffs trophy after leading the regular season in scoring. The bells of First Lutheran Church on Grant Street rang as they passed by.

From the stage, Lemieux thanked the fans who had supported the team through its bleakest moments. The Cup is "right back where it belongs," he said. "You guys are part of our family."

Malkin took center stage and invited his parents to join him. Vladimir and Natalia Malkin had flown from Russia to watch the playoffs, and they had become mini-celebrities for their spirited support of their son. They would share in the celebration, too. "It was very, very special," Malkin recalled later. "My family understood this, too. It's the world's biggest trophy, and when we win it, we win together because my family stayed with me all year." Malkin poured champagne into the Cup and held it tilted over first for his mom, and then his dad, to take a drink.

Crosby took a turn, too, holding the Cup for his parents, Troy and Trina, to drink from it.

Turning to the throng of fans who filled the street, Crosby shared the moment with them, too. "You deserve to be called the City of Champions," he said. "You deserve the Stanley Cup. Today is better than I ever dreamed, better than I think we all ever dreamed."

Mario Lemieux signs a beam before it is raised into place atop Consol Energy Center. (Pittsburgh Tribune-Review, *Joe Appel*)

Mario Lemieux pours melted ice from the Civic Arena over center ice at the Consol Energy Center before the Penguins' home opener in 2010. (Pittsburgh Tribune-Review, *Christopher Horner*)

12

Baptism by Ice
October 7, 2010

In the video, a steel blade scrapes off the final bits of ice from the Civic Arena as black-and-white images of the building under construction in the 1960s play in the background. The ice drops into an industrial-sized funnel, and the camera pans to the half-century-old pipes from the arena's chiller system below the floor, as the old photographs blur into great moments of hockey history that occurred in the team's former home. At the other end of the pipes, a single drop of water rolls out of a narrow trough and falls into a crystal vial. The water drop turns to a trickle, a stream, and finally a frothy torrent that roils inside the glass bottle. As the liquid runs out and the bottle fills, the water slows again until only one drop clings to the edge of the trough before falling. Forty-nine years of hockey, then, have been distilled and collected in that bottle.

As the movie plays on the four 15-foot-tall television screens over center ice at the new Consol Energy Center, a tall man in a dark suit, white shirt, blue tie and ice skates glides quietly onto the playing surface. He moves toward the center of an enormous circle painted with the home team's logo of a muscle-bound cartoon Penguin in skates. As the lights come up, fans in the arena's 18,087 seats can confirm what some might already have guessed, that Mario Lemieux, the hall-of-fame player and team owner, has laced up his skates again.

Spotlights trace across the audience and then converge over Lemieux as he holds up the allegorical bottle with the melted ice from the Civic Arena. On the massive screens, the vial appeared to be more than 10 feet tall, but now it fits easily into Lemieux's hand as he pulls out the stopper, spreads his arms wide, and spills the contents over the blue dot at the center of the ice. As he christens the arena with decades of Penguins lore, fans erupt into a mass of cheering and applause that engulfs the moment. Lemieux lifts the bottle to his lips, kisses it, and then raises his hands in triumph, waving toward the fans. As the lights go dark again, a graphic spreads across the surface, depicting the water from the old building spreading across the entire surface and freezing into the ice of the new one. On the opening night of its first regular-season Penguins home game, Consol Energy Center has had a baptism by ice.

Hours earlier outside the arena's Fifth Avenue entrance, hundreds of fans gathered to watch the players arrive in cars that dropped them at the curb so they could walk across 50 feet of red carpet laid over the sidewalk. People seeking autographs stood behind barricades, holding out Penguins gear to be signed, calling out to every player who passed through the gauntlet.

From the moments when the Penguins started vying for a casino license to pay for the new arena five years earlier, the team owners, executives, hockey staff and players had counted on these fans. The political-style campaign the Penguins' backers started on their own and maintained with the encouragement of the franchise pressured public officials into finding a way to keep the team in Pittsburgh. Until then, politicians had openly admitted they feared losing the hockey team a lot less than they would have worried about the Steelers football team or the Pirates baseball club relocating. Then the fans started to show just how much the hockey team meant not only to them but to the entire city of Pittsburgh. They started appearing at public meetings in black-and-gold hockey sweaters, and they wrote impassioned letters to elected leaders and the state Gaming Control Board to demand that consideration be given to any plan that would build an arena. Governor Ed Rendell was forced to come up with an alternative proposal that would pay for the building no matter who won the slots license. And when that license went to a group other than the one the Penguins had backed, these same fans hounded the governor and other local politicians again until they figured out a way to make good on their promise of an arena when the backup plan fell more than $100 million short of what was needed.

In the bleakest days, those fans had kept the faith that the team would stay, and that losing seasons would lead to high draft picks, that eventually through patience and pressure, the Penguins would find their way back to the top of the National Hockey League. "There needs to be mention here of the people of Pittsburgh, because part of our success really had to do with Pittsburghers understanding that the course we charted was the only course and the only hope to keep the team here for the long haul," said Ken Sawyer, who had served as the team's president and then later as its CEO. "I just felt there was great understanding for that. You see some big hockey markets, and they just can't seem to put it all together because the fans and the media won't let them go to the bottom and dwell there for a couple years. I think our fans knew that if we don't do this, this is a short game."

Now that the Penguins had won the long game, team executives intended to pay back those fans. Morehouse set a goal of coming up with at least one spectacular way of thanking the team's supporters each year. Some gestures would be as grand as giving over the entire arena to high school and college students for a preseason game, passing up $1 million in ticket sales – while others would require no more than common kindness.

In the early evening before Game 6 of the 2008 Stanley Cup Final, the year the Penguins lost to Detroit, Morehouse was walking inside the arena, holding four tickets for seats next to the glass that he planned to give to friends from Toronto who were coming down for the game. When they texted at the last minute to say they could not make the trip after all, Morehouse headed for the box office to return the tickets. Few seats would be better than these, but they likely would go unused with so little time remaining before the first faceoff.

On the way to the office, Morehouse stopped outside to see how many people had gathered on the sidewalk to watch a giant screen where the game would be shown for those who could not get a ticket at a price they could afford. When the team first considered putting up the screen, some executives said it would be a waste of money. The franchise would have to cover all of the costs, and no revenue would come back from fans who watched the game for free. It didn't make financial sense. But Morehouse had insisted it was the right thing to do, that the screen would return dividends that no one could anticipate. From the start, he had been proven right. As hundreds of fans started gathering to watch the games, the outdoor screen created a festive atmosphere on game days. College students started bringing not just folding camp seats but real sofas and chairs from their dorm rooms. On spring nights, an occasional black limousine would pull up in front of the arena so high school students heading to their prom could stop and join the fans long enough to get photographs before continuing onto the dance.

On the night of the Stanley Cup Final, Morehouse stepped outside and saw a crowd of people stretching in front of the video screen and spreading across the expansive concrete sidewalk around the arena. As he stood there marveling at the crowd, a man in the audience recognized Morehouse and walked up to him. "Mr. Morehouse," he said, "I just want to thank you for putting the screen out here. That thing is so great." The man had been outside the arena since noon, holding a spot where he would be able to see the game. He said that he had come every time the Penguins had shown a game outside.

Morehouse thanked the man in return for his support, told him to enjoy the game, and turned to walk away. Before taking a couple steps, however, the team president remembered he had four rink-side tickets in the pocket of his suit jacket. He stopped and turned back.

"Hey," Morehouse called out to the man. "Who are you here with?" The man was by himself.

"Would you want to go to the game?" Oh, the man had never been to a game. He couldn't imagine what it would be like to actually sit inside the arena.

"Grab your stuff and come with me," Morehouse told him. "I'll take you in." The man picked up his small backpack and walked with Morehouse into the arena. A loyal fan who could not afford a ticket – who had been content to watch the game on a giant television on the sidewalk surrounded by other fans – suddenly had a seat next to the ice for the biggest game of the year.

After that night, Morehouse instituted a new rule for the Penguins ticket office: If the team had any seats left at game time, an employee would take them outside, find someone in the crowd, and bring that person into the game. The Penguins did not seek publicity for the giveaways. It was just something Morehouse wanted to do. As a former fan, he knew it was the kind of thing any sports fan would dream of doing if they ever ran a sports franchise. Because he did not come up through the ranks of the sports business, Morehouse still remembered what it was like to sneak into the Civic Arena as a teenager from Beechview. He understood how someone could feel so passionately about a team that they would sit for hours on the sidewalk just to have the thrill of watching the players – win or lose – while surrounded by hundreds or thousands of people who felt the same way. He hadn't been indoctrinated with the thinking that there were certain things professional sports teams simply did not do.

"I was a fan who didn't have a whole lot of money, and I used to think, 'I don't know why they don't do this,' or 'why they don't do that,'" Morehouse said about his attitude for running the Penguins. "I mean, 'Wouldn't it be cool if someone came out and handed me a ticket?' I don't think it's much more complicated than that."

A year after winning the Stanley Cup, the Penguins were ranked by *ESPN: The Magazine* as the fan-friendliest franchise among all of North America's major league sports. For Morehouse, that distinction was nearly as sweet as winning the Stanley Cup.

If Morehouse didn't have any experience running a sports franchise, he did at least grow up in Pittsburgh. As a city native, he knew that he didn't need to look far to find a team to emulate when it came to building a stronger relationship with the Penguins fans. The Rooney family, the owners of the Steelers football team, set the standard for winning championships, giving back to the community and staying humble all along. Art Rooney, who founded the team and was known to family and fans as "The Chief," had been the sort of person who walked the streets around his North Side home with dollar bills in his pockets for neighborhood children and the occasional free game ticket to give someone he just met. When he died in 1988, his eldest son, Dan Rooney, took over the football operation, and then years later went on to serve as the United States ambassador to Ireland. His son, Art Rooney II, started running the team.

There had been a time when some Penguins executives almost resented the Steelers football team, jealous, perhaps, of its winning tradition, its new stadium and its loyal fans who bought all the seats even in the rare season when the team failed to win more than half of its games. Morehouse saw things differently. As a fan of the Steelers, too, he wanted the hockey team to be more like them.

"I look at the Steelers as the model sports franchise," Morehouse said. "They've been able to win consistently more than any other team in professional football, and they have done it the right way, by treating people well, treating their fans well, doing the right things, being humble. They're not running around banging their chests. You don't see the Rooneys running on the field, screaming at refs. You don't see them bragging about their success. They're very humble, and I think they're very Pittsburgh. If there's a patriarch for the city of Pittsburgh, it's Dan Rooney."

When he looked at the Steelers, Morehouse saw that successful teams take extra steps to recognize their fans and to contribute in their communities with sincerity. Even after winning six Super Bowl championships, the Steelers continued to do small things – often without any media notice – like taking a busload of star players to meet with wounded veterans at Walter Reed Army Medical Center in Washington, D.C., on the eve of the biggest game of the year. No reporters wrote about the hospital visit, but it was the right thing to do, said Ambassador Dan Rooney, the Steelers chairman emeritus.

For him, taking the job as ambassador to Ireland was a personal honor that extended the family's reach beyond sports into public service, but it also came with the personal sacrifice of missing games and spending less time with the grandchildren. Rooney's wife, a Penguins fan, stayed in touch with the hockey team by watching occasional games available on satellite in Ireland and by texting with Morehouse to keep up on the latest scores and inside information. What added to the challenge of taking the position so far from home was that Rooney treated the job seriously, visiting 20 of the island's 32 counties during his first year in office. He typically held town hall-style meetings where the occasional sports fan would break out a Steelers Terrible Towel in the audience. Getting that kind of recognition an ocean away from home came from the long-term, deeply emotional relationship the team developed and maintains with its fans – even when the cameras are not rolling and there's no calculated expectation of a return. When the inevitable losing seasons occur, those fans will stick by the team. "You build a structure and you have some chits out there that you've placed when you were good," Rooney said. "When things turn a little bit, the fans understand and they'll give you time to get it in shape. It's just being part of society and caring .... We want to do things that are right and helpful."

The Penguins players, too, adopted a similar philosophy. Every summer, players such as Sidney Crosby, Marc-Andre Fleury and the team's other stars take one afternoon to connect with their fans in an uncommon way by hand-delivering season tickets. When the idea of sending players out to meet with fans in their homes was first pitched in the Penguins' executive suite, some old-timers scoffed at the proposal. It would never work to have players actually come in contact with ticket-buyers. It had never been done, and the Penguins wouldn't make any more money by going out into the community. Morehouse insisted that the team go ahead and try a personal approach. The fans and the media, of course, loved seeing players making surprise home deliveries. What shocked a lot of people was that the players got something out of the experience, too. Inside the bubble of the locker room and the chartered flights, behind the barricades that keep fans at a distance, players can lose touch with the people who spend thousands of dollars on tickets and hang on whether the team wins or loses. For an afternoon, at least, the ticket deliveries allowed the hockey stars to meet the people who support them.

Ray Shero, the general manager, saw the importance of contact among the players and fans during an impromptu meeting after he first arrived in Pittsburgh. Coming in after Crosby's first season, Shero invited the star player to lunch at The Carlton Restaurant in a downtown skyscraper a few blocks from the arena. Shero had asked Crosby to come up with a list of five things the team did well and five it could do better. A lunch that was supposed to last about an hour stretched into three. As they walked back toward the arena, Shero asked Crosby whether he had been to the team's offices in Chatham Center, a separate building from where the games were played. Crosby recalled going into the office to sign his contract, but he had not been back in the year since then. Shero asked whether he would come up for a few minutes to meet the people inside selling tickets, scheduling events and marketing the team. Crosby agreed, and so they went into the building and rode up to the team's offices on the fourth floor. Shero was still new to the suite, but he walked around with the player and introduced him to the office workers. "You can imagine, Sidney Crosby walks in and people are like, 'What the heck?'" Shero recalled later.

As they neared the end of the tour, Crosby stopped outside a small conference room and asked what was going on inside, where a young woman was talking on the phone. She was trying to sell season tickets at a time when games were not yet selling out. One of the executives with Shero leaned in and asked the woman to put the phone on hold. Shero turned to Crosby and said, "Sid, why don't you get on the phone with this guy?" Crosby said, "What?" Shero explained, "You can get on the phone with this guy. We're trying to sell him a season ticket or something like that." Crosby agreed to do it. The woman took the phone off hold and asked the man on the other end whether he would like to talk with the team's best young player. The man didn't believe Crosby was really in the office, but he played along with the offer. Crosby came on the line: "Hi, this is Sidney ... no, seriously, it's Sidney Crosby. I just got back from the world championships. Hi, how are you doing?" Crosby spent a few minutes chatting with the man and then handed the phone back to the woman trying to close the sale. As they walked away, Crosby turned to Shero and said, "That was awesome. We should do that more often."

Delivering tickets to a family in the Pittsburgh suburb of Upper St. Clair in the weeks before the new arena opened, Crosby wore athletic sandals and a black Reebok ball cap pulled down low over his brow as he walked down the street of a cul-de-sac of colonial houses. When he stepped across the lawn of the Koch family's home, the mother, father and three sons rushed out of their front door, all wearing different versions of Crosby's jersey in black, white, powder blue and the red of Team Canada. Crosby talked with them quietly in a tight huddle as television cameras recorded the moment and reporters stood several feet away scribbling into notebooks. Ryan, 13, blurted out that he had just been playing as Crosby in an NHL video game. "How'd I do?" the player asked. "I actually scored a goal with you," came the answer.

Then the boys asked Crosby for a few minutes of street hockey with them in the backyard. The Penguins star already had done his part, and the photo opportunity was secure. He

Sidney Crosby plays goalie as fan Ryan Koch, 13, shoots on goal in his family's driveway. (Pittsburgh Tribune-Review, *Justin Merriman*)

didn't have to do any more. But he did it anyway, walking around to the back of the house where the young boys had a goal set up on the cracked macadam of their driveway. Crosby grabbed a stick with them and played goalie while the young ones took shots on him. Then, when one of the boys wanted to put on his goalie equipment, he asked Crosby whether he would wait a moment longer. Of course. The boys and the hockey star played around with the puck, just as if Crosby had been a young teenager himself back in Nova Scotia.

"It's just a way to say thanks," Crosby said after the pickup game. "It's not an entire day. It's just a couple hours out of our day. ... To meet people face-to-face and thank them is nice."

If the Penguins had left Pittsburgh, those moments would have gone with them. The impact of losing the team would have been great for fans and the city. "Gosh, you think about financially what that would have meant to the city if we lost the Penguins," said Anne Swager, who headed up a community group that evaluated the Pittsburgh casino proposals. "It would have been a tremendous loss."

Even if public officials never really believed the Penguins were going to leave, they weren't willing to take that chance. "I certainly wasn't willing to play poker with them," Mayor Luke Ravenstahl said. "It would have been a bad calculation if we had attempted to call their bluff, only to find out they were prepared to go." As it turned out, the mayor said he believed the Penguins owners weren't really posturing, anyway. After the two sides agreed on the terms of the deal, team owner Ron Burkle informed the elected officials that the agreement to stay in Pittsburgh still wasn't as good on paper as the one in Kansas City, but they had decided to take it anyway because it had been close. "I don't know if that's true or not, but that was the Penguins' position even as they agreed to do the deal," Ravenstahl said. "At that point, once a deal's done, there's no need to keep bluffing. ... It was serious enough, from our perspective, that (relocation) was an alternative if they had to do that. If we didn't give them a building – I shouldn't say give them a building – if we didn't put a deal together, I think they would be somewhere else right now, because the reality is they would simply have to be, based on the economics."

Rendell said he, too, believed the Penguins would have left for Kansas City if the owners had not received a competitive offer to stay in Pittsburgh. Even then, it had been hard for Pennsylvania politicians to compete with a place that already had an arena built. In Kansas City, the hockey team could have started making more money right away by moving into the new rink without waiting the additional years it took for Pittsburgh to open the Consol Energy Center. What they would have lost, however, would have been the loyal fans of Pittsburgh. "In Kansas City, they could make money those first couple years, but Kansas City has never shown an inclination to support a hockey team," Rendell said after the team had committed to staying. "They had no idea, five years down the road, 10 years down the road, what attendance would be in Kansas City. They know – good or bad times – that there's an incredible fan base in Pittsburgh, and their attendance would always be good in Pittsburgh. In the end, the state deal was important, but I think the intensity of the fan base carried the day."

The other key for keeping the Penguins in Pittsburgh, Rendell reasoned, was the legalization of casino gambling. Without the money from slot machines, Pennsylvania never could have afforded to pay for an arena with tax dollars. "Everyone should be clear," Rendell said when the arena opened. "Without gaming, the Penguins are in Kansas City, and the Kansas City Penguins won the Stanley Cup."

Before its first hockey game, Consol Energy Center opened to the public on August 18, 2010, with a Paul McCartney concert. The singer had refused several times to play at the Civic Arena in its final years because the building was too cramped, so Penguins officials touted his willingness to play in the new building as evidence that it could draw major concerts and events on non-game nights.

*From left, President David Morehouse, Allegheny County Executive Dan Onorato, owner Mario Lemieux, Pittsburgh Mayor Luke Ravenstahl, CEO Ken Sawyer and Gov. Ed Rendell shovel dirt for a ceremonial groundbreaking of Consol Energy Center. (*Pittsburgh Tribune-Review, *James M. Kubus)*

For the first of two sold-out shows, Lemieux, Burkle and Morehouse sat together in the owner's ice-level box, Suite 66, a nod to the number that Lemieux wore as a player. Morehouse had been named the team's president when the Penguins were still in the old building, and with Ken Sawyer preparing to retire, he was in line to take over the job of CEO, as well. Late that night, after fans had emptied out of the arena, Morehouse took Burkle and a couple of his guests on a tour. It was a chance for them to appreciate everything that had happened since the owners brought the team out of bankruptcy, very nearly selling it and then almost moving to another city. Here they were, finally, standing in a new building, quietly looking around. "It was just a moment to take a breath and look at it," Morehouse said a few days later. "We weren't saying, 'Look what we did.' It was, 'Look at this place. It's really a fabulous venue. It's breathtaking.'"

*Penguins CEO Ken Sawyer, left, sits next to President David Morehouse and owner Mario Lemieux at the groundbreaking ceremony for Consol Energy Center. (*Pittsburgh Tribune-Review, *James M. Kubus)*

Two months later, on October 7, NHL commissioner Gary Bettman, stood near a podium in the media room at ice level inside the arena, not far from the players' locker rooms and the owners' suite. "Oh, I knew it would all work out," he said dryly, drawing laughter from the reporters gathered around him before the first game at Consol Energy Center. Bettman had been the one who brokered the final negotiations among the owners and local officials, and many of the same reporters had gathered around him on the night in 2007 when the team owners and public officials finally announced they had a deal for the arena in which they were now standing.

Whether Lemieux and Burkle had looked at other cities sincerely or strategically no longer mattered, Bettman said. Ultimately, they had decided to keep the team in Pittsburgh, where they had wanted to be all along. Plus, they had kept ownership when they could have sold. "I actually think you need to give Mario Lemieux and Ron Burkle the credit for sticking by this team and having the vision and foresight to know what could be there, having endured everything they had to go through," he said. "It's a testament to them that we're here tonight, as well as the mayor and the governor and everybody else who participated. But they, and the league, always believed in this franchise and in the city of Pittsburgh."

Two flights up, in the main bowl of the arena, vendors made final preparations by setting out food for the first game as other workers opened boxes of yearbooks and commemorative tickets for each fan to receive as they came through the gates. A ticket-taker named Vince stood near the northwest entrance of the building, wearing a tie under a sweater vest. He had been on the job 49 years, long enough to have opened the Civic Arena, visible across the street through a wall of windows. He recalled how Governor David L. Lawrence, the city's former mayor, had stood at a podium at the opening in 1961, with the September sun melting the ice which had been laid down for a skating show. Of course, the Penguins did not even exist then, with the hockey interest instead focused on the return of the Hornets, a minor-league team. On opening night of Consol Energy Center, Vince figured he had maybe another year in him, as long as his legs would allow him to stand and greet fans on their way inside the new building. That night, he planned to open the place and then go home to watch the game on television.

Some of the first fans inside the new building tried out its gadgets. People with smart phones could use them to watch replays of key moments in the game from four different camera angles, with Consol Energy Center touted as the first arena to provide wi-fi Internet access at every seat. A $2 million Verizon studio tracked Twitter messages from across North America, showing what Penguins-related words were turning up most often across the continent; for a while before the game, Mario Lemieux's name was the most common Tweet coming out of Ontario. Another interactive area allowed fans to pull up videos and stats on players from the Penguins' all-time greatest team and to spin around a virtual image of the Stanley Cup to see the names of champions. "It just makes it seem like we're in the 21st century, instead of the 1970s," said one fan, with the Civic Arena visible behind her through a wall of glass windows.

*Consol Energy Center, right, sits next to the stainless steel dome of the Civic Arena. (*Pittsburgh Tribune-Review, *Jasmine Goldband.)*

From a team that once played in the league's oldest building and had a payroll so low that it could not afford to keep its
best players from leaving for teams willing to pay tens of millions of dollars more, the Penguins had been reborn. Consol
Energy Center provided a strong example of the team's new
life, and it became one of many reasons that free agents suddenly started wanting to come to Pittsburgh and stay there –
even if that meant sometimes taking less money than other
teams might offer. "We've got the new arena," Shero said.
"We've got a good team. We've got committed ownership,
which is important; owners who want to win; a community
that's passionate about their hockey team. There's a lot of good
things."

During the opening ceremony on the ice, each coach and
player had a moment to receive the fans' adulation as their
name was called. On the bench, Dan Bylsma mouthed the word
"Wow," as thunderous cheers filled the arena when his name
was called. Before the players stepped onto the ice, 10 youth
hockey players skated in circles inside the rink and formed two
rows while banging their sticks on the surface to create a path
for the professionals to skate through. Each starting player
stepped onto the ice under a spotlight and then joined his teammates along the center line, from Brent Johnson, the backup
goalie, to Evgeni Malkin, the assistant captain, and finally,
Crosby. The team captain walked toward the ice with his head
down, lifting his eyes and then his stick as he stepped on the
ice and acknowledged the roaring fans.

Moments later, Lemieux and Bettman walked across a red
carpet toward center ice. Burkle was supposed to be with them,
but his plane had been delayed. They dropped the puck for a
ceremonial faceoff between Crosby and Mike Richards, captain of the Philadelphia Flyers, the first opponents to play in
the arena. As he walked off the ice, Lemieux high-fived his
players seated on the bench.

Up in the suite-level seats, Sawyer served as the man of
honor at a small party to celebrate his retirement. Ever since he
joined the Penguins on the day that Lemieux won the right to

purchase the team out of bankruptcy court, Sawyer had worked toward this moment. He had been the one about ready to faint when the team won the rights to draft Crosby, and he had been on the ice when the team won the Stanley Cup. In darker moments, Sawyer also had watched countless public officials dismiss the team's need for a new building, and he had been there through the tough negotiations, right up until the end, when it seemed a deal might never get done. This night, he took the time to look around the new arena. He could hardly believe what the franchise had accomplished, even by its unorthodox methods. Sawyer marveled at the arena's western glass wall, allowing fans inside the concourses to admire the city skyline, and for people walking on the street outside to glimpse the excitement of the activity inside. No other arena could claim to offer that sort of interaction, not even the Civic Arena with its retractable dome. "I must say, this turned out much better than I had hoped," Sawyer said after the experience, "and I had hoped for it to be pretty good."

As the game started, Crosby won the first faceoff, passing the puck to defenseman Brooks Orpik. Fans had little to cheer about after that, with the home team missing opportunities and the Flyers' Danny Briere scoring the Consol Energy Center's first goal at 2:51 in the second period. The Flyers went on to win 3 to 2. Neither the fans nor the players wanted the building to open with a loss, but both had to understand that no matter how momentous the night felt, it would be just one game among 82 that year. Talking with reporters after the game, Bylsma said he looked forward to getting back to the normal routine of the regular season: "There's been a lot of hype and excitement about the building and opening it up."

Burkle, the team's reclusive owner, attended the opener but did not make a public appearance. It might have been odd for fans to see him standing at center ice with Lemieux, anyway. No doubt, he had played critical roles many times in making this night possible – providing seed money when Lemieux brought the team out of bankruptcy, negotiating the fine details of the arena contract, even walking out on Rendell when the governor exploded at the team's lawyer. For now, Burkle had returned to the shadows, apparently content to allow the players and his co-owner to take the limelight.

Lemieux made himself visible but silent for the opener. Even in the days leading up to the opening, he did not say much about the moment. On his 45th birthday, two days before the first game, the team unveiled a mosaic inside the building, made from thousands of photos of cancer survivors and fans that were put together to form images of Lemieux at different stages of his career. For each photo, a donor had contributed $66 to the Mario Lemieux Foundation to support cancer research and playrooms at local hospitals. The mosaic raised $200,000 for the nonprofit. Lemieux stood with his wife and signed autographs for people invited to attend.

Morehouse, the architect of the public campaign that won an arena, the hometown fan who rose up to run the franchise, promised himself one more quiet moment at the first game to appreciate everything that had happened. Many times, the Penguins could have ended up playing in another city or with other owners. Morehouse, himself, nearly walked away from the team and his hometown, too, when Isle of Capri Casinos failed to win the slots license. At every other time in his life, when he had worked for presidential candidates and narrowly lost, Morehouse had picked up, written out a new list of priorities, and moved on to some other challenge. This time, for the first time in his life, Morehouse found himself fighting for a reason to stay in Pittsburgh.

It had been an unexpected blessing to come back home, for his mother to see her grandchildren and for him to reconnect with friends from the old neighborhood. Before coming to work for the Penguins, the hardest moment of his political career had been the six weeks at the end of John Kerry's presidential campaign, when Morehouse had not been home to see his wife and son, Jackson. Child psychology books said the boy would be too young at less than a year old to notice his father's absence, but Morehouse never believed that. As soon as he could crawl, Jackson always found a way inside his father's open suitcase when he was home and getting ready for another trip. Years later, Morehouse suspected the boy still resented him for leaving all those times. On his dresser, he keeps a photograph of Jackson sitting inside an open suitcase. "I have that picture to remind me of how hard it was to leave," Morehouse said, "and of how great it is to be in one place."

After the arena deal, Morehouse considered moving back to Los Angeles and maybe going to work for the Clinton Global Initiative or helping the effort to draw a National Football League franchise back to that city. But when he asked whether the Penguins had a job for him, Lemieux insisted that he stay. His job would be to not only help the hockey team win the Stanley Cup again, but also to keep the Penguins among the fan-friendliest franchises in sports. For 30 years, at least, no one should have to worry about the Penguins leaving for some other city. "Like anything you do, there are curves in the road and things happen for a reason," Morehouse said in the end. "We've had a lot of curves, and that makes it even more gratifying. ... Part of our strength is having gone through all of those things."

Acknowledgements

This book would not have been possible without the support, encouragement and contributions of many people. Thank you all.

My family has endured the writing of this book, through the early mornings and the late nights, from summer vacation through the dark of winter – once, and again. Tania, thank you for believing in me always – from the first moment we met. Your love sustains me more than you know. Noah and Claudia Jay, you bring me joy as you find the words to write your own stories. I am proud of you both, in everything you do. Mom and Dad, thank you for helping me discover my own voice. Elizabeth and Iwan Fuchs, it is a blessing to have you and the boys always near. Pam and Al Miller, you have treated me like your son. Jay Searles, I never will forget your unflinching generosity. Jim Charlton, you inspired me many summers ago on the sun-hot sidewalks of Rehoboth Beach. I hope you take some personal satisfaction from reading this book.

I am grateful to the *Pittsburgh Tribune-Review* and publisher Richard Mellon Scaife for supporting this project and giving me the opportunity to tell stories. In particular, I owe special thanks to Frank Craig: When I was about to give up, you kept me going. Ralph Martin, thank you for backing me up when I needed it most. Bob Fryer, your inspiration lives on in me and many others. Jim Cuddy, Sandy Tolliver and Jim Wilhelm: Thank you for always challenging me to be my best. Rob Rossi, you have been with me from the start, and I am grateful for your guidance along the way. We had many great nights uncovering the story of the Pittsburgh Penguins. I look forward to our next reporting adventures. Jeremy Boren, thank you for reading behind me the whole way. You saved me many times. I cannot wait to return the favor. Jim Kubus, you took me to the top of the Civic Arena, from where I could see this whole story unfold. Thank you for helping get me here – and for lending me your last remaining copy of *Sudden Death*. Karen Price, thank you for sharing your stories.

Brad Bumsted, you know how to open closed doors as well as anyone in the business. Thank you for showing me the way. Salena Zito, you have opened your Rolodex time and again. Hugs. Mark Houser and Mike Wereschagin, thank you for your insights. Laura Gutnick and H. Yale Gutnick, thank you for looking out for me, as always. The Trib graciously allowed me to use photographs from the newspaper's archives, and I appreciate the work of the following photographers: Andrew Russell, who shot the

Author Andrew Conte stands on top of the Civic Arena, taking notes. (James M. Kubus)

photo on the cover of *Breakaway*, as well as Joe Appel, Jasmine Goldband, Keith Hodan, Christopher Horner, James M. Kubus, Justin Merriman, Heidi Murrin, Chaz Palla and Philip G. Pavely.

Many people offered guidance and insights throughout the long process of writing this book. Luis Fabregas, you have been my confidant, my constant ally and my friend. Thank you for making every day a Thursday. Tom Doherty, my publisher, you bought into this project from the first pitch. Thank you. Henry "Bing" Ewalt, I hated your tough criticism, but it made my story better. Jim Dodson, thanks for helping out a fellow ink jockey. Sandy Padwe, Ari Goldman, Ned Rosenbaum, Jack Anderson and Michael Binstein: Thanks for giving me the reporting life. To my colleagues at Point Park University, thank you for encouraging me through this process and for giving me the opportunity to share my craft with the next generations of great writers. DG, writing a book *is* like running a marathon, and you have helped me keep the pace.

Finally, I owe a special thanks to the many sources who trusted me enough to open closed doors and show me how this story really unfolded. You know who you are.